6-3-75

IN PURSUIT
OF MORAL VALUE

IN PURSUIT OF MORAL VALUE

STEPHEN DAVID ROSS

*State University of
New York, Binghamton*

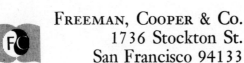

FREEMAN, COOPER & CO.
1736 Stockton St.
San Francisco 94133

Contents

~~~~~~

Preface

~~~~~~

This represents my third book in ethics and, I hope, fulfills the promise of the other two—that of defining the rich complexity of moral decisions and the rational basis of moral actions. In *Moral Decision* (Freeman, Cooper & Company, 1971) and *The Nature of Moral Responsibility* (Wayne State University Press, 1972), ethics was approached from a narrower perspective than in this work. The three books are theoretical, exploring the grounds and nature of moral actions rather than the substantive character of particular decisions. Indeed, my position entails that particular decisions are individual matters, and although intelligent and rational, are not properly of philosophical concern.

In this summary work, it is appropriate that I acknowledge my debt to those who have helped me. My deepest thanks to Douglas Greenlee and to Evelyn Shirk, who read my earlier works and made helpful suggestions, and to members of the New York Philosophy Group who have commented upon a part of the present work. My debt to Justus Buchler is immense: he has read several of my previous works and made important suggestions for their improvement; even more important, he has laid the foundation for many of my fundamental philosophical views—though he is not responsible for the outcome.

Binghamton, New York   S.D.R.
Summer, 1973

IN PURSUIT
OF MORAL VALUE

Introduction

~~~~~~

Certain highly persuasive analyses of moral value bear a fundamental weakness—they consider value to be determinately resolvable in its terminal phases. The two classic analyses of goodness—Plato's and Kant's—both presuppose that moral goodness can be won, by the moral philosopher or the ordinary man. Either the roots of philosophical analysis are inseparable from ordinary conceptions of value, a commentary on the grounds or structure of common principles of action; or principles of value are grounded in a special mode of judgment and analysis, and an authority is suggested. In both cases, the heart of moral values is assumed to have been grasped; only the details of exemplification remain.

The presupposition that actions can be given a firm foundation, even that ordinary moral decisions are firmly based, is so engrained that the abandonment of the presupposition has led not to a more flexible and rational ground for action, but to the repudiation of such grounds altogether. The realization that Being offers no values at its heart—which is but a recognition of the need for human toil as a constituent in value—becomes in existentialism the ground of a fearful absurdity. Since existence without man has no value, neither in itself nor from God, the domain of value is thought absurd, and man must win through this absurdity in every act he undertakes.

Such a view entails the rejection of all rational grounds of action, as if only science could provide rational grounds. It is not often recalled that Galileo relegated perceptual qualities to an inferior realm of existence on no more legitimate basis than that secondary qualities are dependent on the perceiving organism. Hume's scepticism follows from the triumphant sequestration of reason *a priori* to a limited domain of application. It has been overlooked that dependency upon an organism is no different in principle from any relational dependency, and as amenable to reason.

Most puzzling of all, however, is the absurdity that is thought entailed by the death of God—i.e., by the relinquishing of divine grounds for action. Exactly how God's commands could justify a value is mysterious. We must still choose whether or not to accept God's will. A small tag on objects of the world as "good" or "bad" would in no way relieve me of the responsibility for judging whether those labels were valid or not. Kant's repudiation of the theological grounds of moral value depends completely on this recognition. "Even the Holy One of the Gospels must first be compared with our ideal of moral perfection before we can recognize Him as such: and so He says of Himself, 'Why call ye Me (whom you see) good; none is good (the model of good) but God only (whom ye do not see)?' But whence have we the conception of God as the supreme good?" Unfortunately, Kant maintains the preconception that the foundations of value have been settled, and he substitutes the absolute dictates of *a priori* reason for the absolute will of God.

The relinquishing of absolute grounds of value leads neither to absurdity nor even to a naive relativism. Rather, it transforms action from the application of a settled criterion, according to which we make unassailable judgments about what is good and bad, into a continuing *search* for value. The process of evaluation is not a matter of matching an object to dependable criteria of judgment—though criteria may be available and used—but of *finding out* the value of the object. It is quite misleading to think even of the appraisal of a diamond as the determination of a structural property. The appraisal is an educated guess as to the desirability of that particular kind of stone if placed for sale upon the market. Appraisals can fail, if the market is not what it was thought to be. Expert dealers in the diamond trade are sometimes ruined. More important, the diamond market is largely created by appraisals, which therefore contribute to their own future character. Human needs and social practices are an important part of the conditions which such appraisals must take into account, yet both the needs and the practices are significantly affected by the character of ongoing judgments of value.

If this is true concerning the relatively routine matter of diamond appraisal, it is far more significant if we consider the appraisal of works of unknown artists—painters, composers, even dress designers. And it is vital even more if we are concerned with moral values in a society in transition—for the transition marks the unsettling of the conditions of moral value. Evaluation here is action undertaken to provide value where unknown or absent, if only within limited spheres. Every action brings with it a definite possibility of error, of failure, from which stem the peculiar qualities of evaluation. Particularly in moral affairs, where difference of opinion entails an intense commitment to reach agreement, the search for value takes on its characteristic forms of anguish and despair.

The fundamental principle of this work is that to be a moral agent is to engage in a search for value. Our goal here is to understand the characteristics of that pursuit—of evaluation and of valid action. It will be shown to be methodic, and the values which emerge to be the outcome of rational, controlled, yet open-ended methodic activities. The method will be described in general terms, though it is no panacea for moral problems, but is rather the general condition whereby moral action may be given an intelligible foundation. Our present values I will view as temporary resting places—as one who seeks an elusive goal may be temporarily satisfied with approximations and with genuine accomplishments. But the search for value never actually ends. The actions or principles which are the outcome of particular value activities bring new activities directly. New actions are called for however much we may have succeeded or failed before. We live in a value continuum—which is our despair insofar as our obligations never cease, but our salvation insofar as we always have another chance as long as we are alive.

I

Evaluation

~~~~~~

A. The Burdens of Action

If there is any truth to the existentialist claim that Being-in-itself has
no value, it is that we never find values independent of human concerns.
A passive acquiescence in things as they come and go does not bring us to
their value. To Sartre, value has meaning only in the context of human
projects, insofar as we have intentions and find them realized or dashed
into nothingness. Only within our expectations and hopes do things and
events take on goodness and badness. So we are left with our freedom,
first to define our projects and ourselves, thereafter to find that value in
the world which we imposed on it. No antecedent pattern offers itself as a
template according to which we may realize our essences.

Still, the ascription to natural events of a calamitous or beneficent
quality is quite common. A landslide destroys a village; a tidal wave
obliterates a coastal city. Certainly these events are catastrophes, whether
or not stability and order are what is hoped for. Natural events can
support life or make it impossible; they can make gratification easy or
difficult to obtain; they can call forth the highest qualities of endeavor or
promote slackness and resignation. The claim that our judgments are
relative to our projects fails to pay due heed to the fact that our projects
are themselves always defined within contexts of natural events. Such
contexts give form and structure to human projects which can be but vain
wishes without beneficent environmental conditions. The shock of the
realization that Being provides no goods in itself promotes a swing to the
opposite extreme—yet one which preserves the fundamental error at the
heart of the original supposition.

The assumption which underlies both the search for value in Being and the complete repudiation of environmental conditions as determinants of value, is that it is intelligible to suppose that a being could *in itself* (in some imaginable world) possess value. The catastrophes and windfalls of natural events support the ascription of malignity and beneficence to nature; and the realization that nature supports no teleology—at least not as science would have it—renders nature devoid of normative quality. One of the foundations of religious thought may well look to the basis offered by a God to a value-free universe. The Enlightenment faith, that natural law can be the foundation of human society, to direct human aspirations toward their fulfillment, may well be the cornerstone of all religious faith. The view that natural events provide values is without rational support; but one may maintain nevertheless that the only *possible* ground of value rests in natural orders and events, a claim which, however, also cannot find rational support. Faith or sentiment therefore provide the only means of affirming that the natural order or the will of God is the ultimate basis of human purpose.

The repudiation of this faith, based as it is on an external mode of assessment, is a repudiation as well of the possibilities of the natural environment to provide the ground of human aims. "God is dead"—and we are therefore lonely travelers in an absurd world (meaning, one which provides no basis for human actions). Since we cannot rely with security on God's will or on the natural world in which we find ourselves, we will have none of them. We are thrown upon ourselves as the ground of value. Nevertheless, at the heart of our acceptance we are aware of the folly of affirming values without considering the conditions of implementation and circumstances of judgment. We can stand neither to capitulate to existence, since it reflects none of our purpose and provides no basis for it, nor to defy existence, and render our ideals vain shadows of our impotent will. We are doomed to a travesty of self-realization, since by one complete dislocation from the natural order, our wills become devoid of any rationale at all. It is then impossible to discern any basis whatsoever for principles of reason in the moral life.

The fundamental error is the assumption that moral values are immediately available aspects of Being. Although post-Kantian philosophy makes much of the complexities of scientific theory-construction, and emphasizes the complex methods and procedures necessary to scientific knowledge, moral values have remained immune from a parallel realization. The structure of the physical world yields itself to human grasp only upon the application of carefully designed methods—methods which themselves are dependent upon particular characteristics of human observation. Observation is the heart of science; yet observation is not a well-defined activity independent of metaphysical and scientific theories as to what we may observe. We see largely what we look for—and our expectations are defined by our *pre*conceptions of reality. Physical science is the continual modification of the theoretical system that defines our observed world, a system which is faithful to our observations in its own terms. From this point of view, truth is never merely something *found*; facts do not wait around to be discovered. Science is the adoption of methods devoted to a *search* for knowledge; and it is the nature of this quest partly to define its own results. The terms in which our scientific understanding of the world is represented are a consequence both of prior expectations and of observed facts.

That everyday experience is filled with value claims suggests erroneously that evaluation is a well-defined activity, implicitly understood by all of us. This makes no more sense than supposing that because we possess a surface knowledge about the objects of everyday experience, we are deeply cognizant of their characteristics and workings. It is naive to suppose that we have plumbed the depths of what is to be known. Discovery of what is yet unknown is often arduous and time-consuming. A correct explanation of why the sky is blue is by no means obvious. Analogously, a clear understanding of the issues relevant to justifying or avoiding a war—political, moral, economic, historical, etc.—is by no means easy to come by. Moreover, just as many common beliefs are false, so the conviction of many men that a war is justifiable is no proof that it is—any more than that beliefs about the way people behave are more legitimate the more popular they are. Values are exceedingly complex and interrelated, and can be secured only with care and effort. They do not stand out clearly against a background of neutrality—though the appearances of value may. Disagreeable objects are often beneficial; and seemingly agreeable events may have hidden dangers.

The Platonic distinction between appearance and reality, when applied to action, is often paid due heed and thereupon vitiated by too arbitrary a conception of the determination of value. When human projects are conceived too willfully, all grounds of criticism are nullified. The person who would define value by the force of his will alone is left without a ground on which to stand. The Platonic simile of the Good being like the sun rules our preconceptions of value. The sun is obvious in the sky; so do we expect goodness to reveal itself unmistakably. We know what we like and dislike; and we know that very well. Surely that should

provide the foundation of value—but for the fact that others fail to share
with us our likes and dislikes, and attempt to force their judgments on us
as we attempt to force them. When values are viewed as given in
existence, this conflict seems more a war of will and interest than what it
really is—a conflict as to what is truly valuable. It is precisely because
what is valuable is difficult to determine that moral conflicts have the
quality they do.

Even within the bounds of Plato's epistemology, it can be seen that
knowledge of the Good is something won only after arduous and complex
adventures of the mind. The philosopher may indeed leave the cave and
travel in sunlight, but he cuts his chains by unceasing dialectical analysis
of the interrelationship of the various Forms, by unceasing criticism of his
conclusions, and by profound knowledge of the ways in which Forms are
manifested as shadows on the wall of the cave. If Plato's own philosophical
techniques are considered, rather than the metaphors of the *Republic*, then
the philosophical analysis of the Good can be viewed as the adventure in
becoming it is. The detailed analyses of the later dialogues are
exemplifications of the method that must be followed if knowledge of the
Good is to be realized. The love of wisdom that is philosophy is a love of
rational discourse and the give and take of dialectic. By formulation,
counterexample, and reformulation—through attempt, failure, and new
attempt—does philosophy come to realize itself. And its goal, not to be
attained except through the dialectic itself, is the Good.

Plato is sometimes condemned for confusing the making of value
judgments with the philosophical analysis of such judgments of value.
One of his favorite questions arises in an abrupt transition from the sphere
of evaluation to the question of whether the agent who has so judged
knows what he is doing. Euthyphro must answer the question "what is
piety?" to justify his value judgment that his father acted wrongly in
punishing his servant. It is often thought that we have here a shift in
universes of discourse—to the philosophical from the normative.

Such a criticism will be recognized as inadequate if it is understood
that value judgments are not the presentation of a completed activity in
evaluation, but are tentative endeavors in *finding* what is valuable. Until
one has knowledge of the Good (and we may be sceptical whether such a
thing exists apart from the procedures employed in ascertaining it), one is
seeking value, trying to find what is good. Humility and respect for others
would seem to be called for, rather than arrogant and willful action.
Euthyphro is condemned because he is so certain of what is right and
wrong—certain to the point of engaging in dubious action. Socrates asks

him to justify his claims, not by changing universes of discourse, but in order to make him cognizant of the tentative nature of all judgments of value.

The point of this discussion is that finding something good is a complex and tentative judgment, one which we cannot avoid, but whose limitations we must not delude ourselves about. It is precisely the difficulties of evaluation, which permeate our lives and bring us despair and anguish, that are so often overlooked in the oversimplified examples of the classroom. The richness of the texture of life is erased, and moral issues are divested of their relations within the particular cases where they belong. No wonder the conclusions arrived at in such abstract discussion are of little help when the problems become real. No wonder the discussants become convinced either that examination of the issues should bring unanimity—or equally, that no amount of discussion can ground a judgment of value. The presupposition that a conclusion concerning action can be arrived at through the analysis of abstract principles reflects the belief that values will emerge from the welter of confusion surrounding them, once the confusion has been dispelled. Either one finds clarity and a definite value, or one becomes convinced that the whole subject is devoid of rationality.

In reality, an agent must *find a way* to act. He must reach a decision as to what he will do, and thereby implicitly or explicitly will have judged the value of various alternatives before him. But his actions need not reflect a value found and settled upon. Probably nothing has supported paralysis in moral action more than the belief that normative issues are to be settled before action is undertaken. Rather, every human action may be viewed as an essay in attaining some value in human experience. Every such action will redefine the circumstances within which evaluation occurs. And new actions will then be called for, to meet the new circumstances created.

The view I am proposing is that human actions be understood not as responses to values already well formed, but as attempts to bring about values in our lives and circumstances. When a man chooses to act, he intends his actions to *be* valuable, at least to become so, though he may not know in advance how they may. Like a painter who struggles to master a new technique, a moral agent seeks to produce what is valuable based on his experience and knowledge. But the latter guarantee nothing; and he may create a new mode of value in his actions. The analogy between evaluation and artistic creation underlies Nietzsche's scorn for the mediocre. The value of art may not be the same as the value of action, but an artistic creation is certainly the outcome of a deed. The transcendence of value need not be thought of as a rejection of all past systems of morality, but as the creation of new possibilities of value. We ourselves seek to live and act, not to repeat our forerunners' lives—not their successes, certainly not their mistakes.

The Greek playwrights grasped these matters as they intuitively grasped most aspects of the moral life. The *Oresteia* celebrates the creation of a new system of values, without which the house of Atreus would forever be plagued by disaster. Vengeance can be valuable for the preservation of order within a society so structured as to allow ruling families only occasional contact. As a frontier economy grows in size and complexity, a more reliable and stable system of justice must replace the arbitrariness of vendetta-justice. A father has killed his daughter; a wife has murdered her husband; a son has killed his mother. It is enough. But how can a new system of values replace an older one, even when its failures are obvious by their fruits? That is the problem Aeschylus confronts. And if he fails to resolve it fully, it is because he captures the anguish inherent in the situation so well that no dramatic device can make its elimination plausible.

The Furies are often thought to be Aeschylus' major failure in the trilogy. It is impossible for us to take them seriously. Partly this is because our modern productions are relatively intimate and personal compared with the festival celebrations of Greek drama. Even in Euripides, personal emotions are rendered overwhelmingly larger than life, virtual caricatures of genuine emotion, in order that they may move across the footlights without losing their impact. The Furies too might survive a production in which all the transports are magnified. But the key point is that the Furies must, if Aeschylus is to succeed in accomplishing his task of realizing a new morality, become purely external manifestations of remorse. Orestes has murdered his mother, with or without justification—if anything could justify matricide. If that act alone is taken as the basis of the moral judgments to be reached, then he is doomed. Nothing can save him.

But he must be saved, for he represents guilty mankind whose guilt and remorse entail further bloodshed, remorse, and guilt without end. An act of destruction entails further destruction unendingly. The spiral of revenge never ends, but accelerates toward the possibility of the destruction of mankind.

The two-pronged nature of guilt, however, must be coped with in its personal as well as circumstantial aspects. Orestes must be saved; his remorse must not become so overpowering as to ruin him. Otherwise we have no solution. We have not replaced a morality of fairness with a morality of mercy. Aeschylus wisely externalizes the Furies to the point of absurdity, lest they so inhabit Orestes' soul as to entrap him in self-hatred.

Oedipus too discovers something more than his own *hubris* in not more thoroughly heeding the warning of the oracle. He learns that the most rational standards may fail to provide security. The life of man cannot be wholly ordered by reason, but contains threads that can rise up to strangle the most intelligent of men. The quest for truth, one of the greater values in human life, nevertheless is not sufficient for a complete life. By his failure, the most rational man of Thebes awakens at Colonnus to the Dionysian mysteries. Although he is blind the scales have so fallen from his eyes that he is transported to the highest and most mysterious places of the universe. A more explicit rendition of the transcendent quality of a discovered value is difficult to find. Oedipus, blind though he is, "sees" something more than the ordinary man, and his wisdom and holiness make him blessed. The grasp of the limitations of established traditions, when coupled with a profound realization of their strengths as well as their weaknesses, is at once the creation of a new value and a sign of blessedness. Nietzsche's *übermensch* is not a ruler hungry for power—we understand such men perfectly according to prosaic moral standards. He is a man in whose particular life an established value is transcended, as he lives in a way which reveals its limitations. In Nietzsche's eyes, the hypocrisy of Christianity resides in the value of obedience to the will of God—in effect a repudiation of the act of will necessary for a moral agent to accept or defy God's commandments. General principles may provide worthy candidates for goods; but the decision remains of determining just how and when particular principles apply to particular cases. Life is a process of *coming to find* what is valuable, in the decisions we act upon.

I will argue that the abstract possibilities inherent in the principles we consider when making moral decisions help us only to a limited extent. General principles furnish us with facts about human beings in general and the likely prospects of various courses of action. They tell us of the dangers which face us. But we are always left then to make of the concurrence of facts and rules what we can, for there is always the possibility that any particular person, or any particular set of circumstances, is exceptional in significant respects.

Greek tragedy often turns on the unresolvable tension among moral principles and their concrete relevance for different and conflicting individuals. Only within the outcome of action, projected into an indefinite future, can success or failure be realized. The tragedy is ours as well as a tragedy of heroes, for our principles and realizations are always merely tentative, awaiting future determination. An abstract conflict of principles—e.g., to bury a brother or to preserve a stable social order—either is unresolvable or finds its terms of judgment within the circumstances which are brought to pass. A value awaits discovery in terms of those events which promote successful accommodation. Success and failure are more created than discovered, the emergence of new forms in which action realizes or fails to realize human purposes, known or not, even those ends yet to be formed.

It is far from easy to explain success in action. It is much easier to explain failure. But I do not believe that this is because success is less tangible or less intelligible. Rather, it is because the prevailing slackness in human life makes us indifferent to events that do not challenge us. We are not forced to confront our half-successes, only our failures, and a half-success may unchallenged pass satisfactorily. In full confrontation, we may be brought to a definite sense of the quality of failure. But complete success merges with half-success in everyday life, and they become difficult to disentangle. By appeal to the truth that in desperate circumstances no solution will be wholly satisfactory, we settle for a half-success, even for a near-failure, as at least better than disaster. We often acquiesce in not failing, rather than seeking success. The force of circumstances becomes the rationalization of having little. Because we are in dire straits, we must not expect too much. And so the deeper possibilities inherent in the situation slightly elude our grasp. The firm truth that one cannot always have what one wishes passes easily into that form of self-denial that makes one accept the failure of one's wishes to transform the world. Alternatively, too great an expectation of failure can make one unable to distinguish between wishes that have little or no possibility of realization and desires guided by plans that engender the possibility of their own realization.

When a person undertakes a plan, he seeks the realization of some end. He possesses a relatively firm sense not only of his own desires and intentions, but of a method for realizing what he wants. A mere wish can hover, unattached to anything in concrete existence. A goal rests upon plans made and methods possessed. A purpose, then, looks ahead both to considered ends and available means.

However, ends are by no means given in completely determinate form prior to action. Like an artist, who may begin work on a canvas without a definite project in mind, but whose initial brushstrokes exert their own constraints upon the goals implicit in the finished work even to the point of transforming them, so an agent seeks the realization of goals only partly defined as he first undertakes action. In part this is because circumstances elude us and the future remains perilous transcending our controls. More fundamental still, however, is the critical point that our own actions transform us, changing also the conditions of evaluation. In this sense, it is impossible to know in advance what is valuable and thereafter act merely to bring it to pass. The human self is never completely realized at any finite moment or in any finite circumstances. It is virtually inexhaustible in its varied relations, and comes to stand in ever-new relations to its surroundings. It follows that active judgments can only seek the creation of values rather than preconceived and antecedently known conditions of existence.

We search for value in the *world*, it is true, but also and importantly within ourselves. The search is for what *we* truly want, what aspects of the world lie at the heart of our being. The temptations that surround us are varied, and each of them can lead us away from what we most profoundly require. To this extent, I am in complete agreement with the Greek conception of the Good, as what is truly beneficial rather than merely seeming so. I object only to the belief that the Good lies in some intelligible sense external to the soul of each man, and that it is single and unified for all men or even any individual. Rather, insofar as the range of human relations continually stretches into the world through a man's wishes, desires, and imagination, then what is good is constantly undergoing modification. The shifting focus of every person redefines his needs, and transforms what is good for him, adjusting over time and to varying circumstances and conditions. As much as a man may endeavor to capture what is good for himself, and thereafter remake himself in accordance with his model, he may discover only its uselessness to him. It is our misfortune that other men are so much like us that we expect them to share our deepest commitments, when they differ just enough to make that impossible. Siddartha tells Govinda that the pathway to Nirvana must be discovered by each man for himself—for there is no Nirvana but that which is created for each man by his coming to terms with himself. The self that is here realized is not an older one, finally understood or accepted. It is a new self, built out of the old, yet transformed in the very process of evaluation. We seek, in evaluation, for nothing but ourselves, our "true" selves if you will. But our quest can be realized only in an act of self-creation.

B. Self-Realization

The search is for a way to *create* value. It is not for what is valuable timelessly. Goods must be brought into existence—if they existed, no quest would begin. When a man discovers that what is good is common in his experience, he comes to realize not an old value, but a new one; he has changed so that what *was* not valuable has *now* become good. The prodigal son, who travels the world but finds peace and goodness at home where he left them, perceives them with a different gaze upon his return. His experiences throughout his journey have transformed him. If values are antecedent to their creation, it is only as possibilities resident in conditions. Gold at the bottom of the sea is not a good until unearthed. At best, it is the possibility of value that inheres in the remoteness of the deep. The development of techniques to unearth the gold and bring it to light may so transform life that gold no longer may possess the magical quality of instant wealth.

If Being-in-itself is never good or bad, as Sartre claims, it is because values can be created only within contexts of human goals and desires. Natural events possess goodness or evil only in an order of human functioning. The destruction of a village is most likely evil; a moist and warm summer in farm country is probably beneficial. The qualifications "most likely," and "probably" reveal how values depend on persons. The probable values can be realized only in human terms. The landslide that destroyed the village may encourage men to build a more rational and worthwhile place to live. The summer may bring uncontrolled and violent passions if it is overwhelmingly hot. It is not that values are always created *by* human agency, and certainly not by human agency alone. The point is that human beings are necessarily involved in the relations that constitute a value. Every new value involves a change in a man's experience, sometimes of a most profound character. A man who has spent his life on a farm, who is displaced by lack of work, may move to the city and discover a new home and life. In order to find the city good, he must change in his relations to what he does and how he lives. Goodness here is a harmony between a man's feelings and his surroundings.

In the *Republic*, Plato describes just such a harmony in the life of a just man. Within his soul, various constituents are well ordered and harmoniously related. Reason provides direction and control to the appetites, and defines the kinds of satisfaction which are appropriate. But as Plato points out, a just man will not be found in an unjust society, for temptations not controlled by reason are overwhelming. Perhaps the peace of mind inherent in a just soul makes a just life superior to an unjust one even in an unjust society. But that is a purely theoretical notion. For reason to rule within the soul, it must rule in society as well. It is the harmonious relationship between external conditions and the internal order of the soul that makes fulfillment possible. By the proper education—a social function—a man comes to understand what his highest capacities are. When his surroundings are structured so as to permit him to realize these capacities, and encourage only such fulfillments, then we have both a just society and a just man, and internal satisfaction as well. It is when a man stands in a harmonious union of "internal" and "external" elements that he finds what is good. Where the subjective and objective conditions of life meet, there is value.

The theoretical conception of a division within human experience, which must be overcome in the creation of value, is fraught with danger. By dividing the inner soul of a man from his external environment, Plato makes it possible for others to claim that there is no intrinsic connection between inner and outer forms of justice—a claim based on a division between private and public morality. It takes considerable analysis for Plato then to show that the order within a just soul is rooted in social conditions. The appetites must be satisfied in a manner appropriate to them. Only knowledge can provide the means for satisfaction. And it is the same knowledge which stabilizes the social order. A conflict between individual and society is to Plato a consequence of irrationality within either social planning or the appetites of individuals. It is knowledge that bridges the chasm between "inner" and "outer" experience.

Unfortunately, it is precisely the epistemology of Plato's *Republic* that is most questionable, at least so far as the Good is concerned. Plato himself points out that a social order founded on reason is in precarious balance. The concrete decisions necessary to a well-run society demand not only a knowledge somewhat different from philosophy, but a detailed knowledge impossible for any government or person to have. Plato's epistemology depends on a knowledge of what is good prior to its concrete realization. Ironically, Plato's union of rationality in inner and outer experience makes clear that the philosopher-king will be knowledgeable only to the extent that his society is rational and just. But Plato nevertheless supposes that philosophical knowledge is of an antecedent reality. The foundation for action can be determinably reflected prior to undertaking it. This presupposition permeates virtually all moral thought since Plato.

A harmony between inner and outer experience should not be too casually dismissed. The most prosperous environmental conditions can provide little value to a man divided within himself; while a merciless environment can destroy even a saintly and peaceful man. A wide range of harmonious relations seems possible, and that is of profound importance for any theory of value. But the disharmony of experience renders most prescriptions for fulfillment useless.

The most misleading aspect of the discussion so far, however, is the distinction between *inner* and *outer* experience—the very distinction that permits us to speak of the restoration of harmony within experience. Informally, we distinguish easily between physical objects and our feelings about them. Our imagination and the world of science are rarely confused. However, in rigorous contexts of analysis the modes of experience are inextricably related. Our imagination is never free from the influence of objects we have encountered; our feelings have behavioral aspects. Rigorous analysis breaks down the sharp line between internal and external experience—though we must hope not so far as to destroy the point of the distinction entirely.

Worst of all is the implicit conception of a human being—and of any other being as well—as sufficiently determinate to have "inner" and "outer" experiences in a univocal sense. Not only does the distinction between inner and outer experience blur in that each involves the other, but it is a distinction which implicitly addresses the person in a particular respect or situation. The notion of a harmony within the soul, even expanded to include a harmony among one's actions and environing circumstances, suggests quite a univocal and one-dimensional conception of a person. The fact is, however, that men act differently in different circumstances, and are also perceived differently by others in differing circumstances. Are *all* a man's actions to be brought into a unified order? Are *all* his effects on others to be brought into a consistent pattern? It would be remarkable were it so. All our experience speaks against it. The unexpected event, confrontation, or encounter enters nearly all experience. Every man is an alien within some situations, alien in that his actions, his feelings, and the reactions of other men to him jar violently with his "normal" qualities.

On the one hand, diverse facets of an individual's experience are seldom entirely unrelated, but influence each other through their effects upon his character as an agent. On the other hand, the functioning of the person within differing situations leads us not to a coherent and all-embracing self, but—as the literature of the social science reveals—to a sense of *role-playing* wherein the salient elements of an individual's experience vary considerably within different situations. The obvious conclusion relates to variety within one man's experience rather than to the consistency of a single unified person throughout. Varied conditions produce varied responses. All of us experience at different times a sense of being divided against ourselves, reaching extreme proportions in pathological circumstances or where moral conflicts become nearly unbearable.

A human being is at least a physical object who acts upon and is influenced by other physical objects. Often these influences are indirect, even hidden. Events of the remote past may dominate the present, making it impossible to define temporal limits to experience. And the ways in which a man influences the physical world, as well as the events that affect him significantly, are also of indefinite spatial range. Techniques for traveling to the moon may make the deepest recesses of our own planet technologically available. Our radio signals may travel the remotest stretches of space, and awaken unimaginable possibilities in the recesses of the universe. The most confined acts may have the widest ramifications. That is what makes our decisions so precarious, and fills human life with anguish. There is no way to confine the actions of a person to a well-defined region of time and space. A human action draws its conditions from the past and from remote circumstances, while its consequences also have impacts of great range. The narrow situations in which we perceive ourselves to act open into other situations, nearly without limit. Failure is an ever-present prospect because an action defined and grounded within perceived circumstances belongs also to other and very different situations and contexts.

The moral dimension of life depends upon and reveals the indefinite scope of the person. Our most restricted actions may have the widest and least controlled consequences which reflect on our culpability and reveal our failures. From a gross point of view, nothing is intrinsically devoid of moral significance, wholly outside a man's sphere of concern. Distance cannot free an event from moral considerations. My country at war on the other side of the world is something I must face in my actions and decisions. Every death forms part of the sphere of considerations in which I live. At least implicitly, I seek what is good in the shadow of prospects and conditions of indefinite range. The most remote events can burst into my life. Neither distance nor magnitude can make an event morally irrelevant. It follows that the control of events sought in action may be *discovered* to be gained in restricted conditions, but the burden falls upon the agent to justify his limited attention. Successful action generates the imperative to consider whatever might bring us to failure, wherever it might be; and our surroundings are so interconnected that peril is everywhere.

Furthermore, the obligations of a moral agent always stand in a context of aims and standards that impose countless other obligations upon him. Anything can compel a man to respond to it. There are injustices everywhere; evil confronts us at every turn. What seems devoid of moral significance may be the source of important values. A moral agent, if he is to act, must choose *among* his obligations, and he may escape from any of them only by maintaining the superiority of others. A woman who considers an abortion has obligations to her unborn child, to her parents, to the father, even to the society into which she may bring an unwanted child. What she ought to do is never an isolated obligation, but stands in a context of mutually conflicting obligations of indefinite range.

The moral dimension of the human self has no boundaries. In saying this, we note two ontological, not moral, conditions: Every situation is open-ended, interacting with many other situations and domains. In addition, these situations comprise no systematic order, whether of many exclusive domains without overlap or a unified world-order. The contexts for action even within one man's experience—and certainly for mankind collectively—are more a multiplicity of interactions than an all-embracing system, yet a multiplicity which has no permanent and unbridgeable boundaries.

It should not be concluded that a person must consider everything in making his moral choices. That is quite impossible. Nevertheless, at best there may be a strong likelihood that a given event is irrelevant to a man's responsibilities and values. Past events provide the background upon which he must rely for his decisions. Remote events may influence him or form a context of rejection. A man acts as he does only with the implicit affirmation that nothing else is more important. Yet innocuous events sometimes have momentous consequences. An important function of moral principles is to serve as guides to our attention, in indicating directions for our efforts. We are vulnerable before the press of events, which may break upon us unforeseen. Therefore, we must formulate principles that embody the wisdom to guide action. Because principles will fall short of particular exigencies—which are constantly changing— evaluation cannot rely on principles alone. A continual movement is required in action, from narrower spheres through broad principles to wider and more comprehensive values. Principles move from established conditions to the perils of the new and uncharted.

The unbounded scope of evaluation corresponds in a loose way to the unbounded nature of scientific laws and theories, which seek to encompass all time and space in their purview, as evaluations seek to cover all relevant considerations in judgment as to what is to be done—though, it should be noted, no known scientific theory embraces all events, large and small, organic and inorganic. However, in science it is the *theory* that is of critical importance; in morals, it is a particular person and his particular actions. Science seeks facts, and manipulates events to gather information. Action looks to the events themselves; principles are at best means of control. We may disconfirm a scientific theory without prejudice to the scientist who proposed it. But our condemnation of a man's deed includes him within it. A person is at stake in action as he is not in science. Every failure is a failure to *him*—and failure may come from any source. A success too resides *elsewhere*—in given conditions reaching back into the past, to possibilities unknown but available, to the remote future to which the tests of action look. To circumscribe moral issues is to open oneself to the attack that he has overlooked something more important.

Anguish is the consequence of the unrestricted conditions of action. If the human self were enclosed in a finite space and time, then assurance would be possible that one had taken into account everything relevant. But the multiple and indefinite possibilities for every person to realize himself in action bring forth the awareness that nothing can bring security. Though success in action requires unity and control, the human person is fundamentally a multiplicity, complex and usually divided within himself. Man is caught up in anguish as the consciousness of his inadequacy before an indefinite range of possibilities. Sartre conceives of anguish as the consciousness of freedom. I find anguish more significantly to be the consciousness of one's own incapacity in too complex and varied a world. However, I agree that anguish is the consciousness that man can never be secure. No man is God, but he *ought* to be. That is Ivan's cry in *The Brothers Karamazov*: If I were God, then I would not allow so much evil in the world! In reply, however, we may note only that God would have to be quite remarkable to make of the welter of events a coherent order.

Anguish is the awareness of inherent limitations, of the impossibility of finding security within the human condition. There is no hiding place, either in denying one's responsibilities or in repudiating one's being-in-the-world. Mann shows beautifully in *Dr. Faustus* the sickness of soul that enables a man to face his past with moral neutrality. We are called upon continually to respond to the past as well as to the present. We may deny the call only in the context of a greater obligation. The diffuseness and range of our capabilities make every judgment treacherous, and force us to live in anguish. Our desire to circumscribe our world to make it safer is frustrated by both our ideals and the condemnation of others.

If there is a rational solution, it must lie in the realization that anguish is generic to the moral life, and in the mustering of resources to minimize the prospect of failure. The solution to anguish is based on an acceptance of the precariousness of value, with the will to render it a bit less precarious. Through technology, we improve our tools for the betterment of human life, we build networks of communication to learn more quickly of distant events that may influence us—though the same system of communication also increases the likelihood of our being affected by such events. We strengthen our powers, and improve our abilities to control events. This is the constructive acceptance of anguish—the acceptance of our indefinite obligations by strengthening our abilities to meet them.

Yet technological advancement is not enough. The race for power, even over nature, is destined never to be won. Nature receives our contributions and turns them back upon us. Even more important, our inventions and discoveries change the world in which we must act, and what sufficed for the past and for some conditions will no longer do. If we can succeed in action only by becoming powerful enough to avoid all the unexpected, we may spare ourselves the attempt. Control over natural events is vital to action. But the consciousness of anguish is a consciousness of possibilities, and no empirical information about the world can eliminate the prospect of failure. We live with the omnipresence of failure no matter how we struggle to avoid it. The prospect of failure resides within the very condition of all being—not human life alone—of having indefinite boundaries, being open-ended, belonging to many interconnected and overlapping systems, not an all-embracing world order.

It is necessary to bound our failures from the other side. Control of events is vital, but never sufficient. We must also control *ourselves*, if on occasion only by controlling events. Our goals are at stake in our actions with the stubbornness of existence. Only by bringing events into harmony with our aspirations can we reach success. What is created in evaluation is a local harmony between one's idealized and one's practical self. It is this harmony which makes it possible for a man to live with what he does, even through the censure and disapproval of others. It comes about through a creation of *oneself*, the determination of a continuous order through many of the important situations of one's life.

There are countless ways in which a person can fail in his actions. But they fall into two general kinds—a failure to control events so as to bring them into accord with one's purposes; and a failure due to desires that allow no satisfaction. The first failing can promote self-righteousness in defense. If a man has little power over the events surrounding him, he may take refuge in the denial that events are controllable. His desires become sheer wishes; all he knows is the rightness of his aims and the obstinacy of a world that fails him. The second failure in its extreme form becomes insanity; a man may be so torn by internal tensions as to be unable to function.

If the extremes are distinguishable, nevertheless the two modes of failure fade into one another, for the alteration of a man's ideals and wants may bring them in line with his knowledge and capacities; while as he manipulates his environment and gains control over it, his wishes will be transformed by the satisfactions found worth while and the achievements which fade when realized. Too strong a dichotomy between the "internal" and "external" dimensions of a human self is a form of sickness. It is the primary mode of failure; the quest for value is for a means to create consistency and continuity among the various aspects of the person.

If objects gained or which resist us influence our development, while our aims define projects relative to our surroundings, it is theoretically naive to define a man apart from what surrounds him. His character and modes of action are given form by prevailing conditions, available possibilities, and projected goals; nevertheless, his actions leave their trace on his surroundings. Action may be thought of exclusively as manipulation, but agency entails reception: manipulation is assimilated by others and by the agent himself, while what he assimilates influences his actions. All of this suggests that failure is a disparity between projects of manipulation and their fruits for assimilation. The larger view of personality sketched here—of an agent both manipulative and assimilative—coordinates actions in comprehensive terms relative to the broad experiential conditions of a man as agent, rather than in terms of his proximate achievements alone.

The dimensions of a person should not be thought of as "subjective" and "objective." The sense of value as unity in a divided life is as old as Plato. But it is superficial to interpret the harmony between a just individual and a just society as a unity of subject and object. Reason in the soul is as objective as in the State. The respect of each class for the higher class is more subjective (as felt) than objective. No doubt a harmony between feelings and conditions is essential to value. But such a harmony may not itself be valuable. A woman who is sure that she needs a man "stronger than herself" may indeed find one—only to discover that his strength arouses her frustration and spite. We may save the view that we have here a gap between subjective and objective conditions only by saying that she did not know her *true* feelings. But since the only mark of those "true feelings" is the manifest discord, we are complicating the analysis unnecessarily.

It is not that a union among subjective and objective elements is unnecessary. Even in the simplest value, where something is felt to be good, there is a harmonization of feelings and resources. It is rather that not every such harmonization is valuable. A compulsive eater's desires are satisfied by the food he eats, if not by the danger to his health and his unattractive appearance. Everything liked is a union of resources and the pleasure of having them available. When we are criticized for mistaking a momentary satisfaction for a genuine good, it is in terms of a wider context of judgment. Medicine tastes bad; but in the larger context of a person's health, taking it is good. Ignoring one's friends and selfishly pursuing one's own wishes can be rewarding in a narrow context— though selfishness can be harmful in the long run to the agent himself. The Platonic insight is that evaluation involves a movement from a narrower to a wider context—though Plato was limited in restricting the wider context to the civil society. Such a restriction tends to make foreign policy as shortsighted in its goals as is personal self-interest. A wider context permits a larger sphere of judgment.

Evaluation moves to the limits of the person as judge and broaches them. Experience is constantly shifting and expanding, new problems and relations arising to be manipulated and assimilated. Control can be provided only *methodically*, methods which permit rational choice from available alternatives. Yet methods of action are fallible. The multiplicity of spheres of action makes failure a likely prospect. Therefore, such a method must be designed to provide evaluations in ever-expanding contexts, though never within an all-encompassing context. The discovery that something is valuable—rather than merely a candidate for value—is that *on the whole* one can find no better. It completes some sphere of relations for the agent, though at best a relatively wide sphere of action.

Suppose a man, married and with children, spends his working days in routine drudgery. Let us suppose he wakes up one day, looks back at his empty life, and wonders how he could have become so deadened. His wonder may become a quest for value. But what is there to discover? Consider three likely possibilities: of finding a more rewarding occupation; of continuing his dull work out of obligation to his family; or of abandoning them for more enjoyable activities. In each case, if we assume that he finds what is valuable to him, he discovers what he "really" wants, what kind of person he really is, and at the same time *becomes* that person—at least within the range of situations he thereafter encounters. His discovery is a change in his character—in how he views himself, in what he does, and in how he feels about his actions. His discovery of what he values is also a discovery of himself—one he could not make without changing in some important ways. A man who discerns no problem in a situation does not evaluate it—not, that is, in the sense of endowing it with value. He simply acts. He is what he is, and acts accordingly. Evaluation is the bringing of value into situations that have gone awry, in which value resides problematically.

Thus, the anguish of Agamemnon in *Iphigenia in Aulis* is genuine because he does not know what is right. And he never really discovers it. He remains torn and divided. But Iphigenia herself comes to the realization that her life can be fittingly completed in sacrifice to the glory of the Argonauts, and goes willingly to her death. So also, Antigone dies willingly—she knows that she *must* bury her brother, come what may. Creon, subtle in his understanding of what is at stake, nevertheless comes to discover his failure. A value must be relatively enduring. A momentary satisfaction is a passing fancy, unless it endures to govern subsequent events.

The self determined in the creation of value must be armed against failure from two sides. Adequate knowledge of circumstances and prospects is necessary to protect against unforeseen developments. And consistency in one's wants and needs is necessary if they are not to conflict. The agent's goals and means must be so interconnected that time will not tear them asunder. Single-mindedness helps, for it forestalls the possibility of conflict. Yet it can also hide fear—and it will then bring disaster. Self-knowledge is at the heart of evaluation.

It is well known that self-knowledge of a purely descriptive nature may not provide values. A neurotic person, divided in his feelings about himself, may be dissatisfied with all his prospects. One of the obvious lessons of psychoanalysis is that a patient may be articulate about many of his deepest feelings and modes of behavior, yet unable either to accept them or to change them.

It is also well known that under special circumstances, a person may undergo a profound transformation. Dmitri Karamazov gains personal salvation in realizing his excesses, a transformation caused perhaps by fulfillment of his love for Grushenka. Although it is generally true that human beings change little in the course of their lives, there are significant exceptions to this rule.

Such considerations point to the inadequacy of knowledge *about* oneself in value judgment. The knowledge of the patterns of one's behavior does not in itself afford the change in one's person that is essential to the creation of value, to the discovery of what one *must* do in order to fulfill oneself. This is partly because a man may not change as a result of what he knows; and partly because he may change so completely as to nullify much of what he has been and done, when he discovers what has become valuable to him. In realizing what he deeply wishes, he may have to cast off much of his past behavior as false or mistaken.

We must distinguish, then, between a self-knowledge which is the intelligible ordering of one's life in an explanatory sense, and ceasing to be divided against oneself by undergoing a radical transformation resulting in a continuity within one's experience. The knowledge provided by psychoanalysis is of the former sort; and a patient may "understand" the past events of his life in terms of his earliest childhood experiences without being able to change his actions in any significant way. On the other hand, a man who has tried the lowest forms of degradation may awaken to the realization that he can no longer continue. He comes to a relatively coherent sense of himself that directs his purposes and actions.

The two modes of self-realization here have different temporal directions. Knowledge *about* oneself is always oriented to the past. One knows what one has done and felt and why. The consistency that is the mark of evaluation, however, is oriented to the future. One knows what one can best live with. Here the explanation of an action is predicated on one's sense of oneself in the future. This is less a prediction than a project of becoming what one expects and wills oneself to be.

Obviously we can never know the future with certainty, due both to the peril of the future and the inherent multiplicity of existence. The risk of failure is always present in human life, and the search for value unceasing. We struggle to attain a sense of how we must live—but such a realization depends on what we have lived through. The precarious future brings the risk of changing circumstances. Without an awareness of that precariousness, we act blindly and with insufficient concern for the prospect of failure. Insofar as we do not face the prospect of failure and take precautions against it, we risk that failure all the more. We must bring our knowledge of the past into new contexts if we are to protect ourselves against failure. But nothing will guarantee success.

What is to be discussed in the next few chapters is that the ordering of self that maximizes the possibility of success, and which marks value discovered, is the result of the application of rational methods of judgment and action.

C. Methodic Evaluation

In his attempts to determine something valuable, a person seeks to bring a new order into his experience, one that maximizes prospects of satisfaction and minimizes the likelihood of failure. The disorder that prompts the search for value marks satisfaction to be unlikely and failure probable; evaluation is then the *creation* of something new and valuable. The agent does not know what to do because of the unsatisfactory nature of the choices before him and the conflicting tendencies within him. If he is to find what is genuinely valuable, he must change the character of the choices facing him. Action looks to a successful future realized through methodic control. When circumstances prohibit any but unsatisfactory choices, or where disorder prevails throughout the conflicting desires of the agent, then no relief is possible. We act with the realization that none of the alternatives is completely valuable—but we must act. At best we may maximize the prospects of a partial success, satisfied that nothing worse will come to pass. Principles defining acceptable partial satisfactions are essential in such cases.

What is required is the development of methods in action which minimize the probability of failure. No other sense of the search for value is plausible but the quest for what makes failure least likely, though always a prospect. No rules for action can eliminate the possibility, and in some situations, the *probability* of failure. No action can guarantee the accomplishment of a task, nor that it will be found satisfactory if accomplished.

It is this last point that gives to evaluation its particular character, and requires methodic judgment. Caprice cannot be relied on in the struggle to realize future goals. Only rational methods which lead to plans of action based on available information as well as methods of criticism directed toward the expected results of action can provide a foundation for deliberate action. To rely on unfounded or "obvious" presuppositions is to weaken the justification for actions one undertakes, and increases the likelihood of failure. The history of mankind reveals a wealth of principles that were accepted on scant evidence, principles which subsequently had to be rejected for the errors they promoted. Where such presuppositions were fruitful, as often they were, it was because of the range of conditions they fitted, not because of the demands of pure reason. By borrowing alleged *a priori* principles from common sense, one ensures that such principles will have at least partial truth.

Science reveals the hypothetical nature of principles to be beyond question. The most thoroughly confirmed laws of science are qualified by the discoveries made with their help. Once Euclidean geometry became tentative in the light of the discoveries that led to the theory of relativity, nothing in science could be considered beyond question. Once the apodeictic certainty of science was abandoned, and with it the Kantian conception of the categories of the understanding, science could only be viewed as a systematic endeavor to maximize reliable explanation. Science is a continual give and take of theoretical systematization based on available evidence, the criticism of the system by the collection of further evidence, and the modification of the system under the pressure of that criticism.

But science is not alone subject to the alternation of critical perspectives. Even in art, a painter may seek to produce a work of art in terms of a vision or preconception. But seldom will that vision remain intact throughout his endeavors. He must also adopt the role of critic, not only to judge whether he has adequately fulfilled the task he set for himself, but also to judge the task itself in terms of its realization in the work of art. Moreover, the artist is not the sole nor even the most important critic of his own work. The critical function, especially in an extended sense of possibilities realized through a work, rather than addressed solely to whether the work is good or bad, is central to any conception of art. It is in possibilities unleashed that a work of art is realized, and they reside in part within the interpretations given by its audiences.

Action too, insofar as it is the determination of something valuable, requires a critical response. The value created must be submitted to the exigencies of circumstance in order to be proved a value. Accident can undermine expectations relative to any project or event. The impact of conditions from wider spheres of action continually produces unexpected results. Evaluation can be but a partial methodic control of possibilities: unexpected elements can nullify any course of action. Insofar as we seek principles of action, we must consider the event that may abort our desired goals. Here is the imperative in action driving us always toward wider and more comprehensive orders of control.

Method in action is devoted to maximizing the likelihood of success and minimizing the probability of failure. Success and failure will require separate analyses, for important issues are at stake in their conception. But such an analysis must follow a discussion of active methods, since the latter become definitive of their own goals. All self-critical methods define their goals by casting prior commitments into question and by expanding their locus of control. The historical development of such methods is thus central and essential to the avoidance of vicious circularity. Here I shall offer a preliminary account of the notion of failure, to gain entry to the notion of methods of evaluation in action.

Our starting-point is that of an adult human being with conflicting needs and limited resources. Let us take as an example a college teacher with a comfortable income who is offered the opportunity to run for mayor of the city in which he lives. He may desire the higher salary as an opportunity to buy some of the luxuries he has wanted for years. Perhaps his wife has had to work, and he would like to free her from the need to continue. He may welcome the opportunity to put his histrionic gifts to work. He may also have a program whose institution he is convinced would benefit his city. He seeks the decision that will be most valuable. Let us first suppose that the only consideration facing him is what would gratify him most. A failure would be the discovery that his actions produced consequences that did not suit him, did not give him what he really wants. On this simple level of analysis, he has failed when he comes to feel *regret* for what he has done, or when he feels that he has been corrupted or degraded. On this simple level, however, we note that the opportunities available to him must be balanced against resulting costs. However laudatory his motives, his desire for a higher salary must be offset by consideration of the disadvantages of the office of mayor. He may genuinely appreciate privacy with his family, a privacy which is not permitted an elected official. His goals may be compromised by harsh political realities in ways he may not be able to endure. In order to make a decision, he must have a rather clear conception of his own priorities—a hierarchy of his own wishes and satisfactions. If he has no definite conception of what he prefers, he will be paralyzed by a complex choice, or reach it on an arbitrary and perilous basis.

In order to make a valid decision, however, he must possess more than a sense of his hierarchy of preferences: he must possess knowledge of his "true" preferences. He may be quite sure that he would be deeply satisfied by so public a life as that of mayor; yet he may discover to his dismay that he did not know how much he preferred to have quiet times with his family. A musician who wonders if he would like to be a concert artist must consider not only his abilities and love of music, as well as the actual life of a traveling performer. He must endeavor to know whether this life is what he really wants. He must consider the alternatives before him in their various ramifications. He must even consider prospects for the distant future. If the character of his city changes radically, the mayor will have problems to cope with that he may be unequipped to handle. The substance of the arguments Plato gives to show that a just man is a happy man depend upon the claim that anyone who could become just in the society he describes would indeed find that state more satisfactory than any other. All arguments concerning value implicitly make this kind of claim—that among available alternatives, one chooses what *would be* preferred, if one could try the alternatives and see. Plato's claim that every man seeks the good for himself, and that he chooses evil only in error, makes sense only if a comparison can be made among alternatives. Thrasymachus claims that the despot's life is the happiest. Plato's reply, by reference to the myth of Er, is that souls who have tried both would always prefer the life of a just man. The sad truth, however, is that we can seldom directly compare global alternatives of action. We can only surmise possible results, and test them in specific spheres of experience.

The issues at stake in even our simplified example are quite complex, and we require further simplification. A moral agent in his evaluations reaches a judgment about what he will find satisfactory in the future and what he will regret. So much is involved that it is difficult to understand how anyone could evaluate a real situation. Textbook cases are simplified as real choices are complicated. Yet every attempt to circumscribe with assurance a domain of relevance is unjustified, for rather remote events may affect one's life in vital ways. Legal and economic practices in other cities may significantly change the population of the mayor's city. International tensions may lead to radical changes in the distribution of tax revenues. Even so trivial a matter as sanitary practices in a distant country could lead to the spread of disease that would vitally affect the course of a government official's life.

The simplifications that allow men to make moral decisions are the principles of action which define the context within which value judgments are to be made. General principles about human behavior and the possibilities of corruption, moral principles of acceptable conduct, and causal laws which allow the forecasting of likely prospects, all are implicitly introduced in any decision. The agent must seek to ascertain his own tendencies and desires, if he is to have any probability of success. And since no one can be expected to know the details of any particular situation to the degree required, he must appeal to principles that over the years have proved themselves to be reliable in promoting valuable courses of action. Unfortunately, a moral agent must also bear in mind that such principles are only *reliable*—they guarantee nothing—and that his particular circumstances may require treating himself as an exception to the general rule. General principles in no way alleviate anguish. They only permit us to make the dangerous decisions we must.

Two unavoidable complications arise in every value judgment beyond the ones mentioned. The first is that although failure has been defined in terms of the agent's feelings alone, he never acts merely for himself, but is always engaged with others and must consider them in his actions. The second is more difficult to analyze, yet it is central—that a moral agent does not remain constant in his character, but changes under the force of circumstances and the impact of his own actions and judgments. This is why an agent cannot simply find value in things, but must create or determine it through changes in his own person.

Considering other people and their responses to our actions is the major step in the transition to moral evaluation. Let us first elaborate upon the character of decisions isolated from a concern for others. Clearly a wise decision must incorporate judgments as to the relative priority and importance of the various needs and wants of the agent. The question addressed is that of personal benefit; by the proper circumscription of the concerns dealt with an agent can seek his personal goals. He seeks to ascertain what will satisfy him over a period of time. Probably his major effort must be devoted to whether certain short-lived and intense pleasures will live in his memory forcefully enough to endow later periods of ennui or displeasure with enough vitality to outweigh the alternative choice of milder but longer-lived gratifications. John Stuart Mill took for granted that if most men had a free and open choice, they would prefer the "highest" pleasures because of their special qualities and endurance. When a man asks here "what will truly give me pleasure?" then we suppose that he can apply some method for determining a satisfactory answer to the question posed.

Even in so artificially limited a context as this, where one's relations to others are intentionally ignored, evaluation is extremely complex. Rather precise self-knowledge is presupposed in being able to set aside rather intense desires as not beneficial in the long run. The force of a present desire can not only make denying it very painful, but distorts one's beliefs about what is truly important. Tobacco smokers are fond of claiming that a shorter life of pleasure is worth far more than a longer life without the joy of smoking. Perhaps some of them have genuinely faced the prospect of lung cancer, and believe the risk worth incurring even when they come to the direct prospect of an early and painful death. But too many such decisions are made from willful ignorance, and the onset of cancer becomes not an unpleasantness to live through, but the mark of failure. If regret is the mark of a man's discovery that his expectations about himself have not been fulfilled, then regret is a sign of failure. It is not the only sign of such failure, though it is the only one whose impact upon an agent is so compelling as to require reaction.

Even in so clear a case as this, our understanding of failure must be tempered with the realization that a man may come to regret a course of action by assuming the success of an alternative course, without having tried it. Perhaps he would have regretted having lived a long but nervous life. The pervasive effect of the minor envy that makes one prefer what others have to his own, simply because he has not tried it, can generate regret without regard to the relative merits of the proposed alternatives. Such matters must be considered deeply. Here let me only point out that a nonsmoker is far less likely to regret not having smoked than a smoker is to regret smoking when he becomes ill from it. Insofar as we look forward to how we will feel in the future about a decision, the less risky alternatives are far more justifiable. All we can do is minimize the likelihood of regret; nothing can guarantee security and success. When we give advice to a young man to finish his education before undertaking rash action, it is to strengthen his power to deal with future events, and to increase the probability that he will be able to act successfully. Sometimes such advice is misguided, especially for the person addressed. The fate of all general principles of action is to fail in particular instances. Yet not to be loyal to general principles is to be blind to the truth they embody.

The knowledge about oneself and the world required for evaluation in such simple cases, even coupled with the ability to follow the decisions one has made, only touch the surface of most active judgments. We come now to the complexities which other people introduce into action. All but the most trivial decisions involve other people beside oneself, and in at least two ways. Most obviously, our actions affect others, particularly those close to us, and influence their future. A man who undertakes a course of action he knows could mean his death must consider how that would affect his wife, children, and parents. A man may invest heavily in insurance on his life, yet smoke cigarettes unceasingly and be the cause of his early death. The obligations we undertake toward others are often of greater importance in determining our subsequent choices than are our more private decisions. Insofar as men inhabit social orders, their evaluations must take not only their own needs and desires into account, but those of others as well. The deepest self-knowledge cannot help a man to act rightly if he is blind and insensitive to other people. Our knowledge of others may be thought but a part of the knowledge of circumstances required for intelligent evaluation. But it is knowledge of a particularly delicate quality, for it is no less difficult to come by than knowledge of ourselves. Psychoanalysis has shown quite clearly that self-knowledge is often the most difficult to obtain, precisely because it is so personal and threatening.

Adequate response to the needs of others depends on a delicate and subtle sensitivity to them. To evaluate a situation in which others are involved requires an intense awareness of how they will respond to what we do. The husband who undertakes actions without considering his wife's needs—or based on erroneous conceptions of those needs if he does consider them—may find his plans nullified. *The Doll's House*, dated as it may be in many respects, nevertheless captures the complacency inherent in an assured willingness of a man to make judgments concerning his spouse's needs. If the problem of other minds has any but esoteric philosophic interest, it is because we are never quite able to assure ourselves of the desires of others, not even to the limited extent we know our own.

We ask others, then, to make their wishes known. Unfortunately, they often do not know themselves what they really want, and cannot tell us. So our sensitivity and openness to them is essential if they are important to us and we care for them. The life of each human being is caught up with the lives of some if not many others. When we discover, however inadvertently we may have acted, that we have injured those we love, we are hurt ourselves. It is easy to fail in satisfying our own deepest needs. It is far easier to fail to consider the needs of others.

In urging that others tell us of their requirements, we seek to protect ourselves against the risks of our own ignorant actions. If other people tell us what they desire, then we may be able to satisfy them. If they do not tell us, then we may deny our responsibility to them. The irony of such attempts to circumscribe our responsibilities is unmistakable. If those we love do not know their requirements, they cannot tell us. And when they come to realize them, they will act on them whether we have ignored them from malice or not. We seek to discover the needs of others' who are important to us so that we will not fail to consider them when we act, and so that we are protected against their dissatisfaction. But nothing can assure us of success and guard us against the possibility of failure.

The requirement that we know the needs and desires of others can be satisfied in many ways. General principles of psychology, which indicate the probable responses of human beings under various circumstances, are essential to evaluation. Intimacy provides even more reliable insights into the behavior of others—a fact which makes it improbable that the family will be replaced entirely by more casual relationships. Unless the frequency of short liaisons is accompanied by a disregard for the feelings of others, an unprecedented selfishness, men will need the assurance of expectation that only intimate contact over long periods of time can provide.

We can also learn of the expectations of others from them; and this brings us to the second general way in which our lives are entwined with the lives of others. One of the most obvious aspects of social relations turns on the reactions of other men to what we do—in particular, in their approval or disapproval of our actions. We may fail not only in satisfying our own personal needs and the needs of those we love, but we may undertake actions that infringe on others, which inconvenience them, or that they consider wrong. Our decisions and actions, once undertaken, enter a public world, in which they are judged by other men and their defects brought home to their progenitors.

The norms of society, and the censure of others, are essential to any context of action. Without them, evaluation would be without social relevance, or at most with that relevance defined by the consideration of those we love. It is in the unavoidable presence of others that a transition is made from self-interest to morality. Until others make their presence felt as vitally as we feel our own, so that we must consider their wishes in considering our own, we have a context of evaluation which is not yet a moral one. Norms of conduct and the will of other men as manifested in sanctions, censure, and approval compel an individual to consider himself part of a social order even where he would repudiate it. We are compelled by others to consider them. If an individual were both invulnerable to others and completely unconcerned about their wishes, then he might be amoral in his value judgments. But he would not be human. He would be a god or a demon. The essential point here is that active judgments, which look to the control of future satisfactions, depend on the facts of human life.

If the knowledge necessary to evaluation has not yet been proved prohibitive to any assurance of success, we may turn to the second complication in action. Not only must one assure himself as well as he can of information relevant to the judgments he seeks to make—information about himself, other men, and the environment—but he must cope as well with the fact that the actions he will undertake will change the situation in which he stands. It will change the environment, it may deeply affect others, and it is virtually certain to change him also.

Indeed, the more satisfactory a determination of value, the more significantly is the agent transformed by his own actions. He undertook deliberation in doubt, because a conflict or disorder presented itself to him. A resolution of the situation entails a relief from conflict, a sense of doing what he must—though he could not quite tell what he had to do before. What he comes to realize is a discovery about himself, the course of action that most thoroughly fulfills him. That fulfillment is a transformation in his way of viewing himself and his circumstances. Such a transformation in a man's conception of himself alters quite markedly how he will act in the future.

A person who goes to college does not know what it will do to him. Perhaps he will be changed very little; he may change a great deal. Many women who return to school after having borne two or three children find the possibilities in their education of a new life, capacities they never knew they had—for in any but the most rudimentary sense, *they did not have them.* Important activities, like psychotherapy, can provide significant transformations in the lives of those who undertake them. Of course, as in psychotherapy, rational agents seek to direct such changes. But self-transformation, once begun, has its own momentum and requirements. A woman who is willing to enter psychotherapy to explore her own sexual unresponsiveness may find that her discoveries compel her to abandon her marriage and husband. Since she cannot know what she will become, and will become that only after she has undertaken action, she can never quite foretell what she will find valuable. She must live it through to determine it. It is this precariousness in human life that makes anguish so unavoidable.

It does not require so esoteric an enterprise as psychotherapy to make vital changes in a person's life. Education, military service, extreme remorse, or even a love affair can bring marked changes in a man's life and understanding of what is important and what is not. A man who has fallen in love discovers something new and lovable in his beloved. If he had been asked for what he desired in a woman before he fell in love, he probably would have described characteristics quite different from those he would describe afterwards, even when no longer in love. Difficult and trying moral decisions are often transcendent in their effects on the lives of those who live through them. And it is precisely the most transcendent experiences, which change men most profoundly, which are advocated in theories of the good life.

Nearly all the great ways to happiness involve profound transformations to be undergone by him who seeks the way. Peace of mind is thought to come to a tormented soul only by a reformation within. He will find peace *afterward*. His problem is to find a way *to* that peace of mind. Heroes are often portrayed in literature as having always been heroes, which strains our credibility as much as it lifts our hearts. In Ugo Betti's *The Queen and the Rebels*, we find a deeper understanding, of how an ordinary woman can be transformed by the discovery that personal nobility and dignity are overarching values. Lear too comes to the awful discovery of his own arrogance, and it makes him a man too old and sad to live. Trivial events often act as catalysts; but no moral discovery is made which does not represent an important change in the agent, without which he could not have come to his discovery.

We may review some of the gross aspects of method in action. It begins with a question, often provoked by disunity and discord. Without these no methodic evaluation is called for. A man who knows what is good in advance of every situation, and who can determine it without self-examination or self-transformation, does not here determine value. He may have done so in the past. But he has become secure, set in his ways, even rather smug. For human life is such that complete assurance in action is nearly always irrational and indefensible. Only a closed-minded person can suppose he understands enough about human life and the world to act securely in all cases that arise.

Another way to put this is that the situations in which we find ourselves as moral agents pose questions to us which we must answer. And since we are generally not questioned where we know the answers, we must seek them. This is the beginning of the search for value. Where there are straightforward determinations of what is to be done, we have not really been tried. Moral judgment in earnest arises only in true tests of our character and responses.

Put a third way, in acting deliberately, we must resolve a conflict in which we find ourselves by appeal to some principle. We must either be assured of the outcome of a plan of action in its tangible benefits or in the moral qualities inherent in the situation before us. Yet we cannot be secure in either capacity. The situation in which we find ourselves is one that calls for evaluation—in the sense of determining what is valuable— only if specific conflicts inhabit our circumstances. We therefore cannot react automatically or unthinkingly. Every proposed solution to our difficulties brings some possibility of failure with it. Security is ruled out by the very circumstances that began the evaluative considerations.

If a man finds a wallet filled with money in the street, then insofar as he immediately and forthrightly returns it, he is not engaged in value judgment. He acts, but without concern for the range, endurance and intensity of values inherent in his actions. He creates no values, but preserves the ways of acting that served him well before. If there is no question about what he ought to do, then it is unnecessary to determine what is right, only whether he will do what he ought to do. When a set of rules is applied routinely in situations as they arise, then we do not evaluate our actions. We simply obey the rules. Any act may be regarded as a judgment relative to circumstances, and in terms of its control over future prospects and conditions. But not every such act is the result of methodic control arising from an awareness of conflicting alternatives.

It is only when genuine conflicts arise that we are compelled to determine methodically the competing values within that situation— though conflicts may arise everywhere, since there is always the prospect of failure. If the man above desperately needs the money he finds—if his children are ill and require medical aid he cannot afford—then he may (and must) consider whether the particular exigencies of his situation do not require him to depart from conventional norms of behavior. Only to the extent that conventional rules of action are cast into question can he methodically determine what is valuable relative to his circumstances. If he keeps the money, will he regret it? He may discover that the money was urgently needed by the person who lost it. Is his child's operation important enough to him to risk the possible consequences of his actions? Such matters are essential to evaluation.

I have supposed that a man might find himself in circumstances which are perfectly clear to him, and which raise no questions in his mind. I have made this assumption because it is common for men to ignore the complications which reside in the situations which they encounter. Yet I have argued also that to assume a given rule applies without question to any particular circumstances is willful ignorance and self-denial. Every situation asks of an agent whether the situation is one to which a given rule applies, or whether it is an exception. No set of circumstances can be so clearly of a given kind that an agent can without peril ignore other possibilities. The omnipresence of temptation reveals not only that every moral law can be broken by someone, but that every moral law may be questioned under appropriate circumstances. It is always proper to ask if it is not now time to deviate from a hitherto unbroken rule.

Questions of value are not abstract requests for the routine application of some standard, but emerge from situations of genuine conflict. The issue is always one of action, what should be *done*. When we ask what we should do, when we seek an action as yet undetermined, we genuinely do not know; and our ignorance is meaningful only relative to the question of whether our standards genuinely apply, how they do, and whether we may be wrong in the actions we undertake.

In every human action, it is legitimate to ask "why?"—and to expect some kind of answer. Yet the question "why?" is completely open-ended. Whatever answer is given, we may ask "why?" again, though we thereby change the context and function of the question posed. If a principle is appealed to, we may ask for the grounds of accepting the principle, and continue this process indefinitely. Such a regress of interrogation is vicious only where no grounds are forthcoming, where we look not to other actions and their results, but to intuition and magical insight. Methodic evaluation can always be terminated where we need to act, but it does extend without limit, and it extends into ever-new considerations relevant to action. Just as the universal form of a scientific law entails that no finite amount of evidence can completely verify it, so deliberate actions of evaluation are always tentative. The act seeks validity by indefinitely expanding upon a given context of judgment. A perpetual interrogation is entailed in all evaluation. The indefinite future, circumstances we have failed to consider, the reactions of others, our own hidden needs, all may bring us to failure. So may inconsistency of analysis and our unwillingness to face the prospect of changing circumstances.

Any method for action thus has gross application to anything in human life, and involves an unending quest for the determination of value. We seek a way to restore harmonious order to a situation thrown awry. We require knowledge of ourselves and our deepest needs—to enable us to satisfy not only our surface but our hidden wants. We require knowledge of circumstances, to the point where we can reliably anticipate the outcome of our actions. We must know what the actions of others will be, and how they will affect us, for we are social beings influenced by and influencing others. And finally, we must grasp how we will be changed in our actions, so that our deeds will produce no regret. We must know what we will be after having changed under the impact of our own actions and under new conditions as well.

Such forecasting is nigh impossible. It might follow from this that valid action is sheer fortune. However, another conclusion may be drawn—that we are capable of deliberate and controlled action only when we have gained so consistent a sense of ourselves and our surroundings, and have employed such means of action, as to preserve a continuity in our lives sufficient to serve as the basis of value. One argument for achieving a personal order of soul that is relatively free from external influence is that it allows for actions with little risk of personal change. A man who is a slave to his appetites changes with them as they fluctuate. His own actions, as they satisfy or arouse his appetites, constantly bring him to a new wish, and fulfillment is impossible. Only a well-ordered soul, which endures through circumstances, can provide a consistent ground for action. Only a man whose actions represent a continuous and stable character enduring throughout differing circumstances can expect his actions to produce enduring satisfactions. On the other hand, we must note that a man's character is formed by his past deeds, so that consistency in character is not just the source, but may be the result of consistency in action.

A woman who wonders whether or not to seek a divorce can evaluate her circumstances reasonably only if she may expect to preserve some essential order to her life through the events in prospect. If an ugly divorce could destroy her self-respect, could make her hate herself and feel forever guilty, then she cannot begin to face her problems intelligently, nor act with much hope of success. It is on the basis of the conservation of the self, through various circumstances, that validity in action is possible. Yet action always runs the risk of failure, precisely because nothing is entirely fixed in human life.

Evaluation may be viewed from the side of failure. We discover a gap between our imagination and what we can realize. Our expectations cannot be satisfied. Our plans go awry. Our wishes are frustrated. We match our hopes to our accomplishments and realize how far we have fallen short. When our plans fail to come to fruition, or if they are realized without the satisfactions we expected, then we face failure in our deeds and regret what we have done.

This failure is not merely adventitious pain, displeasures that fall upon us. A disease that lays me low for a few days is no cause for regret and involves no failure without a precipitating factor. If the disease is traceable to none of my actions, then I consider it to be an unlucky event, not of great moment. Events which afford no prospects of control must be set aside—though they pose problems for the future. A very different case is an illness caused by poor care or foolish behavior, where I must judge myself to have failed because my actions did not produce satisfactory results. Psychic illnesses are of great moral complexity precisely because they are so much part of what we do and have done.

What is involved in all methodic action is a means for determining valid actions and tests for determining failure or success. A situation poses a question—how shall I act to achieve my desire? In undertaking a course of action, I must have a measure of success in accomplishing my goal. But I must have more than that, for although I accomplish my goal, I may bring to pass many undesirable events as well. I must then not only admit the questions which initiated my methodic concern, but other concerns which arise upon my actions.

Such a general method takes on a life of its own. For once introduced into human life, it brooks no limitations or boundaries. Anything may be interrogated for its possibilities of value and its likelihood of failure. The most trivial decisions can bring disaster, as any husband or wife can testify concerning his actions during a quarrel. The question "will I fail?" is omnipresent, once a means exists for answering it. We may be held to account for our actions and judged for them whether we know it or not. Our most innocent decisions may have dire repercussions. We are at stake in whatever we do. We may always fail.

Even the choice to remain uninvolved can bring failure with it, if what is ignored through such quietism is of great moment. A parent who thoughtlessly brings up his children may be condemned for his lack of foresight. On the other hand, a parent who deliberates too often and hesitates in his actions may be condemned for not knowing what he was doing. The effects for both upon their children provide the basis on which we may speak of failure—a failure quite independent of suspect motives or hidden malice.

We can never rule out any particular subject matter as irrelevant to failure. We are faced with the prospect of failure in everything we do and everything that happens to us. Moreover, we cannot rule out anything in the world as irrelevant to our consideration—for however innocent it appears, it may come to have great moment. A kind word spoken in an hour of need may have powerful effects in the hearer's life. Small ills left unchallenged can wreak destruction.

We have, then, a method with universal applicability, and with no boundaries to its range of concern. We seek to avoid failure. All we can do is to maximize our likelihood of success. Nothing will ensure that we will not fail, however careful we are. Our only hope must be that the means we employ will enable us to gain a control that we may temporarily rely upon, if only a new frame of mind.

The omnipresence of failure is the source of the perpetual interrogation of deliberate actions. It is because we may always fail that we must always ask ourselves how to succeed. A man whose every deed was smiled upon by fortune could never evaluate his actions, for he would never grasp the price of evaluation. If he were very intelligent, he could learn of failure by watching others. But if a guardian angel protected him, then he would not be a genuine agent, choosing, evaluating, and living with the consequences of his actions and the imminence of failure.

The perpetual interrogation of methodic action has two dimensions. One is derived from the fact that the consequences of one's actions never cease to have further consequences, that we are at stake in the remote as well as the direct consequences of our actions. The other dimension rests upon the methodic character of evaluation, the commitment to some mode of rationality. To choose is to act with reason. But reasons too may be interrogated, particularly if they are principles. And this interrogation may be continued without end, or at least until it seems absurd to go on. Although we may break off the interrogation at any point, it is always risky to do so.

Two factors are implicated in choosing to do something as against merely doing it: a method for carrying out the goals set and for evaluating the proposed alternatives; in addition, insofar as the choice is deliberate and methodic it is based on reasons. A person who has *chosen* presumably has reasons for his choice. He has not *merely* acted, but has chosen to act on what he considers adequate grounds. A man who puts his trousers on beginning with the right leg may be asked if he just does that without thinking, or does he choose to. He may do so quite habitually, and admit that there is no choice involved. But if he does make a choice, it is no explanation to say "I just choose to." Perhaps he means that some particular bodily condition makes it feel more natural to begin as he does. The reason is a quality of ease in his movements. With no reason, though, he has not chosen, but has simply acted.

Once a reason is given, however, the natural question arises as to whether or not it is a *good* reason. This question is implicit in every rational explanation. Once it is admitted, the search for justification in action expands without limit. Is it a valid reason for getting dressed in a particular fashion that it is a matter of ease and habit? In such a case, of course, *because nothing else is at stake.* The emphasis, however, shows unmistakably that a matter of whim implicitly looks to the consequences of such an action. Getting dressed seldom has significant consequences, so no deliberation is required. Suppose, however, that an absent-minded man often dresses sloppily. His instinctive preferences are not good reasons for his actions. And if his manner of dress were important—at a ceremonial occasion, for example—then some special care would be obligatory.

A chosen action, then, is based on well-established reasons only to a first approximation. Normally a principle is appealed to that has *prima facie* plausibility. In most cases, dressing requires no more than cursory care, and habit may rule completely. But any particular case may be an exceptional one, where the principle fails to apply. All principles of action admit exceptions and qualifications. Sometimes it is indeed right to tell a lie or even to risk one's life. If I knew more about the situation before me, I might find it to be one of the exceptions.

A principle, then, is not in itself a valid reason. We may move in two directions to ensure ourselves of validity. We may question the validity of the principle. Why is it supposed that premarital sexual relations are inadvisable? Further justifications may be given in only two ways—by appeal to other principles of wider import, which may themselves be questioned; or by appeal to specific factual consequences of disregarding the principle, which may themselves be questioned in a multitude of ways—*i.e.,* as to whether the evidence is sufficient, whether the particular situation at hand is not an exception, even whether the consequences would be so very bad. Justification in evaluation is open-ended: of everything given as a reason to justify calling a course of action good, we may ask whether these reasons are themselves "good" or legitimate. Any terminus is an arbitrary one. We decide at a particular point that it is futile to push the interrogation further—a decision which involves a degree of risk, and which is itself an act to be evaluated for its validity.

Evaluative methods are interrogative and in principle nonterminating. Any justification may be challenged by an appeal to a new principle or unknown facts and consequences; in addition, the principles we appeal to rest on available evidence, while our interpretations of the evidence depends on the principles, and so forth. The fallibility of evaluation is unavoidable, but it is neither vicious nor need it be paralyzing. The situation is no different from that in any science—experimentation is ruled by theoretical considerations which define the mode of experimentation to be employed and the results sought. Yet that same experimentation can lead to the rejection of the theory which gave meaning to it.

The most important difference between scientific and normative methods is that the former address relations discernible among events, and consider particular events only as they provide witness to patterns and laws; in the evaluation of actions, it is the particular event which possesses importance, while principles provide but a means of controlling and defining aims. In scientific experimentation, an error brings only the need for repetition. In politics or morals, an error may be disastrous. Failure in science is a failure in discovery, not in a particular event. Failure in action is always due to some error within a given state of affairs.

Branches of science that lie on the borderline of action constantly grapple with the moral quality of their enterprises. The social sciences constantly face problems of evaluation. Medical research, which from a scientific point of view seeks to ascertain the relational qualities of health and disease, may not experiment on human beings without raising grave moral problems. The science of medicine would ignore particular events and persons except as they provide knowledge of the workings of the human body. As therapy, it must give the best of care to individual patients. These conflicting demands make medical science a treacherous domain, in which a most delicate balance must be maintained between the inhumanity of science realized in impersonal experiments, and the moral concern for a particular patient which would virtually preclude research on living patients.

It is the obtrusiveness of the qualities of particular events and their consequences that defines the peculiar attributes of failure in action. Precisely because these qualities are subordinated in scientific research, the latter risks less and can achieve more. Particular events are brought into a class order, and are regarded as one of a kind. A mismanaged experiment is simply repeated. The researcher is not condemned for his carelessness except in rare circumstances—such as an explosion which destroys property and lives, and which is interpreted to fall in the domain of action, not science. Experimental events are usually far from momentous in any but a scientific regard. In very long-range terms, they may become of great moral value. Science certainly may be viewed as a domain of action in terms of its effects in human life. However, science as action leads to very different judgments from science as theoretical and factual truth. The specific qualities of a particular event are in science far less important than the class of which the event is a member. In this respect, theoretical science artificially isolates itself from its active dimension. With clever management, failure *in science* can be altogether avoided, in the sense that a series of experiments can be designed to yield some relevant information *no matter what the outcome.* This disregard for the specific outcome of events is peculiar to a theoretical science, and wholly alien to active judgment.

Justification in science points to the laws and theories implicated, not to individual events. A particular event which fails to fit an experimental series may be rejected as irrelevant and inconsequential. Something went awry; if irrelevant to the issue at hand, it is of no matter. In action, however, it is the particular event which carries the full weight of significance. Justification here looks to the possibility of avoiding failure in the particular situation, not in the principles or rules appealed to. The rare and exceptional event may well be determinative of failure and produce guilt. It certainly may not be disregarded as irrelevant.

As a consequence, the danger of failure in action is far greater than in science. Predictions are made in science, and we may say that an error in prediction is a failure. But properly speaking, every rigorous but failed prediction teaches us something new, and that is a gain in scientific knowledge. In evaluation, however, we are at stake in particular events. Our goal is as satisfactory a state of affairs as is possible. A mistake may well be disastrous, and we are to blame for our errors.

The perpetual interrogation of evaluation is therefore akin to scientific investigation only to a first order of approximation. In both, the possession of information aids us in controlling the results of activity. But in science, the vicious regress of the perpetual interrogation is overcome by a regard for specific errors either as inconsequential or as sources of information. The discovery of something new in the heavens is not a mark of the failure of astronomy, but a source of its development. In evaluation, however, specific failures are not inconsequential, nor sources of information alone. Though we may learn from an error, it may be too late for those who suffered it. We are engaged in a perpetual battle to control events and to assure ourselves as much as possible of avoiding failure. Yet the chance of failure looms large in every one of our actions.

The specific features of evaluation in action, in particular the nonterminating and open-ended methodic interrogation of events and circumstances, follow from the general conditions of human life coupled with the imperative of avoiding failure and maximizing the prospects of success in action. Specifically, we find ourselves in a multiplicity of overlapping spheres of action, each with its specific qualities, yet related to—influencing and being influenced by—other events and circumstances. The general assumption that all actions and events can be coordinated in a harmonious and systematic relationship—found in Plato and Spinoza—has no basis whatsoever. Every event plays a role in a variety of spheres, with differing attributes in many of them, sometimes with nearly no aspects in common. Failure then may enter from any quarter, the views of others, alien perspectives, or remote and unexpected consequences.

All that can be done within so complex and variegated spheres of action is to search for synthetic reconciliation, to engage in methodic and ongoing interrogation of conditions and prospects within which possibilities of failure reside. Methods of evaluation in action are perpetual and open-ended because they cannot be completed. Anguish is the realization that insecurity in action is inescapable, while our despair is that we are required to act nevertheless. Although there are many spheres of action, they do not form a system; yet on the other hand, no unrelated spheres of action are guaranteed to remain so. Especially, it is a quality of human experience to broach separations, and to impose relations where they did not exist before. Evaluation depends on the movement from narrower to more general spheres of action. But there is no wisest or most comprehensive sphere of action, only a method which incrementally and unceasingly coordinates narrower spheres in synthetic relations.

Evaluation is method devoted to the avoidance of failure in action, to the extent that it is avoidable. As much information as we can obtain concerning the situations in which we find ourselves is required, as is information concerning ourselves as agents and others about whom we care or who influence us deeply. We constantly form rules as to the best conduct available to us and act upon them—only all too often to discover that the rules must be amended as new situations arise. We inhabit a constantly changing world, and cannot be sure of the applicability of established principles of action. All we can do is to appeal to the knowledge we have of ourselves and what brings order and satisfaction into human life. The principles of conduct normative in human life may be thought of as the repository of time-tested wisdom as to the best way to live and act. Yet ever-new situations arise which challenge those principles as inappropriate. Information concerning novel events is thus required, to amend established truths to suit changed conditions. Such information, however, is useless to us unless we have more comprehensive principles available addressing the changing circumstances and the kinds of accommodations which are wisest. These principles, however, also rest on a historical basis of fact, which changing circumstances may again render inadequate to present needs.

This give and take between the circumstances before us and the principles which define our wisest courses of action is unending. And however long it is continued, it can never ensure that we will not fail in our endeavors. We can only try to be as wise as possible, and face failure as it comes upon us. Certainly we cannot abandon the entire enterprise as useless because it can never provide us with certainty. Recurrently in human life, societies change so rapidly as to cast considerable doubt on the most deeply rooted principles of social life, and it becomes dangerous to follow any principles blindly. But the height of folly is reached by lazy-minded people who conclude that they need not concern themselves at all with those principles constitutive of wisdom in human life if they are not perfect. It is sheerest stupidity (as well as culpability) in moral affairs to willfully abandon the moral principles that permeate social life. Without definite grounds for departing from a moral principle of action, we not only increase the risk of failure, but are eminently culpable for that failure when it occurs. Not the barest modicum of excuse remains.

It must be repeated that the process of evaluation is not the discovery of what is and has been valuable, but the determination of value into a life which lacks it. Not only are the circumstances in which evaluation takes place changing under the impact of external events, but the action itself changes the circumstances and the persons involved. The cases in which the mere rearrangement of material in the environment provides value where none existed before are rare and probably unimportant. They consist of circumstances where the agent "knew all along" what ought to be done, and simply had to take proper steps to do it. Far more frequent and more important are the cases where a rather fundamental change is required in the agent himself, making his realized values new at least to him.

A brief summary may be helpful before going on to examine the character of evaluation in detail. Evaluation is the determination of value in a situation which lacks it, usually due to the qualities of both the agent and his circumstances. What is sought is a new state of affairs containing value. The agent undertakes action seeking not to fail. What he must do is to obtain as accurate information as he can about the circumstances, himself, other people involved, and the principles in which reside whatever wisdom we have concerning human conduct. The facts of his circumstances represent the conditions under which an agent must act, and in terms of which he will take whatever steps are called for. Presumably, information of a descriptive and scientific character is what is required. Unfortunately, human situations are not laboratory settings, but are complexly ramified and interconnected. Personal considerations—love and death, for example—have implications for other people. We can never circumscribe the conditions of a given situation so that they will remain fixed. Spheres of action interpenetrate, and alien factors can interfere with the most propitious auspices.

It is a commonplace that facts *alone* do not provide values, that from a given set of conditions *alone* a course of action may not be determined unequivocally. This commonplace is true, but for reasons that have little to do with conventional moral analysis. First of all, the *facts* of a case are of unlimited range, and cannot be circumscribed without peril. Spheres of action intersect and overlap. It is impossible to specify *all* the facts relevant to a given situation. Second, there are no *facts* relevant to a sphere of action that are facts for all spheres and independent of normative considerations derived from a specific past. A falsehood is not culpable if a "mistake," but may be one if a "lie." Motives and intentions are relevant here, but so are the principles of action which proscribe lies. Our moral principles, then, are essential constituents of spheres of action, and their circumstances *include* the principles understood to regulate actions and to represent loyalties within the given situation. Circumstances and principles—the latter including antecedent values—are not separable conditions within a sphere of active judgment. Third, action looks *from* a present situation to its consequences. Here is another function of principles, to project from given circumstances to possible results. Scientific laws are essential—except that they cannot define circumstances for action apart from relevant principles. The principles, however, are drawn from actions of the past, and evoke the peril of new prospects when projected into the future. Principles and circumstances are the sole basis for action, though they are fundamentally limited in their consequences for controlled action.

We have noted explicitly the fourth condition, that action looks to the needs and reactions of other people, both of which are often treacherous and unpredictable. Not only are the facts about other people and their wants elusive—especially when they do not know what they want—but their future reactions depend on what they will become through time, under the impact of intervening actions. Since action is creative, especially so in new and untried circumstances, the human future is especially difficult to ensure ourselves about. Yet not to take given conditions and knowledge of past events into account is foolhardy. Finally, the fifth factor is that action looks to an indefinite future and to the satisfactory nature of consequences and results—satisfactory in terms of someone involved in the later situations, including the agent. Here we may again emphasize that such satisfaction will be a function of intervening action, thus rather difficult to determine in advance. In addition, actions, principles of action, and all the values engendered in the agents concerned, all tend to define what is found satisfactory—taking facts into account as well, but through the impact of prior actions.

The most important principle of action—and perhaps of all method, a fundamental condition of all existence—is that action and control are restricted activities in practice, while separate spheres intersect in ways which are not fully determined from within each of them separately. Methodic action is the interplay of known principles, of known and unknown facts relevant to a given situation, facts which include the feelings and responses of other men and of the agent as well. The method leads to actions which maximize the likelihood of satisfaction defined in the terms posed within the situation and the relevant principles, especially of partial successes to be accepted as satisfactory. However, to maximize satisfaction in given terms is to incur fundamental risks, since spheres of action interpenetrate. A man may act to his own benefit, only to impinge on others who punish him. A man may act to his own benefit taking his immediate surroundings into account, only to fall prey to remote political events. The methodic manipulation of events toward success and away from failure is a projection from given spheres to the unknown. There is then a continual movement from a narrower to a broader and more comprehensive sphere of action—since to act methodically is always to define a larger sphere of action in which principles, goals, and conditions may be interconnected methodically as they have not been before. The primary function of principles is here to define the movement from narrower to broader spheres.

We may deny, then, that there is a world-order, a comprehensive system of the universe, a total sphere of action—and this denial is implicit in our conception of the indefinitely ramified consequences of action. We may understand that failure is not merely a consequence of human frailty, but of the limitations of any manipulative control in an inexhaustible universe. The methodic interplay of feelings, facts, and principles may provide control of a given sphere of action—except that it intersects with others in which control is still lacking, and the intersection itself generates new spheres in which control still remains to be determined. Control of nature breeds the dire consequences of our instruments of control, natural consequences not fully anticipated, and human reactions to these instruments and to social mechanisms that are uncontrolled and dangerous. Action is a continual challenge, but also a continual risk. Rational methods produce the most defensible actions possible relative to success and failure. But actions always transcend the spheres in which they received their methodic justification, and may then lead to failure. Failure is here not only a threat, but generates the need for further effort toward manipulative control, leading to new syntheses through principles and understanding. Were a man fully to satisfy himself in a given sphere, nevertheless he might find implications for other spheres and other people to be unsatisfactory.

One implication of the denial that there may be an all-encompassing world-order is that there may be quite definite determinative relations between past and future in any sphere of action, yet complete determinism relative to any given sphere is quite impossible. Determinative relations belong within a given sphere of activities and events, and are undermined by intersection with other spheres. Were there a comprehensive perspective, a total sphere of activity, then all relations might be conjoined into a total system. We deny that such a total system is intelligible. Therefore, the future comes out of the past, but possibilities remain in every sphere projected into other spheres. Any activity has multiple possibilities. This is the source of novelty, of creativity, and of conscious choice as well. As for human freedom, that is not mere novelty, not merely the prevalence of possibilities, but the control of possibilities through methodic action. Where possibilities are harnessed by methodic control, new synthetic relations are created within human experience over wide ranges of events and conditions. This is the only meaningful sense of autonomy: the methodic selection among multiple possibilities to successful human ends.

Methodic evaluation is the control of a given set of conditions for action in terms of principles drawn from past experiences, the facts of the situation, the known scientific laws relevant to these facts, and including the feelings of the agent and of others. The method can be understood most clearly through the function of principles, and that is how we will subsequently analyze it. Nevertheless, principles function relative to a given sphere of action, yet must be projected into other spheres as well, both in possibility and usually in terms of actual but unknown connections. In one sense, methodic evaluation is nothing but the gain of knowledge relative to circumstances and to projected courses of action—

knowledge in the light of principles drawn from past actions and conditions, and looking to an open future. Action is the manipulation of what is known relative to a given situation and projected into the unknown in terms of satisfactions yet to be realized.

All this knowledge, however, is insufficient. For the ultimate test of action resides in what becomes of the situation and the agent, through the actions undertaken, as the circumstances and the agent himself change. He comes to a discovery about what is valuable, based on what he knows about what he has been. Since it is the very information he unearths about the world and himself that provides the source of his change in being, a moral agent is always moving beyond himself in evaluation. That is the hard truth within Nietzsche's transcendence of conventional morality and Sartre's freedom. A man can never take refuge in what he was, for his very actions to provide security render his life perilous. The only hope in evaluation is for an agent to gather the information he can, and with open eyes and a willingness to face his failures, seek a mode of being (a composite of his feelings, actions, and ideals) that is consistent enough through changing circumstances to be relied on, yet responsive enough to those changing circumstances to meet their challenge.

If the precise traits of methods of action are not yet clear, it is in part due to the diversity of situations calling for action. Nevertheless, through the consideration of the characteristics of failure and success in action, and especially of moral principles and ideals, we may reach a clearer conception of methodic action and of created values.

D. Failure

To this point, I have presented failure in action as a form of *regret* in order to describe the goals of evaluation. The condemnation of others is no proof of failure, for the satisfactions sought and expected may be quite different in character from the agent's. There is some justification for the view that only the agent can fully judge the results of his own actions. The reactions of others are relevant as conditions he must take into account. They may make him suffer and regret what he has done. Nevertheless, room must be found for the heroism which consists in remaining steadfast to one's principles regardless of the scorn and the punishment of others. Considerable further analysis is called for, however, for men are capable of regret only under special circumstances. Either it must be shown that only under such conditions is evaluation possible, or the concept of regret must be expanded and qualified beyond its ordinary meaning. Surely regret can at best be a *mark* or *sign* of failure—a failure which resides in conditions and results, not in feelings alone.

From the standpoint of methodic evaluation, regret is a fundamental sign of failure, however it is brought about. Failure can be transmuted into subsequent action and the transformation of former ideals only through the power of felt regret. Here regret is no longer the mark of failure but the assimilation of failure in methodic control. Nevertheless, we must also address failure in the lives of men who lack method in action, who blind themselves to circumstances or to consequences so as to evade anguish. It may be that no *objective* interpretation of failure is possible—meaning that failure resides not in results as such but in results *assimilated* by an agent, whether the particular agent involved or others. To have failed is always to have been judged to have failed, the judgment an essential component of the failure. If so, then blindness may succeed in avoiding regret, but not the condemnations of others and their judgment that we have failed.

Blindness may avoid regret but not condemnation—and the induced regret that may follow. Openness to conditions and possibilities encourages regret, since it looks constantly to the possibility of failure. It is my position that evaluation proper can only take place when failure is a genuine and considered prospect, and that a concerned agent is open to regret if he seeks value in action. Blindness to the qualities of circumstances can provide an insulation against care while it risks lack of control. At the furthest extreme, a catatonic schizophrenic is immune to events which may threaten his delicate equilibrium to the exact extent as he is incapable of directing those events. He has disengaged himself from care and regret; at the same time he has lost any ability he might have had to bring to pass what he earnestly needs. He so firmly refuses to consider the possibility of realizing his needs that he can only deny that he has them.

Blindness to reality I consider a greater failure than overwhelming remorse. And it need not be pathological to be without value. The refusal to face prospects of failure, which brings with it less control over events than one might otherwise have had, is not a way of avoiding failure as I have defined it, and is likely to increase such failure. It is a form of denial, a way of making oneself immune to events and circumstances by closing oneself off from them. It is rare and pathological that a man may so deny reality that failures will not penetrate his defenses. If the avoidance of failure is significant in human life, it must be an accomplishment realized through an awareness of possibilities pregnant in events, not a limitation placed upon one's imagination. Plato forcefully shows that courage—which is founded on a knowledge of what one ought to fear, therefore on an awareness of possibilities—must not be confused with rashness—which may be but blindness to what can happen. A man who has no awareness of danger may act unhesitatingly in situations fraught with risk. He is not brave, but ignorant, perhaps even rather stupid.

Once we take into account differences in awareness of possibilities among men, and their varying sensitivity to their own failings, then it becomes difficult to let failure be dependent on felt regret alone. What are we to say of men who never feel regret precisely because they are monstrous? We may establish the rule for everyone to "let conscience be your guide" only if we may suppose everyone to have a well-established conscience—a supposition that is certainly false. Even worse are those cases where action brings the agent's death. He cannot experience regret if he is dead.

On the other hand, if we measure failure in terms external to the sensibilities of the agent, we seek a universal criterion of judgment that cannot take sufficiently into account important differences among men. A common standard of value suffers from being too rigidly applied to widely different agents and circumstances. We come to principles of action that are less the embodiment of time-tested wisdom than of coercive social control. Our obligations become the less valuable as they are forced upon us. Our peculiarities are disregarded in the commonality of normative rules that define failure and success. Our awareness of joy and misery conflicts with the rules of behavior which we are expected to observe. The unreliability of subjective awareness becomes an excuse for denying the right of an individual to repudiate a general principle as inapplicable to him insofar as he feels it to be so.

In less complex and less controlled societies, common norms exert control on but a part of an individual's life. Truly his life might be determined from birth to death by external requirements, but not uniformly so. Family, birth, social status, hereditary crafts and name all provide a definite but exceptional order to the life of an individual. The particular qualities of an individual are more apparent, even within a completely structured set of expectations and rules of conduct, than in our larger and more mobile society. In undeveloped societies, an individual knows that and how he is different from others. In modern Western society, it is extremely difficult to determine one's uniqueness amidst an educational system available to all, common entertainments, crowds, and throngs of people who dress similarly, speak similarly, and have similar backgrounds. The same rules apply to everyone indifferently, the same opportunities are available and the same expectations are provided. No wonder our principles of life are almost continuously challenged by young people. They seek to define their individual identities by finding different rules to follow, rules of life appropriate particularly for *them.*

The general solution to such problems is that of mediating methodically between the particular needs of an individual and the common standards he must bring to bear on his judgments. The method inherent in evaluation is common to all circumstances and agents, but it nevertheless pays full heed to the particular attributes of the agent involved to the extent that the agent's particular character, needs, and values are of utmost importance as determinants of success and failure in his actions. Human beings share common goals and attitudes, and certain values seem universal. But their universality is only schematic: particular circumstances modify our conceptions of what is valuable and what we ought to do. The particular character and needs of the agent who must act vary from situation to situation. Success and failure in action are the result of the projection of the agent's character and values from known to novel circumstances. His idiosyncratic traits may be of great importance relative to what is valuable to him and successful for him.

Failure in action—methodic or not—is a disparity between attained results and proposed goals. Action projects from conditions and circumstances in terms of established or hypothetical standards of value to new situations, seeking control over them as measured by the values implicated there, not in the original situation alone. Action projects from a given sphere to another, and the extension seeks the transformation both of circumstances and of the agent involved, his character and his principles. Failure is a failure of control, a disparity within the situation brought to pass, a conflict which engenders further action to attain resolution. Regret is always the mark of failure, a sense of conflict which calls for further action. A failure assimilated in further action is regret in this sense. Nevertheless, there is also a regret of paralysis—a conflict that leads to no action, a sign of failure without accompanying controls. There are also partial successes, which involve no regret but involve an appreciation for achievements brought to pass, yet which must pass into further controls directly. Standards are essential here to determine a partial success not to be a failure. There are in addition actions which lead to death, permitting no regret and subsequent action. Failure here resides in the judgments of others. Finally, there is the defense of blindness to failure, sufficient insensitivity that discordance between expectations and results is unnoticed, the massive conviction that failure is impossible. If such blindness maintains itself, then regret is impossible and so is any sign of failure. Here again, failure resides in the actions of others which may force a man to admit failure by punishment or coercion. The reactions of others may cause us regret, even when we were sure in our convictions—for their reactions are part of the results to which action leads. The heroism of a consistent course of action that withstands the condemnation and punishment of others passes easily into the smugness of self-righteousness and an insensitivity to other people. Punishment here is a means of control, a way to express one's principles and to modify the values of others. Punishment is in some cases a proof of failure. In other cases, if our values are very strong, it is part of the circumstances which test our mettle. The interplay of punishment and action is the source of social values and the arena of justice.

Failure is a disparity within situations brought to pass by action. Sometimes circumstances are such that all possibilities lead to further conflict if not to disaster. Here is the distinction to be made between failure and lack of success. Success looks to resolution and to harmonious adjustment. It is rare and nearly an ideal state. Nearly everything we do is with partial lack of success. But not to succeed is not necessarily to fail, for we may have done the best we could, and may continue to do so. Lack of success is, like failure, a stimulus to further action. It simply calls for modest personal adjustments, for less stringent modifications of our fundamental values and character. Regret at failure can—especially when the result of methodic evaluation—be the source of a total transformation of one's character and values. When others punish us, it is to modify our values and personality. We may not be punished when we simply do not succeed. Punishment is then a sign of failure, not of lack of success alone. Punishment is an act, and is to be justified as such. So also, the judgment that we or another have failed is an act, to be justified in terms of controls and results. Not every lack of success is a failure to be acted upon.

The regret which is the mark of failure in methodic and self-conscious action is far from the everyday feeling that affects most men at various times, the acute displeasure with the results of their actions. Ordinary regret is often spiteful and paralyzing, rather than strengthening our powers of control. In addition, much of what constitutes regret in ordinary circumstances no longer has weight to an agent who has fully faced the circumstances in which he finds himself. This is to be made clear by a careful study of methodic evaluation.

As an initial essay, I shall propose a dialectical transformation of the notion of failure, through a developmental analysis of evaluation. I shall differentiate between failure perceived in methodic evaluation and mere regret by treating the latter as an earlier stage in a dialectical development mediated by rational self-awareness. For simplicity, I will present an idealized account of the genesis of the self-awareness involved in evaluation, beginning with the needs and learned behavior of a child. This is no more than a device to make the domain of analysis clear. What will follow is a conception of the kind of regret that marks a failure to require significant actions in response. I hope to show that this regret is not a "mere feeling," but a methodic disposition, one with rather complex and ramified occasions in the lives of agents who experience it.

At the beginning of his life, an infant is incapable of evaluation; he does not even have "desires" or "wants". To the extent that a desire involves an end to be attained, an infant does not seek. At best, he wants only to avoid discomfort. If we presuppose that wanting has an object, an infant has no wants. He cannot identify what he wants, seek it, nor do more than engage in activities that may produce an alleviation of a primitive urge or discomfort. Yet his behavior is not without structure and organization, and has built into it reflective actions that alleviate discomfort. What is lacking is some recognition of objects which provide comfort.

Most infants learn almost immediately that certain activities and objects provide relief and even feelings of pleasure. In a very little time, babies can be seen to pursue specific objects. They become transported with joy at the sound of their mother's step or the presentation of a nipple to suck. Connections have been made, and child has come to some understanding, however shallow, of the object of his desires.

In as small a change as the one I have described, rather important transformations in the nature of failure have taken place. For the youngest infant, failure has no meaning. Pain and discomfort may be unavoidable, but they do not constitute failure in action. For a child who knows that a specific object usually brings satisfaction, a new kind of failure is possible. Not only may displeasure be unavoidable, but an object which generally pleases may fail to do so in a particular instance. A desire for a specific object brings two kinds of failure with it—the failure to possess the object of desire and the failure of that object to accomplish what is expected. An ill child desires his mother to be near him, but she cannot make his pain disappear.

In time, the desired object may become complete in itself. The joys of securing an object of desire may grow in intensity to the point where it is desired for its own sake. Yet the possibility that a desired object may be acquired and yet fail to satisfy pervades all desire and want. The realization that a loved object may be gained without satisfaction is essential to any effective means for coping with failure.

Unfortunately, it is usually not prominent except at sporadic moments or at times of emergency. The transformations in desire that are brought about by the vagaries of circumstance tend to predominate. Any satisfaction may obscure an original purpose. For an infant, the joy of his mother's presence replaces the hunger that she is known to assuage. Partly, this is all to the good, as the child comes to love his mother. Partly, it can be a danger, as he neglects the continual interaction of needs and acts which provide order within his life, and comes to desire only immediate objects. One of the most striking features of childhood is its emphasis on an immediate object of desire, rather than awareness of the impetus of the desire. Every human being must learn to pass by the obvious objects of his desire and to seek value in remote consequences.

When a person considers events beyond the immediate range of his desires, he has reached a sophisticated level of evaluation and is quite aware of the rich possibilities of failure. He makes plans for achieving his desires, yet realizes that plans do not always bring fruition. Without plans, the failure to realize a wanted object may be but a disappointment; in terms of the original need, it may bring pain. But once plans are drawn to attain a desire, then the plans bring with them their own imperatives. They may fail to bring to pass what is sought, producing disappointment; they may accomplish their explicit goal, yet also bring to pass undesirable and painful events; and they may fail in both respects at once.

A failure realized through an intentional course of action in which a proposed goal is achieved is quite different from the disappointment of unrealized ambitions. The dominant role played by aims in a well-ordered life must be supplemented by a willingness to continually examine those very ends as well as other consequences of activities undertaken. The agent must open his eyes to more than the standards before him at the end of his chosen path. He must be aware of yet other possibilities as well.

The dominance of chosen ends rests upon the focal quality desire brings to its objects. Certain needs—such as for food—create objects of desire which then become independent and dominant. A man seldom seeks *food* when he is hungry—he seeks specific dishes prepared in ways he prefers. Focal awareness is displaced from the original needs to the objects that have satisfied them, and they take on a life of their own. The forms of civilization depend on this transformation. We become of cultivated taste as we learn to desire not food alone, but tastefully and exquisitely prepared dishes; not mere spectacle to dazzle our senses, but subtle and delicate balance. Yet insofar as we are no longer aware of our broader needs, and seek only well-defined objects, we partly lose the capacity to judge them. To evaluate our actions broadly as well as instrumentally, we must look beyond our obvious ends to what they are directed to serve. We cannot recapture our *innocence*—the innocence of those feelings from which desires have grown. Instead, we must seek new and more comprehensive ways of evaluating our ends. By letting ourselves care about larger goals, in ever expanding contexts, we pass on to a new consciousness of failure. By *caring* for what we do, by a renewed feeling about our actions, we become more subtly aware of our failures.

I have spoken about a renewed awareness of failure. Such awareness marks a new mode of methodic consciousness. For men become capable of criticizing their own projects only in terms of methods of criticism. The self-awareness that can make one aware of failures when he has accomplished his stipulated goals would be incredibly delicate and subtle if not accompanied by methods for the control of such awareness. Unless brought to awareness of their "real" or larger needs, men tend to replace them with simple objects of desire. Middle-age dissatisfaction is often a consequence of having realized one's desires—only to discover that they are not sufficient. The walls and defenses which surround most adult human beings can be overcome only by crises or by method.

That very method, however, both depends upon and creates a new consciousness of failure. The mode of self-knowledge that is the result of unremittingly self-critical methods is very different from the uncritical feelings of lower grades of self-awareness—different in its subjective as well as objective aspects. A chess player who has studied the game in depth views it very differently from the most brilliant untutored player. The fund of previous games is with him at all times, ready to be called out in any play. A man who plays chess without knowledge of what others have done can fail only by losing, and will lose only by poor planning. A man who plays with full knowledge of the greatest games of the past can lose, though he is armed against that failure to the utmost. He strengthens his game by his knowledge, but the possibilities of failure for him then become multidimensional.

In the same way, an artist who paints in untutored ignorance of the history of painting may be successful in an intuitive and natural way. He plans his work, but without thought of the reactions of others or the history of his medium. If he fails, it is a simple matter of lacking natural ability or self-discipline. If he studies the history of painting, if he learns to view his work dispassionately and perfectionistically, then his sense of failure is amplified as well. Failure may still be represented by the rejection of others, his inability to sell his paintings. But such failures are now *intelligible:* his self-awareness becomes the basis of judgment. Failure is felt not as a frustration of desire, but as a synthetic realization of all his activities. In terms of his own criticisms, the painter may forestall most one-dimensional responses to his work. He takes them into account in his awareness of what he must do. If he comes to admit failure, it cannot be accompanied by a simple sense of how to improve. He has incorporated minor possibilities of improvement in his self-critical method of work. What is wrong goes far deeper: his entire ability as an artist is at stake. He changes from the regret that he has failed to win a prize to the regret that he has been doing the kind of work he has. A single-faceted failing is transformed into a profound awareness of his inadequacy as a person, artist, or agent.

We may now return to moral evaluation. We have discussed the difference between the failure that is the frustration of a specific desire for a specific object and the failure that considers an object in its relation to deeper and more pervasive needs. However, until a method of self-criticism is developed which reflects objects of desire onto themselves in their relation to a system of needs and aims—until a method is developed to view a person relatively comprehensively—the evaluation of desired objects is at best sporadic and disjointed. A man who finds a desire within himself for dominating women may wonder about his "true" desires; but he will be able to develop alternative possibilities only if he has come to know the source of his desire, enough about other of his needs to see how unsatisfied they would be by such women, and to systematically reorganize his actions in terms of a larger sense of himself. His systematic awareness of failure engenders the possibility of a change in his most deeply rooted desires, a possibility seldom available in the disjointed sense that a particular object is not worthy. It is common for a man in love to know his beloved is not what he "really" wants, but nevertheless to be sufficiently self-destructive as not to cease loving her. If such men are to reevaluate their needs, and change accordingly, they must come to a larger sense of themselves, based on a method of controlling and interpreting their separate desires.

We postulate, then, a transition from simple intentions, plans for the achievement of specific goals, to a self-critical awareness that ends must themselves be reevaluated; that methods of action must be evaluated in terms of their results, reflecting means and ends upon themselves unceasingly; to the point where an individual works constantly to bring the various projects and intentions of his life into conjunction with one another; where his separable desires are reflected upon each other unremittingly. Here is reason at work in the largest sense, where the fruits of every endeavor are extended into every other domain, and the agent's awareness of the possibilities of his actions is reflected into everything he does. This is the gross condition of evaluation in action.

On this ideal level, it may not be plausible that a man might fail. He has taken everything it is humanly possible to take into account in advance. Yet the world is so precarious and multifarious that all precautions fail to protect him fully. His judgments as to what he can expect may be erroneous, even when as well-confirmed as possible. His sense of himself may be accurate, yet the actions he undertakes may change him, and they may be found unsatisfactory from his new point of view. The world is no all-encompassing system, to be fully known and controlled, but consists of shifting and over-lapping systems, interpenetrating in diverse ways. Failure is unavoidable, yet the failure of a methodically self-critical man is very different from any other failure.

For one thing, such a man does not view the frustration of desire as primary. On a simple level, failure is the frustration of desire. On the most complex level, frustration may be necessary to gain what is more important. Here failure is a major disparity of plans and desires. Oedipus does not experience *frustration* when he discovers his condition: he feels *horror* at what he has done. Regret becomes an exquisite and delicate feeling when accompanied by a comprehensive awareness of one's role as directing agent.

The primary element in the methodic self-consciousness that is evaluation is the capacity to respond to various possibilities and to know how deeply one cares about them. This is the source of the conflicts that tear asunder the souls of men of great moral sensitivity. Kierkegaard captures this eloquently in his description of the knight of infinite resignation, who cares too much about the qualities of the situations he lives through to do more than suffer them or resign himself to them. The passionate aspect of action can be eliminated only by a blindness to alternatives. If we are truly to consider various courses of action, their consequences must reside at least partly in care and the possibilities of regret. A man who really cares not a whit for other men could not collapse in self-hatred as does Ivan Karamazov.

The regret that specifies failure in evaluation is not one-dimensional as is sheer frustration. It is not merely a feeling focused on a particular goal and its impediments. A long-distance runner who turns into the last stretch toward the wire can taste his victory. All his being is focused on that wire, on covering the intervening distance. If one of the other runners sprints by him at the last moment, his failure is but a gaping void, an awareness of having lost a particular object and no more. His failure is but a void in his sense of accomplishment. His loss, even if crushing, is no more than the loss of an object, a flat and one-dimensional failure.

A more common example is the loss of one's *beloved*. A man devotes his whole being to make a woman love him, but she comes to love another. The poignancy of the loss may be unbearably intense, but it is not of wide latitude or of multiple ramifications. The focus of an agent on a specific object of his endeavors increases the intensity of its loss, but narrows the range of its consequences. It is true that a man who loses a woman he loves feels he has lost his whole life, because he has come to view his entire life as focused in her becoming his. He cannot but feel his loss as a total calamity, affecting his whole life. And he may be correct; it may indeed affect his life, as the death of a child can shatter the lives of his parents who loved him. A woman and a child may be sorely missed. Yet parents have other children, and a man may come to love another woman.

The regret that methodic evaluation brings when it fails is not likely to be of such intensity nor appear to be of such moment. For one thing, a man who has come to know himself and his surroundings, who has chosen to act with a deep awareness of what he is risking, who knows the likely consequences of his actions, can see upon the failure of his plans how subtle were the distinctions upon which he made his decisions. He has come to know what he cannot bear to live with, but by tasting in imagination the alternative possibilities. If his decision is made intelligently, then it can be no more than plausible. His discovery that it is not right is lessened in intensity by his knowledge of the rich complexities of human life.

More important, his awareness of failure is multidimensional, and essentially without *frustration*. Creon, in Sophocles' *Antigone,* learns of his failure in rather intense and poignant ways, but more importantly, in a context that preserves the complexity of the position he has argued throughout the play. He has maintained the need for social order and the strength of his authority, only to discover that social order is not enough, and that authority is limited. It is a trivialization of his discovery—and I mean the quality of his regret as he experiences it—to say that he misses

his son and wife. There is no frustration of a desire here, at least not with
respect to any antecedent desire whose object is unavailable. Creon has
chosen his course of action knowingly, fully aware of what he risks; and
he discovers his failure in a full-fledged awareness of his own mistakes. He
does not lack anything; he rather knows the fruits of his own endeavors.

This regret is not on the surface very different from remorse—the
sense of having failed oneself. Yet in at least one important way they
differ completely. Probably this has been grasped most fully by Sartre,
who sees in remorse a bad faith. A person who feels remorse for what he
has done in part accepts being the kind of person who would do that.
Remorse has an apology implicit within it. When Meursault is asked
whether he feels remorse in *The Stranger*, Camus has him deny that he
has ever regretted anything he has done. He is *not sorry,* and refuses to
apologize for his existence. It does not follow that he is glad of what he has
done. Meursault is simply not aware enough of the quality of his own
actions to grasp his situation emotionally. He cannot appreciate the fact
that he has indeed killed a man, and that that is unalterable. He himself
faces death, and may well be killed as uncritically as he killed. He cannot
feel remorse if that means that he must apologize for himself. But he
cannot feel regret either.

Regret is the mark of failure for a man who has responsibly chosen to
live with the consequences of his actions. Meursault lacks the capacity to
understand others' feelings, so never really chooses to bear with them as
they affect him. A responsible man defines himself as someone who can
genuinely live with his actions. When he is mistaken, he comes to
understand how wrong he was about what is important to him. His failure
is regret for his actions as false to himself. It is at once a self-denial and a
determination to avoid a similar failure in his subsequent actions. It
reaches out in its qualities to the complex and ordered being that he is
struggling to become. It is no apologetic capitulation to being unable to
change.

When a forty-year-old man awakens to the possibility that his life is
a sham, that he has spent most of his life in unsatisfying activities, that he
dislikes his job, his wife, his town, and even his successes, then he touches
the regret I am describing. Of course, he may simply feel frustrated—he
may not be as rich as he wants to be. Or he may feel remorse for having
sold his youthful ideals for a mess of porridge, and may hate himself for
the choices he has made. But he may come, in his new self-awareness, to
know not only that he has failed but *how*—that is, to know what is *really
important* to him now: not wealth, security, or stability, but the pursuit of

a quality of life. The transition between a sense of having failed and an awareness of what really matters is provided by regret.

A man knows when he has failed in action when he grasps what is at stake in his activities, and especially how he is tested and determined by his actions. Only through a method in which a broad awareness of various possibilities is brought before him can he fail in this way. To ignore possibilities is not to face them, and to blind oneself to what may happen. Evaluation presupposes an agent's willingness to test himself in his deeds and upon his choices, and to discover how wrong he has been.

Methodic evaluation is highly self-critical and interrogative. The consciousness of failure that is regret, if it is nothing but self-hatred, marks the defeat of the method. Remorse as bad faith terminates methodic evaluation, since it in effect is the acceptance of one's deeds as being oneself, and acquiescence in being the kind of person who would do those things. Regret in evaluation must remain within the methodic scheme, based on a self-awareness that will avoid the same error in the future. Perhaps it is this transformational quality that Christians believe is the mark of true repentance. My point is simply that the transformation repentance may bring depends on a methodic willingness to evaluate oneself and what one does; and conversely, methodic evaluation brings a rich awareness of the complex ramifications of one's character and person.

The conception of evaluation in terms of methods which grow out of one-dimensional goal-seeking may be viewed in another light than from the point of view of the feelings of the agent. An agent who moves from a single object of desire to a critical interrogation of the value of that object asks himself about his own dependence on his environment, and seeks to grasp how he is implicated in his desires. He does not merely accept his desires, but interrogates himself to determine if he ought to have them. By looking to the furthest consequences of his actions, he can strive for remote as well as immediate goals. He sees that the range of his choices is immense. He considers other people and the environing conditions to discover how extensive is the range of circumstances which affect him, how remote events can change the character of his life and the nature of his actions. And by choosing and acting, he brings himself under survey, and transforms himself in what he does.

In this sense, evaluation is the attempt to bring order into the disorder of a man's life, or to generate a continuity among the constraints of diverse spheres of action in which a man finds himself. Not to know what to do is not to know who one is, in the various senses of being torn by conflicting principles or conflicting interests, failing to know how one is affected by environing conditions, or in terms of the diverse requirements of different but intersecting spheres of action. To know what is valuable is to know how one *must* act by virtue of being the person one is. A man may have led an inconsistent and disordered life, but his discovery of what is truly valuable is simultaneously a discovery about *himself*, how he is to be consistent in his actions. A successful act preserves the continuity within a man's life from one sphere of action to others. A failure is a break within the continuity he has established in his relations with his surroundings.

Here we have implicit the solution to both blindness and to the death that can make regret impossible. Failure, as I have described it, is the condition which urgently compels modification of the agent's values and character as an agent, and is the sense of having inadequate principles, convictions, and wisdom to act in diverse circumstances. Failure is common for most men insofar as they encounter their limitations and as the variety of obligations threaten them. Methodic evaluation is the only justifiable response to insecurity in action—the deliberate strengthening of one's powers of control through the development of instruments and secure and consistent values. Blindness escapes regret, but at the expense of powerlessness. It transforms a regret at one's weaknesses into a regret at the inclemency of the world. But failure intrudes forcibly even upon those who would repudiate it by blindness. Even were they to succeed in their blindness, we would note their incoherence of values and of attainments. Action projects control from the past to the future, from the established to the prospective. Failure is a break, a discontinuity, inadequate control in terms of one's resources. Total valuelessness appears to be a state where nothing can threaten—were it truly to be attained. Even so, it would be impotence, since it controls nothing but emotion, letting everything else pass. The main argument against it, however, is that control is required for creatures with values, and that is what we are.

As for those values which bring us to death, regret is then impossible, and so then is that sign of failure. A dead man cannot change. In this sense, failure is for the living. Others can only make their values known to us, but they cannot prove our failures. Alive, only regret can signify acceptance of failure, the need for self-transformation, for abandoning former values. What others do simply must be considered within our spheres of action. To say another man has failed is no more than to act punitively toward him, with the end of affecting his future actions, or to strengthen and reenforce our own ideals. A judgment of the failure of another person is itself but an act, with all related complexities.

A heroic death is an exceptional case, one where regret is impossible even if justified and legitimate. Here we must turn from failure to success. Failure is not meaningful to a dead man, and that is why death is often so much easier to face than life. To die is to escape from the perils of action, and to do so permanently. Failure and anguish are both dissipated. Nevertheless, death may not be a success. The values of the agent may be violated. A heroic death can never be a full success, though it may avoid a sense of failure where it is the best of the available alternatives. Action projects from given conditions, from standards and ideals accepted and circumstances available, to new possibilities. If actions bring a man's death, nevertheless they may be discontinuous with his values and character, inadequately comprehensive, abortive and in vain. Success can be achieved through death—where one's values brook no endurance of evil, perhaps. If a man does what he must, death may be inevitable. It is not here a sign of failure. There might be a greater success—to attain a continuity among events which does not require death. But a heroic death may be better in some cases than a mediocrely successful life—depending on the results attained.

The critical point here is that failure is itself a judgment relative to action. An agent who judges his own deeds to be failures regrets them, and must learn from them. An agent who judges another's failure also learns from it and takes an attitude relative to such actions—a punitive one perhaps. To condemn a death as a failure is to deny its value and applicability to one's own or to others' lives. It provides no values comprehensive enough to serve. A heroic death, then, does provide such a value. Ideals can bring us to death, if that is the best we can do in the circumstances. If we die in vain, or as but a weak achievement, where far better and more effective alternatives might have been found, then our death is unnecessary and thereby a failure. Nevertheless, circumstances often conspire against us. Too often we lack control over our conditions and our surroundings, even over ourselves.

Failure is always a significant incoherence within one's life, either in internal or psychic conflict or in one's relations to circumstances. A German who discovers that his support of immoral laws led to monstrous crimes learns not only that sometimes laws must be opposed. He learns that there is a species of moral corruption that is obedience to law. He may continue to obey the law most of the time thereafter, but if he genuinely regrets his past actions, then he admits the need for civil disobedience. He becomes less automatically bureaucratic, less blindly a servant of authority. His regret is at his *automatic* obedience, which is a form of blindness. In effect, he learns how dependent he is on unseen events; and by becoming alert, may bring those unseen events into closer accord with his own moral requirements. Regret at having failed, coupled with methodic evaluation, brings a man into a larger sphere of action, one encompassing his prior conditions as well as those which have brought failure. Successful action then is the generation of a larger continuity in a man's relations, a continuous extension in time and into new conditions, a growth in understanding and control.

Evaluation is the methodic attempt to gain unified control over oneself within the world and to bring one's needs and relations into a coherent order with external circumstances. It is an attempt to achieve a harmonious relationship between circumstances and personal needs. Failure is regret at disorder, the sadness that one has yet much further to go in one's continuous relations with one's surroundings. It differs from frustration—for the latter comes from too great an emphasis on a single facet of a person's being; and from remorse—for that is an acquiescence in incoherence. Regret is a discovery of disorder which engenders a new possibility of order in action and control.

E. Success

I have discussed failure in some detail, because it is so often the basis of our actions. We come to awareness of alternatives by becoming aware of our failures. In middling circumstances, which neither forcefully reveal our inadequacies nor reach satisfactory arrangement, we may settle for "the best we can have" in an imperfect world. The press of circumstances compels us to accept much that could be improved, if we only had more energy or more time. Where we have not failed, we may be content—but we may not have succeeded either. When we fall short of the ideal, we may well be satisfied, for none can live unremittingly with a sense of failure. A middling accomplishment is no mean feat. We may view an avoidance of failure as all the success we can gain. Moreover, we may not succeed yet not have failed either, if circumstances are very difficult. It is, however, useful to consider success, if only to hold it before our eyes as an ideal for which we may strive, always to fall short.

In evaluation, an agent stands before his world in an interrogative posture. He seeks to answer the questions circumstances pose to him. The American pragmatists emphasize the problems in experience that lead to evaluation. However, they over-emphasize the biological origins of these problems, to some extent neglecting the methods in which questions arise. Although some problems have sufficient force to break through the most complete indifference, men can live in closed routines that give rise to few questions. Methodic evaluation presupposes a profound awareness of oneself, a self-critical awareness of how a man is implicated in the events that bear upon him. Evaluation presupposes an interrogative attitude and a concern for questions as well as a search for their answers.

The interrogation of the world and of ourselves has two dimensions, which represent our acting and being acted upon by our surroundings. A person may be viewed as the focus of processes in space and time. Like a river rushing between two banks, the personality of a human being moves in directions given by its prior forms, continually challenging its boundaries, threatening to break out and to take new paths. Habits rule its form and direction, but the banks of habit can become worn, opening new directions. In this process, a man's personality takes the forms that are given to it, yet also shapes the environment to its own purposes. In John Dewey's words, man is continually *doing* and *undergoing;* he is always acting upon his surroundings and being acted upon. It is absurd that he should cease either, quite as absurd as that he should cease to experience and still be a person.

The interplay of manipulation and assimilation (doing and undergoing) is the experience of a person; the forms of this interplay constitute his personality. A man learns from his environment in the role of assimilator; and he can control it only by manipulation. Moreover, however powerless he feels, he manipulates other things; and however powerful he feels, he assimilates the influence of things upon him. His habits are forms simultaneously of assimilation and manipulation; and the various ways in which he shapes and is shaped by his environment are revealed in the habits he possesses.

We may view a person as the variety of modes of assimilation and manipulation that constitutes his life, the forms of which constitute his character or personality. In evaluation, distinct modes relative to action are coordinated within the order of personality. When a man's values are successfully coordinated in action, they reflect a consistent manner toward his surroundings, ordering events of great and minor relevance according to his character, continuous throughout his many roles and needs. By coordinating his past relative to its outcomes, an agent can learn from history and influence his future. Nevertheless, nothing is outside his possible concern, for it may be the source of failure.

In his actions and submissions, a man bears witness to unlimited prospects of experience. Most often, his various activities form no coherent and unified whole. For example, a man may actively isolate himself from others, and treat them so they will ignore him. Yet he may also be deeply affected by them in his thoughts and behavior. His intentions are to become independent, but they are not reflected in his actions. The aspects of a person's life may be inconsistent and disunited. He then cannot know what is valuable to him, for he is torn and divided about it.

This division is by no means what is called "internal" or "subjective". A man who seeks above all else to become wealthy, who dreams constantly of discovering gold in his travels, whose entire life is the search for a mine, but who finds none—possibly because he looks in the wrong places without knowing it—suffers too from a divided being. He lacks the means to realize his ends. A man's personality and character reside within his relations to his surroundings, especially within his actions and goals. His character is the general pattern of assimilation and manipulation in his experience. What a man does and what he receives may be totally at odds. His actions are then devoid of value. His failure is reflected within the forms of his activities. He seeks the success that would bring coherence into a divided life; but circumstances do not permit him this success.

Success in evaluation coordinates in dynamic and changing relations the assimilative and manipulative dimensions of a man's experience. A man's actions may be directed against himself or include abortive efforts to change. A man may struggle to change his surroundings to suit himself or to change himself to gain greater ease in his actions. When his struggles are vain, his attempts are not fulfilled, his manipulations and assimilations fall apart. He assimilates what he cannot control, though his efforts seek control. In this sense, what he wants and what he can realize are continually at odds, and that is the mark of failure. A course of action which brings the agent's death is in this sense not a complete success, especially if he desires not to die. Yet it may be the best of all the alternatives available to him. As the best of the prospects before him, it is no failure; but it is no successful control of the future either.

The primary discontinuity in human experience is given by the precariousness of nature. Life in pretechnical society was insecure, subject to countless vicissitudes of natural life. Disease came and went; the seasons brought unexpected changes. Droughts, floods, winds—man was prey to all of them, enduring what was little within his power. In such times, the most obvious problem of action is to bring nature under control, to subdue or at least make known her dangerous variety. Technology and science provide the means for harnessing nature at least partly to our will. By discovering and improving order within nature, man becomes more powerful. Technology provides means of manipulation and control. In this sense, evaluation depends upon knowledge of the physical world as a tool for the manipulation of the environment. It depends on instruments employed as means of control. The goal is freedom from the precariousness of the natural world. With the discovery of fire, men could travel to places barred from them before, could remain awake by firelight when they desired, and could cook foods to their own pleasure. Technical discoveries bring assimilation more under human control.

Nevertheless, the improvement of techniques of manipulation does not suffice to bring unity into human experience. Most obviously, we are not able to gain complete control. The precariousness of life intrudes itself upon us, with equal or greater force because less expected. Imagination is expanded and so is the stress of choosing among possibilities. Insecurities are more apparent and more influential. Death in a subsistence culture is taken for granted more easily than death in a prosperous and well-organized society. Technical control alone cannot restrain our expectations and desires to what can technically be provided.

The second factor, then, is that human desires are not easily controlled with the means at our disposal. As we gain control over natural events, and bring them into harmony with our simple wishes, we discover that our expectations and "needs" have grown too. The gulf remains between our desires and our capacities. One of the most powerful restraints upon human expectations is their impossibility of fulfillment. As men gain more, they expect still more. External means may provide greater control of the conditions of assimilation, and some continuity within the dimensions of experience may be secured. But a new gulf opens, of virtually divergent trends within the personality. A man can significantly control his environment, but his goals are not given by the means of control. The impulses and forces within the personality, which direct its activities and characterize its assimilations, are diverted from realization. The goals of manipulation shift with the means, and a wide disparity remains between the forms of manipulation and assimilation.

The third factor, which may be most important in civilized society, is that the technical means of manipulation transform the environment, and create new conditions of assimilation. An industrial society may produce enough food for everyone, but its economic instruments may not accommodate equitable distribution of goods. The individual instruments require new forms of labor that may widen the gap between manipulation and assimilation in the lives of the men who work upon them. Human powers are social, and manipulative instruments which provide increased control over the environment may also make life harder to assimilate for individuals. A life in which one's labor is mechanical and unthinking, while one's leisure is viewed as the goal of life—leisure to act freely, with maximal control over one's activities—is divided and fragmented. Experience can be discordant also in its temporal aspects, where the projects an agent undertakes are disparate, disconnected, and of wholly different characteristics at different times. Men seek to coordinate their separate activities and responses, even—though in vain—their entire lives. Civilized society has brought new divisions into human life virtually in proportion to the control it has gained over nature.

Two paths may be followed to resolve the discordancies of civilized society. One is to direct rational control to nature, whose manipulation is the object of technology, but also to the instruments of manipulation themselves as they become part of the conditions of life. Rational technology must seek not only specific means of control but implicitly address the wider aspects of human manipulation, to provide harmony with the assimilative dimension of experience. Strong controls on specific activities can create uncontrolled consequences. Such restricted rationality may well be the height of irrationality. Rational means of industrial production have engendered abominations of social life—ghettos, unemployment, hatred, disease, the perversion of the environment. As Marx pointed out, the gulf within the social lives of men created by the rationalization of production under capitalism was far greater than what preceded it. Only rational control throughout society, directed toward the assimilative consequences of manipulative control, is likely to bring man's social life under his control as he has brought nature. Control over a part of nature widens and deepens the range of events we must manipulate. Nothing proves more forcefully that the human self is unbounded in its range than the continual extension of rational concern our technology demands of us. As we seek to manipulate events to our satisfaction we discover not only that the range of our interests expands without limit, but that the very means of manipulation we develop compel the invention of new methods for their control.

The other path to the surmounting of the gulf that is created by technical means of manipulation is by control of *oneself* as assimilator, rather than by rational control of environing conditions. If modes of manipulation and assimilation are disharmoniously related, we may seek control of assimilation as well as the technical instruments of manipulative control—though it is worth emphasizing that control of assimilation is always through manipulation. In terms of a narrow view of the human self, this is action devoted to changing oneself rather than the world. However, a man never changes merely within himself, nor merely within the environing world. A man and his various roles together define his personality—what he is related *to* as manipulator, what is related *to him* as assimilator. Assimilation and manipulation are distinguishable but inseparable, together constituting the agent who acts. What is critical in particular cases is the emphasis given to manipulation or assimilation— whether our instruments of control need improvement or whether such controls bring about satisfactory accommodations. Ultimately, though assimilation and manipulation interpenetrate, it is to action and manipulation that we must turn for control, manipulation which looks to the assimilative consequences of deeds performed. Here we should emphasize that assimilation, like manipulation, has forms and character. It is not mere feeling, but the manner, style, even *methods* whereby the impact of events is realized. Manipulation and assimilation are correlative dimensions, disharmonious where manipulation generates lack of control in assimilation, or where assimilation is chaotic and uncontrolled despite great manipulative efforts.

By virtue of the interplay of the manipulative and assimilative dimensions of experience, it is impossible to change the forms of one without affecting the other. This point needs constant emphasis. It is easy to find advocates of one or another program for the improvement of human life who neglect the interplay of the dimensions of experience. Marxists often view social planning wholly from an institutional perspective, and neglect the modes of individual assimilation. Revolutionary leaders are often the last people we may wish to have as leaders of society after the proposed revolution. On the other hand, the repudiation of political activity as personally suspect, the quest for individual peace of mind—whether by psychotherapeutic, chemical, or religious means—pretends to assimilative transformation without control of the larger conditions of manipulation. Unfortunately, the limited successes of both distortions of the complexity of human experience lead to even greater gaps within human life, promoting a monstrous divergence on strategy between groups of people dedicated to the same goals—the improvement of human life.

Nevertheless, an emphasis on one particular aspect of assimilation and manipulation can sometimes be valuable. Rational control of nature and society through technical means has the limitations I have described. It also has the further limitation that technical powers in the hands of men divided within themselves or ignorant of what is of supreme importance in human life can be monstrous. The earnest intentions of government officials of limited vision, whose understanding of themselves is small and whose comprehension of human ideals is distorted and impaired, are capable of working unmatched destruction in a technically advanced society. The stunted and unhappy citizens of industrial society suggest that concern for the inner hearts of such men is at least an act of charity and love, and may provide the roots for the betterment of human life. We are so powerful technically, though the failure of life surrounds us at every turn, that the plausibility of finding a solution in the assimilative dimension of experience is overwhelming. Men who can feel and love, who are open to experience and who care for other men, may be men who can use technology rationally and constructively.

This concern for the emotional side of life has taken many forms in the history of mankind. At all times, there have been men who urge that true values are not to be found in mere activity and control. When primitive men sought to gain stability and security within natural events, their inevitable failure suggested that through acceptance of an unknown but significant order and unity, men could live peacefully and well. Early religions provide both a means for manipulation of events—by sacrifice to the gods—and the acceptance of an order provided by a superior being. Unfortunately, manipulation of the gods does not provide control over nature; and the assimilation of events as meaningful does not coincide with their destructive capabilities. The great conflict between science and religion has been little concerned with opposing theoretical attitudes. Rather, the compelling issues have concerned the means to bring order into human life. Religion emphasizes acquiescence in assimilation, often coupled with acceptance of an inexplicable order. Science challenges not the acquiescence, but the divine order. Science leads to technology and to rational methods of control—but also undermines the acceptance necessary to peaceful assimiliation. Science, by perpetually seeking to advance, is a challenge to existence. For most men, such a challenge promotes frustration and unfulfilled expectations.

Peaceful modes of assimilation have always been equated with quietism and resignation. Laotze admits his quietism gladly—and it takes a modern interpretation to couple manipulative control with peace of mind. The paradoxical qualities of most quietistic moral theories arise from the fact that resignation and control are often incompatible. A way of life that assures men of peace of mind is either delusive and ignores the need for control over nature and social institutions, or proposes a paradoxical fusion of manipulation and peaceful assimilation. Chemicals do not avoid the same difficulties; they may provide peace of mind, but by limiting the energy available to rational control of human life. People who are convinced that peace of mind and rational manipulation are compatible seem to live in the extremes of optimistic folly.

But this is so only when peaceful assimilation is isolated from methodic control within an agent's life. What I wish to show is that a unification of self provided by a value methodically determined may provide both peaceful assimilation and the rational control of events as well. The critical factor is the generality of the method employed. All too often rational evaluation is construed narrowly, particularly by neglecting the assimilative dimension of evaluation. On the other hand, emphasis on harmonious assimilation without a method for the control of the conditions of life is mostly vain, and where successful entails the neglect of the manipulative controls that make the assimilation harmonious with the material conditions of life. No doubt there is something valuable in the realization that disciplined study of yoga can make a man relatively free from the urgent demands of his body—the same value realized in Thoreau's arguments that a man does not need to be enslaved by the social conditions of life. But unless the independence gained by realization of these possibilities strengthens our ability to control our lives, it is but a passing candidate for value.

It follows from this that, in paraphrase of Kant, harmonious assimilation without controlled manipulation is blind, while controlled manipulation without harmonious assimilation is inhumane. Evaluation must be an explicit union of assimilation and manipulation if it is to be capable of organizing the elements of a man's life. This suggests that we may begin our methodic analysis at any point, to uncover the unified dimensions of assimilation and manipulation. Unfortunately, it is not so, primarily because the application of a method is never wholly abstract, but involves concrete decisions and actions. The assimilative dimension of experience is too diffuse to provide sufficient direction. A good or wise man may intuitively grasp the specific actions required in the situations before him; but his followers may understand only the quality of his special purity, unable to serve it in action. Moral goodness resides in specific actions. The spiritual purity that provides the basis of action for a wise man can be corruption in his followers. Although manipulation and assimilation are correlative dimensions of human experience, in evaluation we are called upon to assimilate *through manipulation*. The latter is prior. All this means, of course, is that our concern is with action, not with feeling or thought. The latter are subordinate in action.

This will be clearer if we reconsider methodic evaluation in its assimilative and manipulative dimensions. We seek the integration of the various dimensions of experience in the constitution of a self consistent throughout many of its spheres of action. The various situations in which we act constitute the framework within which we seek value. Whether we act forcefully or abstain from specific action, it is the consequences of what we do that provide the test of our achievements. Things can always be made worse. On the other hand, we cannot bring anything whatever to pass, but must work within the conditions given to us.

The knowledge required for action is virtually unlimited. Conditions and situations are interrelated in complex and ramified ways, and we continually discover new forms of ignorance. Every boundary we cross threatens with the new and dangerous. Relatively insignificant events in a man's life may have vital consequences for the future. Virtually nothing can be neglected if we are to realize our desires. *Chance* and *fortune* remain on all sides to threaten us, though perhaps diminished slightly in magnitude by what we know. We seek the complete technological control over our environment, and we always fail. Yet action to produce value requires knowledge of consequences and instruments. Knowledge is our only tool for manipulative control.

Knowledge of material conditions is not sufficient, however. A human being not only seeks to manipulate, but is himself affected by his manipulations, assimilates them, and redefines his own goals. Often we struggle furiously to produce results with which we are not pleased. We must anticipate not only the material results of manipulation, but how we will assimilate them as well. Self-knowledge is required for evaluation, knowledge of how events will affect the assimilative character of experience. We must know how our own actions exert direct or indirect influence upon us, to make significant our plans for the future. Our deepest needs are often hidden and unknown. The satisfaction of our strongest desires does not serve when we have changed with their realization. Broad and specific self-knowledge is essential to evaluation. Yet assimilation and manipulation have indefinite and expanding boundaries. In this sense, evaluation extends indefinitely into the world.

Knowledge *about* oneself as a manipulative agent and assimilative subject is not sufficient for evaluation. Plato claims that men always pursue what they think is good; and claims also that if men could only know the good, they would not choose anything else. Unfortunately, one of the most obvious abilities of men is their ability to lie to themselves. Their actions belie their assertion as to what has value for them. One of the most obvious effects of psychotherapy is that patients are able to explain their neuroses, yet are unable to modify their actions. Knowledge about oneself and the world does not produce the changes in action and feeling that are essential to successful evaluation.

Until a man is literally transformed by his knowledge, he has not determined what is valuable for him. A man who feels divided in his yearnings does not attain consistency merely by knowing of his ambivalences. In fact, explicit consciousness of ambivalence can produce even greater divisions within the self, as an outcome of the torment generated. So also, when men discover the impossibility of achieving their desires, they do not automatically relinquish them. They may instead become cynical, frustrated, and spiteful—like Dostoievski's Underground Man.

What is needed for evaluation, above and beyond a broad knowledge about himself, is the skill that enables a man to change in accordance with his decisions. And since we constantly find ourselves projected into new situations, such a skill depends on the methodic extension of understanding and control into new and more comprehensive spheres of action. A man aware of being divided in his desires must be able to neglect some of them, to become less ambivalent, or to accept his divided nature and to harmonize distinct elements into coherent forms—for example, in terms of different roles at different times. A man who has extreme longings for fame, but who requires privacy as well, may settle his ambivalence by giving up one of his wants, or by organizing his life to satisfy both desires at different times—provided he knows what he is doing. However, to the extent that he is genuinely aware of his conflict of interests, then he can determine what is truly valuable for him only by a significant change in his personality—that which eliminates the conflict. Such a change can be accomplished only through control over the environment. If the environment is recalcitrant, he is doomed to failure.

The knowledge a moral agent possesses of himself in his manifold relations is the basis on which he may change himself. Peace of mind isolated from assimilative relations is self-deceptive and fruitless. But where a man knows as much as can reasonably be expected of his dependence upon his surroundings and how he can influence them, then the methodical transformation of circumstances to his ends is all that can be done. Once embarked on the methodic project of the continual expansion of understanding and control into new situations and more comprehensive spheres of action, a man can find a failure but the source of new wisdom and means of control—provided he has taken the greatest precautions possible. Here cynicism and spitefulness serve only one purpose—to prevent the agent from realizing even his limited possibilities. On the other hand, the realistic appraisal of possibilities, based on knowledge and accompanied by power to change oneself, is a quieting force. The harmony provided by self-knowledge and methodic evaluation does not come with knowledge alone, but is provided by the development of the power to implement one's decisions.

Evaluation is the maximization of the probability of success and the minimization of the probability of failure. Nothing can guarantee success; but by manipulating events, one can certainly affect probabilities. Yet unless one's abilities to undertake action conform to the knowledge possessed of consequences, one cannot actually bring order into his life. Evaluation is thus self-reflective, not only in self-knowledge, but in its control of the assimilative dimension of the agent's experience as a consequence of his own manipulations. By acting so as to gain control over his environing conditions, he gains control as well over himself. Evaluation brings changes within his modes of assimilation that coincide with the control he can exert on external events. This is the harmony that is brought by successful evaluation.

A successful action is the methodic extension from a given sphere of action to a more comprehensive sphere, especially to new conditions of assimilation and manipulation. Where the manipulative extension pre-serves a continuity of expectations as well as instruments and powers, so that control within the given sphere is continuous with the control required within the larger sphere, in terms of what is assimilated there and in terms of the personality and character of the agent, then we have success. A successful action is a continuous extension through manipula-tion to a larger sphere of action. The self projected from the narrower to the broader sphere by the action is assimilated as continuous and coherent in its different roles and needs. Success organizes manipulation in terms continuous with the requirements of assimilation as defined by the character and principles of the agent, and organizes assimilation in terms of powers developed for further action—since a temporary success may well lead to eventual failure. Success is the continuous projection of powers into new situations that are assimilated both as satisfactory and as the development of further powers for future control.

There remains the possibility that the self-determination I have proposed as the goal of evaluation is but another form of resignation.

What is it to accept one's prospects of action when they are limited by circumstances except a resignation to imperfection? Can a man who lives in a society which breeds poverty and misery really come into harmony with his circumstances and environment? Can one do anything but struggle to oppose evil, and angrily work to bring a better world from the old? Am I proposing an ideal that has no basis in an unjust world?

Such questions fail completely to touch the compatibility of manipulation and assimilation I have described. The continuity of self involved is not necessarily a form of contentment or pleasure. In fact, a man may decide that conditions permit no contentment while there is misery in the world. His projected values generate a permanent struggle against injustice in all walks of life—but a struggle which is both self-affirming and which provides him with strength, with persistence, and with satisfactions. Principles are evolved which define partial successes to be very satisfactory in terms of available resources. If a partial success is not a full success, in that events elude our full control, nevertheless it may be a great achievement given the poverty of our resources. The partial nature of such successes is no cause for condemnation, but an impulse toward greater comprehensiveness in spheres of control. There is a complacency which is the conviction of having done everything possible. But there is a peace of mind that rests upon the same conviction. The difference between the two depends on how adequate is the knowledge one possesses of what must be done and how to do it, on the unremittingly interrogative method employed.

A successful action extends the self continuously from one sphere of action to another, coordinating the manipulative and assimilative dimensions. Nevertheless, an action has remote consequences, the self projected into ever wider spheres of action. The complex and ramified interplay of spheres of action and experience entails that no action will be successful for all situations, in terms of all its future consequences. Methodic evaluation seeks such control, but must define our expectations modestly enough to promote satisfaction. Action seeks control; in addition, it extends the self continuously in terms of prior standards and skills into new spheres of action; third, principles and ideals define both the character of the agent and his values, but also the expectations and standards of success available. A successful action is never a permanent success, but evokes the challenge of its future consequences. Partial success is here a satisfactory result in a given sphere, but one leading to further actions looking to other and more comprehensive spheres as well. In this sense, a completely successful action is either only a partial success;

or, instead, it is bought at the price of complacency. Complete success is at best an ideal relative to an action in a narrow sphere—only to evoke the perils of failure relative to other spheres subsequently.

Methodic evaluation presupposes an unremitting interrogative posture. One is at stake in everything one chooses to do, and everything that happens as a result. This continual testing of one's actions is all that protects us from smug complacency, but it is quite enough. Complacency is the conviction that one cannot fail. Successful evaluation is the conviction that one has done the best one could, predicated upon a profound awareness of the possibilities of failure, and validated in terms of the larger sphere of action entered. Complacency is a blindness that prevents a man from expanding his horizons and the comprehensiveness of his understanding, so that he regards all situations alike, failing to discern the differences within them that call for synthetic realization. Complacency and blindness may produce satisfaction, and may avoid regret—but by insensitivity to circumstances. A man remains *inert* through vicissitudes and through conflicting demands. Success is bred of methodic action, generating a new self continuous with the old, but in control of a larger sphere of events and conditions, either by manipulating events, by changing within oneself, or most often, by both together. A successful action is an expansion of the self in its manipulative control and in what is assimilated. It broadens the reach and the identity of the agent as determiner of his own destiny. In this sense, it is autonomy and the mark of a responsible and praiseworthy moral agent.

F. Anguish and Despair

If men look to success in their endeavors, nevertheless the press of circumstances and the imperfection of life often place that success beyond their reach. Failure remains their nemesis. At best they may avoid failure; they cannot often achieve success. They may not regret their lack of control when they have done the best they could; but they may also gain no continuous extension of control within larger spheres of action. Life here remains disjointed. The struggle with conflicting obligations brings little chance of satisfying relations. All a man can do is to act as he must, and to choose among the wealth of conflicting imperatives that action which most suits him, most realizes his character and needs. If he has done well, he will not fail—though he will not necessarily bring about a unified order within his conflicting tendencies. To know that one has done what one had to, so completely as to be without regret, need not imply that one has rendered consistent the dimensions of his experience. Of course, if a man feels inadequate where he does not fully succeed, then he will fail. Moreover, sufficient control to provide partial success may not make a man free from conflict.

The possibility of failure haunts life; the struggle to avoid failure is the main impetus to methodic evaluation. Yet even a man who has given himself completely to methodic interrogation to determine what he must do in terms of his ideals and circumstances lives with the constant threat of failure. The blindness that protects a man from consciousness of failure only increases the probability of failing. The sensitive alertness that permits a man to consider every possibility of failure and to accommodate it in his deliberations both protects him, yet fills his life with pain. The anticipation of failure is anguish. The only escape from anguish is by flight into blindness, with its attendant increase in the likelihood of failure.

The attempt to escape from anguish is in vain—though not for the reasons Sartre gives. To Sartre, freedom is the essential property of consciousness—its ability to negate its past and to redefine itself. Whenever a man considers himself a thing, particularly as an excuse, he is in bad faith. He denies his essential nature—which is to be nothing until self-defined. Men cannot face their freedom, and flee from anguish into an acceptance which would excuse them for their failings. The basis for Sartre's claim that the repudiation of responsibility is always in bad faith is the freedom at the heart of consciousness.

Even if we neglect the difficulties inherent in existential freedom, there is a major problem in Sartre's view of bad faith. It is essential to any analysis of responsibility that the capacity of men to delude themselves be taken into account. Men rationalize their transgressions almost without limit, and devise complex explanations of their failures based on ignorance, blindness, or elements of character. Sartre develops a metaphysical ground for the analysis of self-deception. But his analysis entails that no one can ever sincerely excuse a failure. Sartre moves from a metaphysical ground for freedom to the assumption that men are always conscious of that freedom—at least pre-reflectively. Therefore, when they deny their responsibilities, they are lying to themselves as well as to others.

It is difficult to make meaningful claims about pre-reflective experience. Moreover, even full-fledged moral agents, willing and able to accept responsibility for their actions, often feel constrained by the pressure of events. Sartre argues that a man under torture can always last a bit longer without divulging information—and thus is both free and responsible for capitulating when he does. There is an interesting theoretical point here—though I do not believe that Sartere draws the correct conclusion—but surely there is substance as well to the prisoner's sense of constraint by other men and their devices. Perhaps the claim "I couldn't help it" is not quite accurate—a man can always act a trifle differently. But it is false to say that he could have withstood the torture.

Men do lie to themselves—that is clear from ordinary experience, and is detailed exquisitely in psychoanalytic case studies. In fact, the main consequence of psychoanalysis for moral analysis may well be the compelling realization that men act blindly and censor information essential to rational evaluation. Men seem purposefully to lack self-knowledge. And once a man has repressed what he ought to know, we seem committed to accepting his ignorance as an excuse. If anguish is essential to responsible action, what are we to do with men who are not aware of anguish? Sartre claims they are in bad faith—*everyone* experiences anguish, at least pre-reflectively. But such anguish is out of awareness. Sartre's solution is no solution.

If anguish is essential to responsible action, we must find a basis on which to hold that men *ought* to feel anguish, and also to accept the consequences that follow for men who lack moral awareness. Sartre's wish to maintain that men are always responsible for what they do even leads him to distort the role of rationalization in evaluation, by claiming that it is always insincere. The striking thing about rationalization is that it may be perfectly effective and thoroughly genuine, yet still fail in its purposes.

It is precarious to define the function of rationalization and self-deception. Nevertheless, it seems apparent that the giving of excuses, and the defining of circumstances so as always to have excuses, have as their primary function the avoidance of remorse, of condemnation, or in general, of a sense of failure. Anguish is the consciousness that failure is always a possibility. By rationalizing that one did the best he could (considering the circumstances, his history and character), he may obliterate anguish from his awareness. He may deny that failure is a possibility for him. Men have continually sought to find such complete grounds for action as to make failure impossible. Unfortunately, that assurance is itself impossible; so that a man who concludes that he *couldn't* fail is simply wrong. Yet he may be quite sincere, if rather misled.

All the techniques available for denying the prospects of failure entail some kind of blindness—the willful refusal to entertain some possibilities.

Nevertheless, it is to be blind in such a way as to make conscious realization of failure impossible. A man who views life as but a series of arbitrary and willful actions may act capriciously and disconnectedly. He cannot fail, for he has accepted no standards by which to judge failure. Analogously, a man who views morality as a system of rules which have routine application in his life is thereby protected against the possibility of failure, so long as he conforms to the rules. The consequences of his actions do not matter, for he refuses to take them into account.

Such forms of blindness achieve a felt security, yet also increase the prospects of failure, especially when judged by any other standards. Inertness to new circumstances avoids the conscious sense of being unable to control them. The continuity attained here is of inert insensitivity to one's surroundings. The willful refusal to consider any purpose to one's actions may eliminate all awareness of the prospect of failure. Yet a man who lives in such a manner cannot intentionally satisfy any desires. If we suppose that he in fact has no purposes or desires, then he has eliminated the possibility of failure, and lives without anguish. So also, a man who acts according to a clear set of moral principles may ignore the consequences of his behavior as irrelevant. If he is indeed without concern for the harm produced by his blindness, then he may be free from anguish. In both cases, the freedom from anguish depends on what is true about the agent's desires, intentions, or concerns. In both cases also, freedom from anguish is attained through an almost total lack of control.

These flights from anguish are founded upon an arbitrary completion of rational evaluation. Dostoievski's Underground Man quite explicitly denies all rational grounds for action. He *will not* accept any argument that would circumscribe his freedom. He does not prove that he will not fail, but refuses to engage in the consideration of failure. Ironically, he is by no means emotionally secure against the failure he intellectually disregards. He is miserable and wallows in futility.

Our inability to make our desires consistent with a flight from anguish is important. However much we may flee from the possibility of failure, we can succeed only by not failing. The presumption is that we know ourselves and our surroundings well enough to escape failure. An agent can justify the conclusion that some blindness is beneficial only by first considering various possibilities. Such blindness, based as it is on clear self-knowledge—for example, that one cannot tolerate details of suffering, and would rather not hear of them—is by no means the naive and willful rejection of the possibilities of experience we have been discussing. It may be indeed true that too heightened a consciousness of failure may produce paralysis and misery. But this truth must be based on a profound consciousness of alternatives if it is to be grounded. One may flee from anguish only by having faced it—which is no flight at all.

It is indeed possible to live without consciousness of anguish, and to flee from the possibility of failure. But either this is a state reached without control and intention, or it is based upon the explicit realization of the possibilities of failure. Moreover, once a man has considered failure in its various aspects, then it is difficult to see how he could rationally choose to live blindly, when that blindness brings an increased likelihood of failure. Once a man faces failure in his actions, then the possibility of failure can be seen everywhere, and there is no possibility of escape. If we consider the possibility of failure, then we live in anguish. If we deny the possibility of failure, then that denial will increase the prospects of failure.

If failure is everywhere, and anguish the consciousness that it cannot be avoided, then anguish itself must be evaluated as relevant to the likelihood of failure. Here it is obvious that too heightened a consciousness of anguish—the poignant awareness of one's limitations and futile prospects—produces a passivity and self-loathing that produces additional failure. Principles which define partial success are essential, so that we may gain in power and control by conviction, and not lapse into a sterile sense of the omnipresence of failure that inhibits action. Blindness is an escape from anguish that brings failure to pass unnecessarily. Acceptance of modest and limited goals does not eliminate anguish, but rather moves from it to greater effectiveness in action and control.

The poignant anguish that is contempt for being helpless must be transformed into a consciousness of failure that is not self-loathing but self-control, not passivity but the impetus to action, not frustration but affirmative decision. The methodic aspect of evaluation makes this inevitable. We are speaking here of methods of action inspired by a consciousness of failure, methods devoted to controlling and eliminating failure. Only a full and sensitive awareness of possibilities can make such a method successful. But also, only a rich and effective self-discipline, as well as ease with oneself as an agent, can enhance prospects of success. Only by a profound awareness of the possibilities of failure, and also the strengthening of one's abilities to cope with the conditions of life, can successful control be attained. It is the transformation of anguish from a destructive to a motivating and inspiring force that harmonizes the assimilative and methodic dimensions of human experience. We assimilate the results of our actions only on the basis of self-respect, motivated by the consciousness of the possibility of failure to act to the best of our abilities.

Methodic evaluation depends on a heightened awareness of possibilities of failure, the awareness which is anguish. On the other hand, evaluation is not theory but *action*. The need for action, when coupled with anguish, produces "despair"—the awareness that *we must act*, though we may fail. To live continually with anguish may produce a horror at the omnipresence of choice, at the unavoidability of action. What evaluation must produce is an anguish free from despair. Only then can action be deeply effective.

Despair is the paralysis that anguish can bring to the need for action. Nothing a man can do will assure him of success; everything he plans may go awry. When his deeds are of little consequence he can still be appalled at the insufficiency of the grounds on which he must act. In times of moment, the calamitous force of events is overwhelming. Nothing can mitigate the possibility of disaster. Anguish becomes despair; and the needs of men become Furies confusing them, rather than impulses to action.

If despair is the paralysis of will before the need for action in a precarious world, then hope is its antidote. Hope is the quality of anguish when action is welcomed. Despair is the quality of anguish when failure inhibits action. Hope is anguish as the impetus to action, where failure is the ground of decision. The omnipresence of failure can paralyze the will in despair. But even the paralysis of action can bring failure. The habit of decisiveness in the face of the perpetual possibility of failure is the only defensible response. Despair is a focus on failure and the insecurity of life; hope is a focus on success as the possible outcome of rational action. Submission to the insecurity of anguish is despair; the realization of possibilities through action rests on hope.

Smugness is not hope, nor is hope blind and unquestioning faith. Faith can illuminate a man's decisions with a false light as if of hope; but where no method provides a way, the light of faith leads to untimely fall. Hope is the other side of anguish from despair, but it is deeply rooted in the possibility of failure. Hope is realized where the risk we face is known, and we use all the means at our disposal to bring events to fruition. Faith is surrounded by ignorance and is often thought to move beyond reason in what is known. Hope is the fulfillment of rational method, the completion of evaluation in the action that can bring satisfaction. Hope is the affirmative quality that all evaluation must have to generate goodness from the vale of misery and disorder that is life.

Despair is the negation that consciousness of failure can arouse. Faith is the affirmation of success on insufficient grounds, based on ignorance and willfullness. Hope is the affirmation of success that can come from rational judgment directed to the avoidance of failure. Despair is the horror that the limitations of reason can arouse. Hope is the fulfillment of whatever order is *possible,* the promotion of whatever peace can be found, the discovery of what is intelligible amidst the seeds of irrationality. Faith is a submission to the bright lure of Dionysus, the lure that makes it akin to the light of Apollo. Despair is a submission to the dark side of Dionysus. Hope is the affirmation of the light of Apollo—as the day comes out of the night, not as day is thought to rule supreme forever.

Moral Principles

~~~~~~

A. Function

To this point, I have made only passing reference to the role of principles in action. Yet it is obvious that principled judgment is essential to evaluation. In fact, it is difficult to comprehend the notion of a value that does not involve an appeal of some sort to principle. An action that is not subsumable under a general rule is arbitrary and not *valued*. The moral significance of Sartre's existentialism is opaque precisely because its ontology leaves no room for action ruled by principles. The radical freedom Sartre espouses makes every principle a form of bondage. Principles having no *clear* foundation have none at all other than that of a willful choice to observe them—which in effect leaves them with no function at all as principles. If principles serve any function, they in some sense govern the actions taken in accordance with them. The problem is to make sense of the notion of rule-governed actions which does not reduce them merely to instances of a general prescription. For if evaluation is nothing but the observation of rules, then it loses the quality of risk that is present in every concrete act—that the consequences may prove failure. The most plausible relief from anguish is in principles of action to which one conforms without question. It is also extremely perilous.

Kant's analysis of the principles of morals as grounded in *a priori* reason provides the only possibility yet discerned for a system of value based on principles of absolute worth. The laws which practical reason prescribes to itself generate both freedom and their own absolute rule. The perpetual problems of reevaluation are terminated in the principles *constitutive* of reason; while the formal structure of such principles, insofar as they are necessary to moral judgment, allows an escape from anguish in the security of law. Unfortunately, the price paid for eliminating the risk of failure is the grounding of action solely in the will. Consequences which cannot be reduced to formal principles are considered of no *moral* consequence. Kant so fully incorporates the rule of law into moral judgment as to render it secure; but the perils of action remain in the conflict between prudence—which considers the consequences of action in their relation to the agent's desires—and morals—which is wholly subject to *a priori* principle. Either men should *never* let prudential considerations outweigh moral law; or every evaluation must balance moral against prudential considerations—and we have not eliminated the complexities of evaluation. We have simply distinguished them into two theoretically separate, but concretely inseparable categories. Moreover, we wholly lack a basis for weighing the demands of prudence against the rule of moral law. By basing moral judgment on reason *a priori*, Kant in effect renders evaluation in the large—the judgment of the place of prudence in any concrete situation—arbitrary and without foundation. Kierkegaard's sense of the absurdity of evaluation is a natural consequence. Hegel's movement from the realm of law to the particular case is even more plausible—except that it casts in doubt the rule of principle, since the richness of every concrete situation may obviate the application of any principle. It is a simple step to the Nietzschean abandonment of principle.

The fundamental problem of the role of principles in action is that of locating the possibilities of failure properly. An arbitrary or disordered residuum remains within any sphere of action. Principles may conflict, they may fail to reflect changing prospects, or situations may overlap in complex and ramified ways. The danger is of distorting arbitrariness in action by misplacing it in relationship to law. Kant so conceives of the function of principles in moral judgment as to make concrete failure impossible, if law has been observed. Moral judgment becomes completely rational and free from arbitrariness. But actions themselves, which involve both prudential and moral concerns, are then wholly without foundation. The price Kant pays for eliminating the risk of failure in morals is of rendering complex political actions nearly without intelligible foundation. Political judgment, viewed as a union of expediency and moral values, is irrational.

On the other hand, in Hegel, Marx, and Nietzsche, the grounding of action in the concrete richness of situations is based on laws of their development. The rule of moral principles at any given time is treated as a transient result of developing forces. Principles entirely lose their rational authority. They preserve a degree of substance, in defining the context which must be surpassed. But they cannot theoretically govern situations and judgments. Even in Dewey's careful analysis of the continuum of means and ends, the experimental nature of value judgment tends to predominate over the legislative capacity of principles. The force of the concept of habit is constitutive, not regulative. Dewey cannot satisfactorily define a role for principles that both is regulative *and* allows for the possibility of surpassing those very principles. Habits are significant constitutive factors in situations which call for action; but the action itself surpasses, or raises the possibility of surpassing, the principles involved. Dewey stresses the fact that the intelligent reappraisal of principles is not the same as abandoning them. But he never quite captures the governing power of principles in his concern for reinvesting them with a vitality relevant to the situations in which they are employed. Of all philosophers, Kierkegaard alone seems to have captured the terrible risk of abandoning a moral principle, coupled with the awareness that some particular situations make it necessary. It is precisely because principles both regulate and constitute actions and their values that failure produces anguish and despair. Anguish is the gap between the force of law and the consequences of action. Our acceptance of a principle can bring disastrous consequences; our abandonment of principle can turn us wholly into instruments.

Principles have a three-fold role in evaluation. They are at once regulative, constitutive, and substantive. In the interplay of these functions, as well as in their outcome, we may find the clearest sense of methodic evaluation. Yet there is more to any situation than its lawful aspects; and in the last analysis, evaluation must consider the concrete nature of action also. Every situation calls for a transcendence in value within the context of regulation by law. The character of this transcendence will be made clear by the consideration of the various functions of principles in evaluation.

1. Substantive

In all action, new conditions are created from the old. In methodic evaluation, the agent redirects his energies, reconstitutes his environment, and brings diverse components of his life into a continuous and consistent order. Among the various constituents of situations that call for evaluation, and which must be brought into coherence, are the various principles which play a role within the situation. And it is within principles that we may look for the unifying capacity of intelligence in action. Where principles and actions remain incommensurate, evaluation must fail. Where principles are erroneously applied, under conditions unsuitable to them, where actions bring new affairs without control or satisfaction, and where principles conflict with each other, allowing for no intelligent integration, we have no possibility of success. Principles define the very character of evaluative situations and set the grounds upon which values rest. They define the means of synthetic encompassment in terms of which success may be realized. But it is action that is the test of success and failure. Principles are exhausted in circumscribing the context of judgment. Action completes the evaluation in the development of new states of affairs.

The function of principles is three-fold. Their most obvious function, and the ground for their other functions, is *substantive*. A principle appealed to in evaluation provides what has been learned in the past about means to success and the avoidance of failure. Evaluation is grounded on principles which carry whatever wisdom the past can offer to the present. One reason why a child is not a full active agent is that he has not lived enough to have practical wisdom—the wisdom inherent in attempted efforts and attendant failures, and in the related principles of conduct that mark general means to success.

Apothegms and saws have the force they do in human life not because of their humdrum quality, but because they contain the substance of timeless wisdom—if only we can grasp their message. "A stitch in time saves nine" pointedly captures the need for taking action early—a lesson which men keep in mind when doing business, but tend to forget when faced with moral difficulties. If political pressure is to be exerted on a repressive government subject to diverse pressures from various interest groups, one must not wait too long to undertake the campaign. If we wait too long to oppose evil, we may find that it has grown so powerful in the delay that opposing it runs a far greater risk than it did at the beginning.

Sayings usually come in pairs. "A stitch in time saves nine," but "haste makes waste." Simple truths are not of great value when taken literally or followed unthinkingly. Every maxim of action, however true, demands both qualification and interpretation in particular circumstances. When we are cognizant of both sayings of a complementary pair, we are warned to consider both of them, that no simple rule will suffice for the determination of what is valuable. We gain in wisdom the more completely we grasp the substance of such rules of conduct, though we must interpret them for our concrete circumstances.

Maxims and saws provide us with relatively trivial principles of evaluation—trivial because they demand so complex an interpretation by the agent that he must virtually reject the substance of the maxim to respect its wisdom. The more seriously a man believes that "All that glitters is not gold," the more deeply he must consider whether he is about to let a major opportunity escape by requiring too conclusive a proof of value before he acts. For anyone who thinks even a moment about following them, saws tend to provide the consideration of the opposite point of view. For this reason, old saws are not a significant contribution to evaluative situations. Their substantive wisdom has the quality of respect for considered judgment, so much as to nullify the possibility of regulative acquiescence.

When we turn to more important principles, particularly to moral laws, we find the same substantive character, but with a far more significant and serious role. Consider first, before looking at specifically moral principles, the principle "power corrupts, and absolute power corrupts absolutely"; and the analogous principle concerning wealth, implicit in Plato's *Republic:* "wealth corrupts, and great wealth corrupts greatly." Here we have as vague and unqualified principles as we find in saws and sayings, but with far greater substantial truth. Such principles may be violated only at great risk, though violation is often necessary. A man who seeks to gain political power from the most laudatory of motives must face the fact that his character is at the mercy of the instruments he must employ to hold power. Men who deal with other men in positions of authority do not remain untouched by what they do. Richard III's deviousness is a natural consequence of the means he has employed to gain power. Lear's foolish expectations follow easily from his position of power. The possession of authority can render a man blind to many alternatives and to the consequences of methods he must employ.

The wisdom embodied in principles of conduct provides to an agent aware of them a tool he may employ in his actions, and dares not disregard. Men who take power are transformed by what they undertake. Every moral agent must know the likelihood of his undergoing so gradual a transformation that he will be unaware of it taking place. The general rules of conduct that permeate our understanding of honor and of human psychology provide us with substance for our actions. Whether we accept a general rule or set it aside as inapplicable to ourselves, the wisdom contained within it may not be overlooked.

The substance of general rules of conduct is in many respects what we seek when we make moral judgments. For this reason it may be called "wisdom"—a wisdom to be found in discourse and deliberation, if not the wisdom of action. What we seek in action is a means for rendering our situation secure and satisfying, for eliminating discordancies, for channeling our activities productively. Without general principles, men would be literally unintelligent, forced to develop procedures anew in every situation. Fortunately, we often encounter situations alike, in our lives and in the lives of others. General rules in their substantive function represent the tried and tested procedures—or the repeated failures—that we may call upon again in our actions. When we ask ourselves what we should do, general principles represent what we may choose from, on the grounds that such principles have proved valuable in the past.

Knowledge drawn from past successes and failures, and projected into future expectations, constitutes the only knowledge we may have of how to deal with events before us. If we ever have justification for our actions, it is by reference to actions and their consequences. Actions grounded in knowledge all share this same characteristic, whether obviously moral and profoundly normative, or whether relatively technical and straightforward. Knowledge is coordinated in the general principles of how to act to accomplish goals. Action without knowledge of general principles and of relevant facts is blind.

Of course, since principled action can at best project principles from established conditions to new situations, the risks of failure are not eliminated, though they may be minimized. The crucial point is that intelligence can *only* be rooted in general truths based on past actions and their successes or failures. Principles in their substantive role *summarize* the ways to avoid failure, as realized in past actions. The projection into new situations, required in all action, is perilous. Moreover, it requires also the continual reexamination and reformulation of traditional principles, so that they may represent more comprehensive relations emerging through time. Only by coordinating traditional principles with new conditions, and representing a larger sphere of action—larger at least over time and inclusive of a more comprehensive range of historical conditions—can action move from narrower to larger spheres, to reach whatever continuity of personal integrity and satisfaction is possible for the agent. In the end, it is as principles become broad ideals, adhered to faithfully and with integrity, but interpreted appropriately with respect to varying conditions, that actions become generally successful.

A man who must make a moral decision can but refer to the general

principles of action and general facts that are relevant to his circumstances. Antigone, in burying her brother against the commands of
Creon, appeals to a principle relating the burial of corpses and the
fortunes of their shades in the after life. Creon attacks her actions as
socially ill-advised, referring to the need for social order and respect for
authority. The discovery to which Creon is brought in the end comes also
under a general rule—that rational control of events is not without
danger; and *especially,* that traditional moral principles may not be flouted
without danger. This latter *fact* is the most general substantive principle
of moral action. Precisely insofar as moral laws embody wisdom, to
disobey them even on rational grounds is to court disaster. This is partly
due to the regulative function of moral principles. But it is also due to the
wisdom implicit in such principles which cannot always be made
completely explicit.

One of the most telling lessons a child must learn in becoming an
adult is how much substantive wisdom is embodied in social conventions.
Many adolescents find it necessary to challenge and even disregard the
conventions of their upbringing in order to learn which they must accept
and which have little or no foundation. This is one of the adaptive
mechanisms by which a society adjusts its principles to its own realities. It
is not uncommon for young people to avoid responsibility, to try extreme
forms of self-indulgence, to see how satisfactory such behavior proves to
be. Their parents tell them that a good job is important in living well—so
some adolescents willfully refuse to work. They are told that sexual purity
is beneficial, that sexual license can lead to degradation and loss of
self-respect—so many act licentiously and wantonly, to experience for
themselves the results of violating common norms. If fortunate, young
people learn some of the wisdom embodied in moral conventions without
permanently harming themselves. At times when the forms of rebellion
are extreme, many young people are not so fortunate. The worst
consequences of such arbitrary rejection of traditional standards come
about when an equally narrow or narrower standard is substituted for a
traditionally established principle. Experimentation with traditional norms
is of value only where it establishes a larger continuity of action in a more
comprehensive sphere of control.

Rebellion is a necessary part of maturation. The wisdom of social
conventions is not obvious or easy to confirm. General principles are
never quite as subtle or sophisticated in their formulations as we would
like, and we must interpret them to suit our particular circumstances and
needs. Thus, it is difficult to defend the wisdom of self-control to an

adolescent who is prey to powerful emotions and vulnerable to an experimental environment. To make no distinction between sexual and any other behavior can be degrading and destroy a person's capacity for feeling. But complete chastity can be equally repressive in a sexually charged environment. A man can never know exactly where wisdom ends and repressiveness begins in the vagueness of general rules. Some experimentation is necessary to make sense of these rules in one's own terms and for one's own life.

More important than this is the fact that general principles are not exhaustive for action and evaluation. They often conflict, and an agent must ascertain how they are to be reconciled in his concrete actions. Chastity can be based on self-respect and be a good; but so are love and intimacy. It is wrong to tell lies, and dangerous to the teller; but courtesy demands daily trifling with the truth. Honesty can be a deadly weapon. Everyone must experiment with general rules to fit his own circumstances. Whatever the wisdom of the principles we live by, we act individually and personally.

The final reason for the rejection of the wisdom of general principles is based more on their regulative than their substantive function. So long as general principles are taken automatically to represent wisdom, and to regulate our conception of what is valuable, we avoid the overwhelmingly personal character of action. Yet principles often conflict, or require interpretation in specific cases.

Evaluation transcends all boundaries of judgment, by using them rather than by casting them off. The acquiescence to rule without thought is the abdication of judgment. It results in a perpetuation of parochial and limited standards within spheres of action that have expanded drastically. It may well bring about the most severe discordancies and inconsistencies in life and action. This will be dealt with in our discussion of the regulative function of principles.

2. Constitutive

Where the substantive function of moral principles is considered alone, an action may be viewed as a decision based on adequate knowledge and nothing more. Either the agent knows the principles that apply or he does not. The fundamental act of choice is thus trivialized and reduced to the routine application of a known rule.

However, the transcendent aspect of action arises from the function of general principles not only to provide wisdom gathered from past enterprises, but to *constitute* the elements which call for action. Without general principles accepted as determinative and constitutive, moral decisions are not possible. A man might ask himself what he ought to do to gain benefit. But without principles which define the benefits available as well as the means which define possibilities, he can at best make abortive sallies that fall short of genuine efforts. Control can be sought only where principles obtain which are sufficiently comprehensive to define such control broadly throughout relevant spheres of action.

Only trivial decisions can exist without general principles to define the terms of judgment. Even in defining justice to be the interest of the stronger, Thrasymachus assumes the application of some general principles—vague ones to be sure—concerning the nature of interest and its relationship to justice. He assumes that force is an instrument of rule, and allows that fact to constitute his conception of what is right. What is essential is not that any *particular* principles define our judgments, but that *some* must. To attack one principle in terms of another is important and common, but to undermine the entire rule of principle in evaluation is at the expense of incoherence and unintelligibility. Nietzsche's unintelligibility stems most from his wish to deny the rule of *any* general principles.

Consider a relatively trivial decision—a man considering whether to drive his automobile to work or to take the train. On the surface, general principles which refer to convenience, relative efficiency, comfort, and punctuality seem to be nothing other than the *substance* of his judgment. Nevertheless, insofar as he has a specific goal or a coherent hierarchy of goals, they constitute the terms of his judgment. The rule that he ought to be on time to work defines the substance of his judgment, but constitutes it as well. If his work is tension producing, and his convenience and ease are paramount, then his judgment will be different. The general principles that represent his operative values constitute the situation, one which requires judgment and action.

As we move from situations in which principles are primarily substantive to those in which principles function constitutively, we move more toward the moral sphere. Moral principles are overwhelmingly constitutive and regulative, to the point of nearly obliterating the substantive qualities such principles possess in human life. This is one of the reasons why moral principles seem so odd: they regulate decisions, and constitute possibilities of action, yet their wisdom is often obscure. It is easy to feel constrained by rules that define and regulate the circumstances of action when the wisdom inherent in such rules is not clearly apprehended. Freedom appears to belong within possibilities beyond those provided by circumstances, rather than within the range of possibility belonging to the domain of regulation and wisdom.

Thus the principle that one ought to seek the satisfactory use of one's powers in productive activity, a principle that represents the wisdom of many men's lives, becomes an onerous restriction when merely constitutive in a young man's life. His plans for the future are not free, but circumscribed within the possibilities defined by the principle of work. If a man sincerely doubts the value of the exercise of talents and skill, wondering whether pleasure and indolence are not the highest values in life, he poses a complete challenge to the principle of work. His incapacities generate no need for action, especially in a highly propitious environment. Without a principle constituting spheres of action to need talents and skill, a man cannot be led to action except by failure. The claim that many men have found their fulfillment in productive activity is not clearly proved, nor does it clearly affect him. He is left with virtually an unrestricted domain of choice, to do whatever crosses his mind. If no principles constitute a range of possible action for him, he can do anything and therefore *must* do nothing in particular. He then can find no clear way to determine value within his circumstances.

To accept no constitutive principles is to abandon any basis for action in any given sphere—for the sphere is defined by those principles relevant to it which constitute it as one calling for action. Constitutive principles define both the boundaries of a sphere of action and its primary values. Nevertheless, since action always projects established principles from one sphere of control to another, constitutive principles are nearly always in question in methodic action. Though we can act only within a situation defined by constitutive principles, a satisfactory action is a test of these very principles and their applicability. Only by accepting the risks of action and of failure, and accepting *both* the constitutive power of moral principles and the need to transcend them in action—the two separated sometimes in time, sometimes only theoretically—can methodic action be undertaken.

In moral decisions, principles become almost determinative, so powerful is their constitutive role. A war ten thousand miles away is an object of *moral* scrutiny only under the rule of a moral principle—for example, that one ought never to kill another human being. The inconvenience of war—in increased taxes, shortage of essential materials, and the like—is significant, but often without moral impact. Although we might wonder whether productive activity does indeed provide fulfillment, we cannot as reasonably wonder if killing is rewarding in the same way. All general principles have a substantive function; and the prohibition against murder too contains a kind of wisdom about what must be prohibited if men are to live peaceably together. But the overwhelming function of such a principle is to constitute the moral character of the decisions we consider. This tends to submerge the substantive function of such principles.

Nevertheless, the substantive function of principles and rules is primary in one fundamental sense. That is, that *if* one places a moral principle under attack, the sole ground of validity rests in its substantive character. It is because principles have substance that they can become regulative and constitutive. On the surface, this may not appear to be true, for one may accept a rule that has no ground in past experience. We may accept the rules of a game without acquiescing to a ground of substantiated wisdom for those rules.

But morals is not a game. This is another way of saying that moral situations are constituted by principles quite differently from games like chess. One may play chess only according to rules which both constitute the game and regulate moves within it. A method may be constituted and regulated by principles that have no substantive function. Such a method or activity is never coercive—that is, one rather arbitrarily or capriciously chooses to adopt the method or not. If one does, one accepts the rules which constitute it. Otherwise one does not. Rules of a game constitute the game for a player who has agreed to play. But a man is not compelled by the rules to play the game.

When principles have a secure substantive quality, as they do in moral affairs, then they gain a second constitutive power, virtually a coercive one. That is, they compel an agent to accept a situation as falling within their purview. Put another way, they constitute a situation, one which must be regulated by themselves. It is this mode of constitution that I consider essential. The weaker constitutive function of principles is primarily one dependent on the methods at work and situations at hand. The stronger constitutive function of principles is the power possessed by moral principles to force upon a given state of affairs the use of specific methods and a conformity to certain rules. Constitutive principles here become regulative. A situation constituted a moral one is regulated by moral principles. Either such principles then constrain spheres of control through prescription, so that change then is arbitrary and impossible to justify, or the constitutive function of principles within a situation must implicitly be based on substantive considerations. However, principles may conflict, thus undermining their regulative powers. They remain constitutive, however, since in conflict they define the situation to call for action in the light of their constitutive powers. Principles may justify this power only through their substance as embodiments of rational aim. Arbitrary rules define a game, one which cannot exert coercive force unless substantive content is presupposed.

The device used in psychoanalytic theory to describe the coercive force of principles is *internalization*. The point is that principles can be internalized only if they have had *external* effect, and if they continue to embody some external value. Otherwise they become arbitrary and irrational, which is to say neurotic and idiopathic. The difference between conscience and obsession is no more than substantive quality. Moral principles suggest their own wisdom, and refer to some aim. The Greek principle that all action aims at some good is preserved in the substantive function of principles. Without this, their regulative and constitutive properties become pathological.

Thus, the attack on a constitutive principle is always an attack on its substance. And it is an attack that aims at undermining its entire function as a principle. When Creon denies the effectiveness of Antigone's action in burying her brother, and urges her to consider the social order and the consequences of her actions for others as well as herself, he is denying that the situation is one constituted by the principle she appeals to. If it truly has substance, and represents an adequate means of control in human action, then it is relevant and must be considered. So long as the principle that one must bury one's brother is in force, it defines the situation to be of moral conflict. To attack the principle's substance, by overriding it with pragmatic considerations, is to undermine its other functions as well. If there is no divine truth embodied in the principle, it has no hold on action. Either there is a situation of conflict constituted in part by the validity of a principle or there is not. No middle ground exists here.

A principle is constitutive within a sphere of control if it governs the deliberations relevant to action and if it represents a necessary condition of the validity of the action. A constitutive principle must be "taken into account." A substantive principle may be ignored, though true generally, if irrelevant. A constitutive principle is necessarily relevant—that is its constitutive role—though the nature of its relevance may remain in question. A regulative principle may stand in conflict with another, incapable of regulating action without qualification. Its constitutive function maintains its relevance, even where it will be repudiated altogether. The constitutive function of principles asserts their relevance to the sphere of action which they constitute.

3. Regulative

The constitutive function of principles in evaluation passes easily into the regulative function, which is dual and complex. Constitutive principles define spheres of action; regulative principles define the actions called for. The two functions are distinguishable only theoretically. Principles are regulative at once in providing control of evaluation by circumscribing its conditions, and also in providing those conditions. Nevertheless, such conditions are never quite sufficient for the specific needs of action. A tension always exists between regulative principles and substantive requirements of action.

The regulative function of principles is their most obvious and powerful role. No evaluation can be valid unless it affords a maxim or principle. Kant perceived one of the basic characteristics of the regulative function of principles: actions have moral worth only insofar as they are regulated by moral laws. The formal conditions of actions are embodied in the regulative function of principles. A maxim is a moral law for Kant if it *can be* a moral law—i.e., if it is of a form appropriate to moral laws in their regulative capacity. If a principle *can be* obligatory for everyone, then it *must be* so obligatory.

Kant's claim that moral laws cannot be substantive as well and still carry moral force for everyone is an essential part of his conception of the regulative function. It does violence to his whole conception of principles to impose substantive functions upon them. It can be argued that Kant's sense of the function of principles is based on an unwarranted belief that a secure *ground* can be provided by principles. No unquestionable ground can be given for principles in their substantive roles; but one can be found for regulative principles. If we regretfully relinquish such a ground of moral principles, then the regulative function of moral principles can be expanded, and the substantive function defined.

The regulative function provides the unconditioned aspect of moral laws. "Thou shalt not kill" has in itself virtually no regulative power, in that it is unconditioned without affording a clear substance. "Thou shalt not commit murder," however, in its role as a possibility within situations of violence, regulates the character of such situations and our expectations within them. The possibility that violence may bring death inhabits all cases of violence. It is a possibility we may not overlook. A man who feels no pang of concern at another's death lacks moral sensitivity—precisely that provided by the regulative control of moral principles. Meursault in Camus' *The Stranger* has no feeling for the death of his mother. His life is not regulated by moral concerns, but by the immediate urgency of sensory experience. Aristotle remarks casually that men who believe that happiness is a life of pleasure are slavish—meaning, I take it, that to lack standards of nobility which regulate life is to lack the barest elements of the moral life. A precondition of moral discourse is the regulation of judgment by principles.

The most essential aspect of the regulative function of principles is that they are *principles* or *rules*. Pure relativism, or the refusal to admit the force of any principles whatsoever, degenerates easily into unintelligibility, and always entails an obvious arbitrariness. No ground of value can be found, nor can inconsistency be criticized. Without principles, the making of claims remains a personal activity lacking rudimentary modes of appraisal. A claim admits of linguistic analysis, of criticism, of logical analysis. Without the regulation of principles which define each of these modes of analysis, claims are but meaningless strings of ciphers or sounds.

Moral claims go a step further, however, in surmounting the relativism of sheer taste. The essence of taste is its freedom from coercion. If I appeal to norms in justifying a claim of good taste, my declaring my judgment a "matter of taste" destroys the *regulative* effect of these norms. My taste may have substance and be constituted by principles of judgment, but such principles exert the weakest regulative control.

Moral principles, however, exert the strongest possible regulative control. A valid moral judgment is coercive in possessing validity for more than its proponent alone. This is the essence of Kant's discovery—that the regulative function expresses the coercive public character of moral principles. One can never be an exception to a relevant moral law. If one is regulated by rule, then one is part of a structured order with other men. The regulative function of moral laws expresses in the systematic interrelationship of such laws the togetherness of men as part of a social order. If men have different obligations by virtue of their class differences, the principles of obligation form a system that regulates the class structure of that society. Otherwise we have sheer incoherence, both in our moral understanding and in the social forms of behavior. The basic mode of consistency in action is found in the system of regulative principles governing a sphere of control.

The regulative function of principles is the *prescriptive* quality they possess. A substantiated principle possesses force only as a *description*, indifferent to action. Until a description has been suffused with purpose, it can have no prescriptive force. Hume proved this beyond the possibility of challenge; Kant took it over. Scientific knowledge provides no ground for action—or, more accurately, provides only a partial ground independent of commitment to principles. These principles, therefore, constitute the basis of action by virtue of their regulation of the conditions of judgment. In such a role, they prescribe to judgment; they are not conclusions of judgment. They are valid by virtue of the conditions they provide for evaluation. They are not themselves evaluated.

The dichotomy between fact and value has its roots in the conditioned aspect of value judgment. The logical conditions of discourse define the possibility of proof; they are not themselves open to proof. Principles define the conditions of evaluative judgment; they are not themselves open to evaluation in the same sense. Either they have no justification, or they are self-justifying. Arbitrariness or intuition. No other alternatives seem possible. Even Kant's reason *a priori* has the quality of intuition or self-justification: the intuited validity of a principle either is irrelevant to the specific conditions of action, or bears no influence on the will.

The alternatives proposed for the justification of principles suffer from too great a purity—one akin to the purity of motives which is the luxury of impracticability. The achievements of science mock the insecurity of analysis. The absence of an absolute ground for scientific principles is overcome by the stubbornness of scientific discoveries. Principles which are an expression of faith bear the fruits of that faith in their achievements. Substantive discoveries of science become regulative principles without challenge—or, if challenged, reply in new substantive discoveries. Philosophical scepticism is a vain and empty challenge to the powers of science.

But it strikes the very heart of moral judgment, not merely because of the cognitive weaknesses of moral analysis, but in the importance of moral issues. The single event in science is submerged in the enterprise of discovery. The progress of science is all; the particular event passes and is gone. Its success is a contribution; a failure is of no moment. One cannot say the same of morals; a failure is the essence of concern. We address the particular event, not the principle which governs it. In science, the particular event makes its contribution to the system of our understanding, and is of no intrinsic importance. In evaluation, the event is all-important.

The challenge to a ground of value strikes to the deepest core of action. Principles contain the fabric of evaluation; but they are not the goal of that judgment, which seeks control over individual events. If the gap between principles and actions is unresolvable, our judgments are treacherous and insecure. We seek security in action; scepticism shows us that nothing can give us security.

So it does. Let us no longer challenge the sceptic. Failure haunts human life. Nothing—I mean *nothing*—can eliminate the possibility of failure. But let us not conclude from this that no methods are superior to others, no principles are more valid than others. Wisdom is not certainty, and provides no total security. But it can give us reliability, and maximize our likelihood of success.

Fallibilism is not unpopular, but only with respect to substantive matters. All claims to truth possess an inherent incompleteness within them, a residual possibility of falsehood that remains no matter what ground is provided. Moral principles as substantive wisdom are seldom thought to represent assured truths. As generalizations from experience, they are taken matter-of-factly to be of limited value.

The question is, how can regulative principles be so dubious and ungrounded? If principles which condition judgment are themselves of questionable legitimacy, does anything remain but sheer obstinacy and glorified arbitrariness? Such a problem arises only if the regulative function of principles is thought to be absolute and to provide a complete ground for judgments of value. However, principles are under test, even in the situations they regulate. The regress or circle suggested here is not unique to value principles, but is inherent in all cognition, and is not in the least vicious—though it is fallible. I will take up the details of this process of justification in a moment. I am more concerned here with the possibility of regulation under such circumstances.

Principles prescribe to moral judgments by defining the only conditions of appeal for such judgments. The ground of any action lies in a maxim of action. Without regulative principles which prescribe to actions, no distinction can be maintained between expediency and morals. Kant emphasized this point but sought an absolute ground for the distinction. Setting aside that ground, we may define the distinction in terms of *loyalty:* a principle that has prescriptive force is one to which we are loyal, which transcends its substantive limitations and becomes obligatory, which represents for us an *ideal* of action. The transition from the substantive to the regulative, from the descriptive to the ideal, is the transition upon which morality rests. Principles without binding force are not moral.

Moral life is not simple. The cases in which principles to which we are loyal determine our actions are overshadowed by the many instances in which obligatory principles conflict. Such conflicts are made even more common by the systematic impulse of reason towards consistency and order. Instances of different times and places, ruled by different obligatory principles yet which seem similar, can raise indirect conflicts of consistency; either the circumstances were different, or the same principles ought to have ruled. Loyalty can rule supreme, but it is often dominated by an urge to order. Continuity of standards within larger spheres is required for successful action. Out of the fury of the conflicts between our principles does deeper knowledge of the good grow.

The regulative function of principles is essential, but it is limited. Principles regulate action; but they cannot replace it. Partly this is due to the conflicts which arise between strongly held but vaguely conceived principles. Partly it is inherent within the multiplicity of functions of principles of value. Whenever principles are challenged—either on a substantive basis or where conflicting loyalties arise—a chasm lurks of irresolution and incompleteness. One way of putting this is that principles of judgment can never be given a complete ground. A more telling description is that the generality of principles always makes them incomplete within any specific application.

The critical point is that no action is in itself a case for the application of a general principle—at least, not where we admit the possibility of exceptions. It is this possibility, which cannot be denied in any of our actions, which makes the possibility of failure omnipresent. General rules are prescriptive, but only for all cases of a certain kind. "Thou shalt not commit murder" clearly proscribes murder—but it does not, and cannot, define murder. We must determine whether any particular set of circumstances falls under a general rule. The individual is left with a decision that he alone can make, one which transcends all principles, all assurance from others, all authorities, perhaps even all justification—except for the fact that we expect reasons for his decision, and recognize it as important. An action always transcends the sphere of dominance of a regulative principle, if only by widening its range of control.

Here the force of the loyalty to principles is to be found. Without loyalty, one could maintain that any particular instance might be an exception to a general principle. Without the commitment that loyalty provides, one might succumb to the scepticism of fallibility, and shrug off events as unknowable. Without the regulative function of principles, one could refuse to observe them, on grounds of scepticism. As Dostoievski puts it in *The Brothers Karamazov*, without loyalty, *anything is possible*. If philosophical scepticism is not to become evil, it must be founded on a strong and secure loyalty to moral principles.

But this loyalty equally must be tempered by the truth embodied in the scepticism—that loyalty is not enough. For loyalties may compete; while every particular instance may be an exception. The delicate balance amongst these opposing strains is the core of the good life, and seems hopelessly impossible of achievement. An alternative is to conceive of the balance between loyalty and challenge as a dynamic tension among the substantive, constitutive, and regulative functions of principles in action, one which is constantly shifting and turning back upon itself. The interplay of these functions is the source of expanding spheres over which we maintain control, providing a continuity among the assimilative and manipulative dimensions of experience. This will now be examined.

B. *The Ground of Principles*

Ultimately the ground on which principles rest is substantive, but substantive considerations are often remote and overwhelmed by the proximate ground of principles in their regulative and prescriptive functions. The substantive aspect of principles of action comes to the fore only where regulative principles conflict, where their regulative capacity is undermined by irresolution. At such times we must reconsider the principles which regulate action in the light of means and ends. The substantive basis of rules of conduct is of pragmatic value only when their regulative and ideal qualities have been abrogated.

For this reason, it conforms more to actual practice to consider first the ground of principles in their regulative and constitutive capacities. We undertake actions of moral force only insofar as we appeal to principles of an overriding quality. A value possesses moral quality only insofar as it is constituted by principles of quite general purview—though the exact range of generality is difficult to determine. The constitutive principles which define an action to be moral also regulate the action unless other regulative principles preempt the agent's loyalties.

We are here on a level of routine morality—routine in being constituted and regulated by law. Kant's ethical theory represents such a morality and its regulation by law to an extreme, and quite neglects the substantive basis of principles. Nevertheless, Kant does recognize the central role of law in action, that where moral laws have genuine regulative capacity, they are *categorical.* "Thou shalt not kill," in well-ordered times defines for righteous men the basis of their thoughts and actions. A moral sense is a loyalty to principles of such regulative force as to prescribe without concern for consequences or antecedents. A virtuous man does not think through every situation in terms of specific interests. His virtue consists in his loyalty to principle. To Kant, this is the whole nature of the moral life. To Mill, it is the ideal of utility translated into a love of virtue for its own sake. Dewey emphasizes its habitual aspects. Aristotle casually dismisses those who have no loyalty to something higher than their own pleasure as "slavish".

Aristotle's condemnation of men who lack ideals reflects the particular priority of the regulative function in action. The substantive function is logically prior, in being the ultimate ground of principles. Therefore, regulative priority is of a unique nature. It is a priority in method, defined by the role of principles in action. Unless an agent accepts certain principles as regulative and constitutive, he cannot methodically evaluate his actions at all. Until interest has been suffused by standards which capture his loyalty transcending any immediate situation, an agent fails to grasp the regulative power of moral laws and lacks a moral "sense."

Here the regulative function of principles provides its own ground. Substantively, no principle can be valid beyond question. Amidst the urgency and complexity of moral difficulties, the incompleteness of substantiation brings no ground for action in particular cases. It is the regulative function of principles which bridges the gap between wisdom and practice by prescribing a ground in the principles which command our loyalties.

The ground created by loyalty, though an unquestionable foundation of action, is undercut in particular circumstances both by vagueness of formulation and conflict of application. Although in theory loyalty to principle commands complete assent in *some* situations, in most situations no single principle is of unquestionable applicability. Regulative principles tend to conflict; moreover, all principles have exceptions. Here the substantive function becomes paramount. The principles which constitute and regulate our actions always allow for particular deviations. "Thou shalt not kill"—except in self-defense, in war, or in punishment. The exceptions cannot be precisely delineated. Yet principles do not lose their regulative power.

The key to the regulative power of principles, when based on a theoretically indeterminate substantive ground, is found in the nature of conflicts among principles. A man completely loyal to several principles cannot but find cases hopelessly opaque to resolution. "Thou shalt not kill"—but what if a man will kill another unless I prevent him, even by taking his life? To what is our loyalty given, to the purity of our own motives or to the irreducible worth of human life? All our actions have both immediate and remote consequences, and we must consider not only direct threats to life, but remote possibilities of harm inherent in our neglect of preventive measures. In war, we are forced to kill or to be the instrument of the enemy, no matter how we would avoid either. Our regulative principles, to which we are utterly loyal, collapse in the realities of practice.

Let me hasten to add that the collapse of principles is not encountered in all situations. This is of critical importance to the regulative function of principles. A chaotic world might allow no stable situations in which general rules bring satisfactory resolution, in which loyalty provides adequate reward. Our experience, however, is moderately well-ordered. The principles to which we commit our loyalties can be reliable sources of satisfaction, not alone in the passionate joy the commitment itself brings, but in the resolution provided by action. This is the ground of the substantive function of principles.

In a purely logical sense, every moral situation brings with it a conflict among regulative principles. A moral judgment is called for only if a principle constitutive of morality conflicts with another, or at least with self-interest in some narrow sense. In calling forth action, a principle always engenders the possibility that another principle, even of duty to oneself, should prescribe to that action instead. A man who finds a wallet which contains a considerable sum of money must implicitly weigh his duty toward the owner against his own need for the money. His choice to seek out the owner is obedience to a principle higher than his duty to or love for himself.

The critical function of regulative principles is to transform the implicit irresolution of all moral situation into action. Principles stand in hierarchical relations—though only partially in most men's lives. The notion of a "system of values" refers to a hierarchical order among regulative principles. By virtue of the systematic nature of principles, and the capacity they have to interact in particular situations, a rational impulse toward systematic clarity and consistency is generated, however inadequately it is realized. The possibility of conflict in judgments, once recognized, virtually demands resolution in a consistent system of principles. The regulative dimension of principles, when submitted to the control of rational powers, generates a loyalty so systematically ordered as to render determinate situations which in theory are irresolvable on substantive grounds alone. Ideals to which we are supremely loyal override principles which command a lesser loyalty, and allow for assured action. Regulative principles bridge the theoretical indeterminacy of concrete situations by the force of loyalty and the systematic interrelationship provided by reason, and generate assurance in action. This is the quality of ordinary moral life. It is a characteristic of whatever continuity may be attained throughout diverse spheres of action in a complex world, qualified by the perilous demands of action.

However, we live in an intractable world, one which transcends the possibilities inherent in regulative principles. The world need not have been so unruly; in a more ideal time, it may cease to be so. A well-ordered society of men who live according to well-defined principles of mutual trust and respect is by no means theoretically impossible. A society which is successful in generating regulative principles to which all its citizens conform can be stable and endure indefinitely. This may well be the ideal of conventional morality—the stability generated by regulative principles which raise no substantive conflicts. Kant is the spokesman for this possibility. But he neglects the hard facts of moral life in its capacity to generate evil as well as despair. As Kierkegaard shows, there are times when a good man *cannot* know what to do—and by virtue of his goodness. Regulative principles are undermined by the pressures of particular circumstances.

Consider a woman in a concentration camp asked to choose which of her two children shall be killed. Nothing could possibly help her to decide. Her overriding maxim of action is one devoted to protecting her children; but she must in effect kill one to save another. Shall she choose to save the one she loves best?—how could she face her guilt thereafter? Shall she refuse to decide or kill herself instead?—perhaps they will then kill both children. Moreover, can she trust the offer made to her—or will the soldiers do just the opposite of what she chooses?

This is an extreme example, so extreme as to transcend not only the regulative but the substantive dimension of moral principles. Nothing can provide a ground for action in such circumstances. Here we find the limitations of principles, that some circumstances undermine all justification of action. The world we live in allows for only partial control. If we are to manage with the rest, it can only be by a personal resolution of an intransigent conflict in terms of our deepest sense of ourselves. Within every moral situation is the possibility that the limitations of principles in all their powers will be reached. Yet moral decision is still required, in a crystallization of one's sense of oneself and what one must do to persevere. In the last analysis, a moral agent stands alone amidst his principles, his wisdom, and his self-knowledge, none of which suffice for his decision. He must go beyond all grounds—yet he cannot give up in sheer arbitrariness.

It is not yet time for this discussion—let us return to a less extreme conflict of regulative principles. Consider a physician caring for an old lady who is mortally ill. The physician believes it is wrong to lie, but also knows that many people who believe they are dying often lose the will to persevere. He does not wish to hasten his patient's death; must he lie to her about her condition? Here we have a conflict of regulative principles. What, after all, is the ground of the principles which are in conflict?

Substantively, principles represent the standards men have found it best to live by. Lying promotes distrust and hatred. Lack of respect for life creates disorder and distrust. Peace and fulfillment seem to be the goals of human life; respect for truth and life are essential to peace and stability; respect for truth is one of the fulfilling drives in human life. Moreover, the physician is committed professionally to saving life. His overriding principle of action is that of the ideal of life. Nevertheless, he must consider the effect of lying on his credibility and effectiveness. If he too casually lies to his patients, particularly to one who genuinely wishes to know the truth, his ability to help such a person may be subverted.

Still within the context of regulative principles, then, this physician may reevaluate the respective relation between his ideals of truth and life in their substantive aspect. He must determine what is truly wise for him as a physician to do, considering above all the well-being of his patients, but seeking as well the most defensible position he can take with respect to the preservation of truth. Perhaps he will formulate a new principle, based on his substantive reconsideration, that it is justifiable to lie if he clearly can save a life, or if telling the truth would only make his patient suffer without providing her with compensating abilities to cope with her extremity. If he can, the physician must reach psychological judgments about the character of his patients. If he cannot, he will have to develop a different principle, one which is far less likely to provide satisfactory results.

It is not quite correct to say that the substantive role of principles is instrumental. For one thing, the ends of action cannot themselves be defined by instruments alone. A continuum of substantive appraisal is presupposed in which the continual submission of principles to test by the consequences they generate determines a set of principles most satisfactory to live by, *generally speaking*. These represent our wisdom, our knowledge of the best ways to live—*generally speaking*. We must be on guard against possibilities in a changing world which call for the reformulation and even the rejection of our principles. Substantively, all principles are in continual reevaluation, and we are constantly faced with the possibility that they may no longer be valid.

However, by virtue of their constitutive and regulative function, moral principles form the conditions of judgment as well as substantive conclusions. We have here a complex and ongoing process of reevaluation, in which conclusions are transformed into conditions, and in which conditions may themselves be subsequently reevaluated. A war physician will not consider the lives of his patients of the same intrinsic value as will a physician in a peaceful and stable society. His soldier-patients are instruments in this war to victory; that is a principle he cannot but tacitly accept, and it will affect his judgments. It would be unwise for him to neglect the circumstances of his role—*even if that role is itself not morally defensible*. The balanced outcome of his deliberations must take his actual circumstances into account, however he does so.

The wisdom of substantive principles is the wisdom generated by a tradition of test and evaluation. Such a tradition exists whether explicitly acknowledged or not. In the course of time, the principles men live by and which regulate their lives must meet the exigencies of circumstance and the trial of application. However vaguely, the principles of a society are tested in the lives of the members of that society, ultimately in the satisfactions those principles provide. It is important to realize that no principle can be substantively judged alone, but as part of a complex system of principles and norms. In their everyday lives, men live the results of principles that become social norms and legal codes. Inconsistencies give rise to confusion and inequity; principles grounded in *a priori* convictions inadequate to human experience generate frustration and impotence. The norms of a society are constantly on test in the ability of that society to endure and to satisfy its members. Principles which affirm the irreducible worth of human life represent the conviction that men are the final ground of all value, that without subjective approval, all evaluation is for naught. Consideration for others is valuable in its affirmation of the respect we give to ourselves in principled form. As substantive principles become regulative, they take on an inexpugnable generality in terms of which their substantive basis is evaluated.

The substantive ground of principles is in the last analysis hypothetical, as are all empirical claims. Substantive principles represent the most general goals of human life, the "good" toward which all men aim in their actions, whatever this is taken to be, and however different it is to different men. Ultimately, substantive principles represent the means to maximal fulfillment of our aspirations and ideals.

The regulative function of principles, however, cannot be avoided in substantive evaluation. That principles become regulative is the basis of their substantive function. In judging whether the principle "thou shalt not kill" represents wisdom, we must consider that it is a regulative principle, and determine whether it represents wisdom *as* such a principle. In the final analysis, a valid moral principle is one which represents the most satisfactory principle to which men may commit their deepest loyalties. Mill grasped the importance of this truth in his acknowledgment of a version of rule-utilitarianism: principles of justice are evaluated for their utility *as principles*. It is only as they represent rules for life that principles allow substantive appraisal. For this reason, it is ideals which possess the greatest substantive value in the overriding order they provide to a man's life and to society as a whole.

Even more important, the regulative function of principles enters forcefully into the very goals adopted in substantive judgment. The evaluation of principles in terms of their ultimate possibilities of fulfillment must accept the terms of fulfillment defined by those same principles—or at least by principles of the same system of norms. This is why substantive evaluation cannot be carried on piecemeal. In effect, the entire system of principles and ideals that form the ground of regulative judgment is evaluated in terms of its own ends. Failure can be due to radical incompatibility of principles or a radical disregard for the facts of human life. A materialistic society may fail in the inconsistency of material goals with deeply spiritual aspirations. Men may turn away from achievable material results to higher ideals of spiritual life. A materialistic society may also fail in the realization of its own goals, in the dissatisfaction of its successful members. If prosperity does not bring fulfillment, then we may deny its substantive value. Materialistic goals gain their meaning from ideals of personal fulfillment. These ideals may necessitate the rejection of material prosperity, if personal fulfillment is not provided thereby.

Aristotle's position that happiness represents the supreme fulfillment of human capacity is preserved in the substantive function of principles. Kant's emphasis on the regulative function of principles is preserved in the tests available for substantive evaluation. The prior condition for the determination of happiness is the nobility of character defined by regulative principles. The regulative and substantive functions are conjoined in the realization that evaluation is a never-ending process, where principles are evaluated substantively in being good *as* regulative principles, but evaluated also in achieving the greatest fulfillment possible in terms of these regulative ideals. The interplay of tests of principles and of results is the projection of substantive values from spheres of action which they regulate to wider and more comprehensive spheres also as regulative principles, there to serve adequately, to maintain their continuity of integrity, or to bring about schisms and conflicts. This complex mode of appraisal cannot occur in a single moment nor be finished in a single trial. The world changes and so do the men in it, under the impact of social norms and environing circumstances; systems of ideals may require modification under new conditions. But even apart from the changes in men's lives, the regulative power of principles, when coupled with their incompleteness of formulation, tends to create a dynamic imbalance, calling for a constant reappraisal of norms pushed to extremes. Life-styles lead to extremes; good things are overdone and lose their worth. Substantive evaluation is dynamic in the deepest sense, a process of continual readjustment of ideals under the impact of extremity and overenthusiasm. The movement to larger spheres of action and understanding is predicated on the dynamic challenge of action and adjustment. The golden mean, for societies of men, is not a point of harmony, but a dynamic expansion of balanced powers. This, it seems to me, is what Dewey means by both the continuum of ends and means and the notion of social experimentation.

The continual process of substantive appraisal does entail that no final determination is possible of what is good. There is suggested, then, an infinite regress. But this is unnecessary. For one thing, the continual need for reevaluation may be no more than an affirmation of fallibilism— that we must consider the possibility of error and commit ourselves never to become hardened in assurance. More important, the dynamic process of reevaluation may crystallize certain principles as essential to all moral judgment, providing the substantive and regulative ground for moral life. Sufficiently general principles may define values consistent with all our obligations, broadly continuous throughout the diverse spheres of action and concern. These principles then become the ideals we live by, as well as the wisdom of goodness. Yet they remain, in their interpretations, subject to the same continual imbalance I have described, calling for continual reinterpretation. Ideals serve to harness and direct energies, not to fulfill expectations.

C. Ideals

Ideals are principles of utmost generality to which we commit our utmost loyalties. They represent the continual movement toward greater generality in control over spheres of action, the widest reach of our values and commitments. Their extreme generality enables them to guide action without suffering too direct a confrontation with unpleasant reality, and to constitute the regulative ground upon which maxims of action are based. Concrete maxims, in representing means to accomplish ideal ends, always have a significant substantive aspect, and allow for regulation on the basis of definite facts. Ideal principles, at the remotest distance from application, have the greatest regulative force, and possess their substantive value in the system of which they are the heart. If concrete maxims of action within a systematic morality collapse almost entirely in their substantive applications, then the ideals basic to that system must be abandoned. The gap between the reach of ideals and the maxims found to serve in particular spheres of action measures the gap between our manipulative values and our assimilative capacities. An honor-based morality, though successful in a class-stratified society, may not be defensible in the context of more egalitarian modes of social organization. The ideal of honor, of great value in preserving individual integrity when life is precarious, may lose its substantive force when medical science and social stability bring relative security in life.

The systematic hierarchy here proposed is itself an ideal, one not commonly accepted. Ideals may be principles, and perhaps ought to be, but they are seldom so in fact. Kant's categorical imperative is an ideal principle, particularly in its second version. The conception of men treated as ends only, never as means, is ideal both in that all maxims of action are claimed by Kant to flow from it, and in that its interpretation is seldom quite clear. The foremost characteristic of ideals other than their supreme regulative function is their vagueness, both in formulation and in applicability. The ideal of life, represented by the principle to which almost no one quite subscribes—"thou shalt not kill"—is a supreme value with no precisely determinable meaning. From it flows not only the justification of capital punishment but also a refusal to consider taking another life in extreme duress. To some extent, the vagueness of ideals is eliminable, and it is the goal of rational morality to render ideals as precise as possible. Mainly, however, the vagueness is a distinguishing character- istic of supreme ideals. Ideals extend the purview of our considerations at the expense of specificity in action. To narrow the gap, to bring ideals into consonance with specific constraints of action, is to advance in methodic control. Nevertheless, to sacrifice ideals to the needs of specific action is to narrow to an extreme our domains of understanding, in effect becoming blind to far-reaching possibilities.

We have considered in detail the irreducibility of individual differences inherent in all evaluation. Upon the most rational grounds imaginable, men may and will come to different conclusions about what is right and wrong, not in every case nor without a common denominator, but in the possibilities of action that remain after deliberative considera- tion. It is not that reasons fail at some point, to be followed by arbitrariness, but that reasons are grounded in the agent's unique circumstances and qualities. In the final analysis, principles are interpreted by the agent as best he can, but not precisely as anyone else will interpret them.

It follows that ideals cannot be precisely formulated and continue to serve their ideal function. As ideals, they represent supreme loyalties; and to a man who is loyal to them, they must have the same force for others. We may accept the interpretations of others of common ideals, and tolerate their differences in the name of individuality. But we expect our ideals to accommodate themselves to the individual differences among men. They represent common spheres of action, a community attained by lack of specification. As ideals, they define what is best for everyone. They cannot do so and be precisely formulated. The ideal of the supreme value of human life must, at least in the concrete applications of today's world, govern both peace and war, both commonplace and emergency situations, or it is of little value as an ideal.

It should not be concluded from this that ideals may be so loosely drawn and vaguely conceived as to permit men to do anything at all. If ideals functioned solely as substantive truths, their vagueness would make them worthless. It is in the overwhelming regulative power with which principles are endowed that their ideal function is preserved amidst vagueness. The compulsion exerted by moral ideals is not to obey a rule however one interprets it, but for men to follow it with agreement. The standard of perfection an ideal represents is one we believe, insofar as we are loyal to it, that other men should be loyal to as well. Pacifists interpret the supreme value of human life to entail that the taking of a human life is always wrong, and that everyone should agree. The man who interprets that ideal to entail capital punishment also believes that everyone should agree.

Ideals represent the widest principles of control available, attaining their breadth at the expense of specific details, and leaving room for individual interpretation and action. Nevertheless, ideals represent and define the widest spheres of control in which values have been determined. In this sense, they represent not the moral or ethical—understood in terms of individual decisions—but the *political*—understood not merely as the social but as the *general*. Action moves from established to wider spheres, seeking control through ideal principles and known facts. Methodic evaluation is committed to the ongoing extension of prospects of control, a never-ending movement from the established ideal to more comprehensive possibilities of order through action. If ethics represents the established range of individual values, then the existence of other men and of new conditions of life—technological, economic, social, even theoretical and scientific—call for the continual reappraisal of established ideals in action. Politics is here the mode of methodic action, the sphere in which individual controls are intersected in social institutions, where the great variety of forms and structures of human life interpenetrate in directed and controlled avenues. Ideals define not ethics *in contrast with* political expediency, but the largest values yet found to be tested in the arena of collective action.

A given society may succeed in generating agreement among its members concerning certain ideals and their precise interpretation. Every successful society does so to a certain extent. An authoritarian society may be defined as one whose authority can generate mutual agreement on ideals through the interpretations of the authority. The point is that ideals do not interpret themselves, however precisely they are formulated. Every generalization is challenged by particular exceptions; individuals are forced to consider their own specific acts within their ideals. Only by arbitrary limitation can principles be made secure. Ideals in their applications in concrete circumstances by different individuals will have different interpretations, all equally legitimate. Methodic evaluation entails an ideal of tolerance—one which itself must be interpreted and appraised in varying fashions. When ideals are conceived precisely and rigidly, they may cease to possess an ideal quality. If we seek a ground for ideals, regulatively and substantively, then we must affirm as well the importance of individuality and the need for accepting some differences. Ideals can be supremely regulative and perfectly precise but without any foundation; or they may be substantively grounded, and of great regulative force, but allow for individual deviation and subjective appropriation.

The natural subject to consider here is that of religion and its determination of moral ideals. For religion is capable of supreme authority over men's lives in the determination of the ideals they live by and their modes of application; yet in fact religions make available ideals of a most vague and unintelligible character.

We may take the extreme view that the determination of ideals is the sole function of religion. A religious man has made a supreme commitment, represented perhaps by a sense of the divine, but basically to be found in the *supreme* quality of his loyalty. Piety is acquiescence to the uncompromisable supremacy of the will of God, an ultimate allegiance to divine ideals. One of the peculiarities of ontological proofs for the existence of God is that they fail to define divine ideals. To accept such a proof is to know nothing about God's perfection, merely that He is. We have no particular ideals defined—of justice, mercy, or love—which is to have none at all. The ontological proof—with all other proofs of God's existence—fails not only in its ability to prove what is unprovable, but in defining our ideals. Divinity is first of all *supremacy*, not the supernatural. We may infer from the supremacy of the ideal that it must be unchanging, self-sufficient, and therefore not a part of the natural order. The greatest of philosophers have always realized the poverty of such a conception of the divine.

In terms of the ideal, piety and morality become one, though apprehended from different sides. Morality demands loyalty to ideals, the organization of life within an order subservient to overriding ideals. A righteous man is supremely loyal to ideal values that regulate his actions and define his purposes. The pious man too is obedient to a supreme Being which defines his life and guides his actions. His piety is the acknowledgment of the supremacy of the ideal in everything he does.

The union of piety and righteousness in their allegiance to the ideal suggests that they are the same. Dewey attempts in *A Common Faith* to develop this notion as a theory of the religious. An ideal arises in intelligent conduct, and comes to arouse our emotions and command our loyalties. On the other hand, Kierkegaard finds in faith the transcendence of the ethical, its "teleological suspension." If the essence of morality resides in principles, even ideal ones, then the religious here is supremely *subjective,* and represents a truth higher even than our ideal moral principles. God is always particular, and so is man's relationship to God.

Two explanations of the different emphases can be found, both touching on vital aspects of the function of ideals. Both Dewey and Kierkegaard are correct, but toward only a part of the ideal. Though both the religious and moral attitudes entail allegiance to ideals, it is from different sides—the moral from the side of substantive wisdom, the religious from the side of regulative supremacy. Dewey views ideals in their moral function primarily, as representing the wisdom garnered in action. Kierkegaard emphasizes the supreme loyalty that a regulative ideal commands. For Dewey, ideals guide our hopes and organize our passions because they have been tested and found worthy of doing so; moreover, they continue to be evaluated in the affairs they promote. Ideals not only *merit* loyalty by virtue of their substantive foundations, but they are constantly affirmed and grounded anew in methodic evaluation. Political action is the other face of loyalty to ideals. For Kierkegaard, the ideal transcends any possibility that it may be judged. The divine becomes an ideal incapable of examination, a comprehensive ideal which is no attainment but rather postulated on faith alone.

More important is the difference between the stages of moral judgment emphasized by the two philosophers. Dewey stresses the substantive role of ideals, and therefore the intelligence in which they are grounded. Ideals are the supreme act of intelligence in providing the most general truths by which to live. They represent our striving after comprehensiveness, emerging from methodic efforts and rational exploits. Politics is the arena in which ideals are forged and in which our loyalties are substantiated. Kierkegaard stresses the regulative function of ideals in particular situations, comprehensively regulative though they may have no substantive foundation. Ideals bridge the gulf between thought and action, between the general and the particular. To Dewey, ideals are objective truths realized by intelligence in its activities; to Kierkegaard, faith is the subjective transcendence of reason in particular applications. Dewey emphasizes the general principles which make evaluation possible; Kierkegaard emphasizes the abrogation of these principles in action.

Here we see the difference between piety and morality. Religion comes to the ideal through regulative faith without concern for rational wisdom. Piety is the faith that one has conformed to the will of God. It represents the conviction that there is a Supreme order and all-encompassing ideal. Euthyphro is attacked by Socrates for claiming that he "knows" that he is pious. Socrates' attack is that one may "be" pious, but one can never *know* it, for piety is a state of allegiance without a substantive ground. Piety is loyalty, but it is not wisdom.

On the other hand, moral wisdom is the rational urge to ground action in the fruits of failure and success. Unfortunately, wisdom can find no ultimate ground within itself, but must presuppose an absolute loyalty. This absolute loyalty is either open to rational criticism, entailing a never-ending process, or is not, and collapses into piety.

All that remains is the development of methods where the substantive wisdom embodied in ideals and the supreme allegiance they command fuse together in dynamic interchange. Ideals command our highest loyalties, and represent our piety and our faith. But *as* such ideals, they afford substantive appraisal as to whether they succeed in representing our greatest satisfactions. And they are in continual development as we expand our manipulative capacities and the comprehensiveness of our spheres of action. Individual concerns give way to the larger spheres of political control, engendering wider and more sophisticated ideals. Yet individual assimilations provide the ultimate basis for evaluating any ideal. We seek those general principles which represent the best ways men have found over the centuries to live. But these principles can be judged only as ideals, commanding supreme loyalty. The tension within the ideal between the regulative and substantive dimensions is the continual tension of the spiritual life, and the source of a permanent conflict between piety and morality. It is the tension so often—and incorrectly—thought to be the conflict between morality and expediency. Piety seeks loyalty, and tends toward intractability; morality seeks a rational ground, and tends to promote criticism and undermine loyalty. A noble man is both pious and moral, and overcomes the tension within his life out of the goodness of his soul. His limitations are circumscribed by his humility: he seeks comprehensiveness, but expects the continual peril of failure. He is loyal to the widest ideals he can find, but seeks unremittingly for more comprehensive principles of action, always concerned for the social, the political, the broader consequences of any action, yet in terms of the individuals affected.

III

Self-Determination

A. Interest

A one-dimensional account of moral duties cannot easily handle the problem of interest. It is assumed either that interested parties are not "objective" enough to pursue their duties at their personal expense, or that a permanent and unavoidable conflict obtains among different personal interests. The founding of morals in law makes a mortal enemy of an agent's self-interest; the founding of morals in self-interest makes others antagonists. It is of no help that the subjective element in morality has a personal taint—for that only enforces the sense that others oppose us. In its most extreme form, the emphasis on the personal components of interest suggests that a man alone has no moral concerns, that morals are solely a fruit of the social accommodation of conflicting interests. The model of laissez-faire capitalism, the democratic reconciliation of opposing interests, is brought easily into the realm of morals. How one can then be loyal to his own interests and also to the interests of others, or to some over-arching ideal, becomes unfathomable. Thus, Nietzsche must cry out against the blunting of a man's strength by the mediocrity of the herd, the corruption of excellence by a concern for others. Mankind needs its self-interested heroes who forge history out of their personal concerns. A tension is generated that is unending and which has no resolution. It should never have begun.

Aristotle calls man a "social animal." Modern man, unfortunately, has little notion of the Greek sense of the person, and conceives his personal well-being to be in continual danger of compromise by others. We live in a society to satisfy some of our most important interests; in order to meet these interests, others must be sacrificed. Life is a tension of opposing interests and compromises among them. This view carries sway from laissez-faire capitalism to the dim pessimism of *Civilization and Its Discontents* where Freud sees the war of opposing interests carried on within the personality of civilized man. Here man is a social animal because organized society meets some of his needs and satisfies some of his interests. The entire relation between a man and what satisfies him is an accidental one.

To the Greeks, however, and to Karl Marx, man is not accidentally a social being, whose needs happen to be partly met within an organized society. To Marx, human identity is determined within an order of social production of goods. Man is a *producer;* and production has social forms. How and what men think is given form and substance by social determinants; what a man will become is provided by social constraints. Man is a social being because he could not be anything else and be man. A hermit sells his birthright as a man for the porridge of an inhuman life. Perhaps his interest is served by the trade, but it is not a human interest to be so served.

Man is a social being in that his characteristically human and personal traits are largely a product of his relations with others. In this sense, the individual character that is the basis of assimilated satisfactions merges with the character of his social environment, and individual values tend toward the comprehensively political. A man's earliest years manifest the microsociety of his family, and his personality reflects—though not without distortion—the qualities of his family life. Language, mores, expectations, possessions, with all the characteristics of their function in social life, are the fabric of individual identity.

But not its seams or pattern. Man is a social being whose identity and character are defined by social forms. But he is also an organic being, an *individual.* The norms of social interaction, the expectations inherent in social organization, the organic needs and dispositions of the body, are all given peculiar focus for each individual. Personal identity has its unique aspects—that is what individuality means. The character of human life is formed grossly in social molds; but the fineness of a decision is rooted in a specific and personal integrity. The decision to extend control from established to new conditions is one made *by* an individual, relative to his particular character and requirements, and cannot be the same for all men—if only because some of their characteristic traits differ, and they are relevant to specific actions.

Let us not waste time on one point: each man indeed possesses a

specific identity and personal preferences. That is of greatest importance
for the ultimate irresolvability of moral questions, and is the source of the
irresistible relativity in action. Moral problems have no univocal or
universal resolutions. That is vital to our understanding of moral
principles and the nature of action. However, it is quite irrelevant when it
comes to opposing interests and the tension between individual concerns
and the needs of others. Moral judgments reflect the nature of the judge;
but his judgments must coordinate multiple interests in a single decision
to have moral force. The multiplicity inherent in moral judgment is a
consequence of a plurality of agents. Conflicting interest is not.

The Platonic distinction must be stated categorically, so we may
move on: a man may not know what is in his interest. He may be
mistaken about what will benefit him. Even if we grant that men look out
merely for their own *self*-interest, we have said nothing without
knowledge of the extended nature of the self involved. The alleged gulf
between social and personal interest manifests the romantic personality in
its isolation and uniqueness. However, romanticism may well be absurd,
and is certainly mistaken. It is impossible to defend from a general point
of view. Individuality entails difference; but existence entails relatedness.
Neither of these metaphysical "facts" has a direct bearing on self-interest.
It is as simplistic to argue that a man's "true" interest is served in loyalty
to a supra-personal order as that his "true" interest is private and
irrefragable.

The term "interest" brings into moral analysis nothing new, except
for its pecuniary connotations. The natural phrase in which we speak of
serving the interests of a man seems to allow for three interpretations: (1)
A man's interests are what concern him—in two senses, subjectively or
objectively: what is *felt* to be or what *is* of moment relative to the
character of a man's experience. An interest is what is important. (2) A
man's interests are what is to his advantage or benefit. This allows for the
same distinction between the subjective and the objective, but not as
naturally. To Plato, the question of *true* benefits is the critical one, and the
first and second meanings of interest are conflated: what is of benefit
depends on what is important to a man, given that we are capable of
understanding his nature. Here there is no natural conflict among the
interests of men, for (a) what concerns all men equally is a stable and
rewarding social order whose interest harmonizes with that of individual
citizens; and (b) it is of true benefit to individuals to consider the welfare
of society and to be just. Unfortunately, this kind of analysis is gross, and
offends our sensibilities by its omissions. Even if we accept the general

character of Plato's analysis and agree that the interests of men tend to harmonize, it is obvious that in detail they may not. It may be of personal benefit to a man to be just; but even in a just society, individuals may find themselves in opposition. The *general* formula that interests conflict is undercut by the reply that true interests tend to coincide. Nevertheless, the omnipresence of conflict in moral life and its details are lost in this formula.

(3) The capitalist sense of interest then easily comes to the fore, in the notion of interest as *profit.* Here we abandon, with capitalism in general, a humanistic interest in mankind, and emphasize personal acquisition. The conception of a "true" profit is not altogether lost—witness: "what shall it profit ye to win the world and lose your soul"—but it becomes as extrinsic as the claim that capitalistic enterprises should have a social conscience. Capital seeks profit—that is its essential nature. (Wealth may not.) Perhaps the consciences of individual capitalists may move them to charity; or instincts toward self-preservation may move them to ameliorate the most severe forms of inequity in social organization. But they need not be so moved as capitalists. Profit stands opposed to benevolence; and self-interest conflicts with moral duties and an altruistic concern for others.

The argument that a "true" self-interest does not conflict with the interests of others is still possible within the framework of presuppositions of profit, as the Biblical line above intimates. Nevertheless, the onus is on the man who would show true profit to lie in justice and personal harmony. When the apparent conflict of interests is confounded with the necessary plurality of valid personal judgments, then the personal and the social stand permanently in opposition. Thus, Sartre regards the personal quality of judgments to be threatened by all other men, before whom an agent feels guilt, remorse, and fear. He then may seek to destroy them or subjugate them to his will. But the subjugation of others cannot eliminate the plurality of perspectives. Even Sartre realizes this, in showing firmly that it is the *possibility* of others' looks, not their actual responses, that is a threat. Total unanimity cannot protect us from the threat of failure. By presupposing a beginning in the *cogito,* which isolates personality from its social conditions, an agent is torn from his surroundings, hostile to all other men. His interests are imposed upon by others, but are incompatible with them. Harmonious social interaction and social controls are made impossible. The beginning is inadequate. Let us, then, not make that beginning.

If the notion of self-interest has a primary meaning, not rooted in a particular economic system, it refers to what is of essential importance to a person—in what he is at stake. A person's interests lie in what is of greatest importance to him, what affects him in critical ways, what has implications for the course of his life. In a rather natural way, we may say that a man's self-interest is his interest in him*self*. The notion that a man's self-interest conflicts with the interests of others, or his moral duties, stems from the hidden presupposition that his interests are mercenary and acquisitive. Merely addressing the self implicated in self-interest casts into doubt most views of interest as limited, even specious.

The word "interest" has two distinct meanings, as well as a host of subsidiary characteristics. These rather loosely represent a distinction between "subjective" and "objective" elements, and may vaguely be correlated with "apparent" and "true" interests. The latter versions, however, presuppose epistemological commitments to be avoided. Let us then distinguish the *affective* quality of interest inherent in felt concern from the *personal* interest inherent in events and things which shape a man's life and person. What a man is interested in, when he shows interest and pursues an object, has an emotional or affective quality. Sometimes affective interest is nothing but desire; sometimes it can be a focal center of activities which coordinate desire, without being a desired object itself. Thus, a man may be interested in a particular horse, or he may be interested in riding. In both cases, the impulse to action and the devotion to specific activities are emotional. Affective interest is intrinsic to education, embodied in the commonplace that men learn only what they are interested in, or else learn only through inducement in terms of their interests—through threats of punishment or reward.

Affective interest is often distorted into a concern for objects of desire rather than coordinated activities. Personal interest is usually (though also mistakenly) embodied in objects rather than actions, and easily confused with affective interest in objects. The view that men primarily seek pleasure makes interest an acquisitive impulse, directed toward specific objects and possessions. If men seek pleasure above all else, then actions are means to pleasure rather than objects of emotion in their own right. Marx's conception of man as a producer suggests an appropriate counterthrust: men *necessarily* produce; and their modes of production determine their interests. Here activities become primary, while specific objects of desire are a means of generating activities. The activities men undertake, in which they pursue their major interests, define the goals they set for themselves. A skier continually needs new equipment. His desires are determined by the activities in which he participates. It is true that his activities embody goals, but often not goals of acquisition. The sense of art in Plato's analysis is always of an activity with standards of control and accomplishment, not of acquisition. This is the source of the Aristotelian sense that happiness, to be a complete goal, cannot be an acquisition, but is an activity *in* which goals are set and realized, not itself a realizable fulfillment.

Affective interest is the quality that coordinates activities willingly undertaken, whether or not objects of desire are thought important. The pursuit of a desired object implicates a man in activities of rich and varied ramifications, and may utterly transform his goals. The pursuit of gold entails a life of prospecting, which defines the life-style and the further interests of the men who undertake that life. The analysis of affective interest in terms of objects of desire is blind to the activities implicated in such interest. It is true that men often undertake activities of little interest to them in order to attain a goal of utmost interest. But objects and activities are continuously related whether one knows it or not. Affective interest can be transferred from an object to an activity, and from an activity to an object inherent within it; and such a transfer is natural to men who seek to render their lives palatable. But it is the activities undertaken that have the greatest force in the lives of men. Ends and objects of desire are stimuli to activity. Richard II desperately wanted a horse—within an activity of battle, by no means in itself. Control is attained through intentional and directed action, but by no means always in terms of specific objects to be acquired. Far more often, it is the attainment of some state or the completion of some activity that is sought. It is a distortion to emphasize the emotional concern for objects in human life. Desire is ephemeral and blind; it is the activity entailed by a desire that provides structure and control. Affective interest is the emotional quality that implicates men in procedures and methods, that defines the character of a man's life in the activities he undertakes. What a man is interested in is part and parcel of what he does (and of course the reverse). Affective interest is parasitic on the more fundamental notion of *concern.* What ultimately concerns a man, in being a reflection of the character of his life, is expressed in his particular activities and affective interests. Affective interests provide the shape which is imposed on spheres of action as they are projected into new spheres to be controlled by actions undertaken.

We move, then, to the central notion of personal interest, to what is *important* in a man's life. A man's interests lie in what has importance to him, in what has influence *upon* him. A man is self-interested when he is interested in himself. Although a man's self is always of importance to him, it is by no means obvious just how, in what way. Certainly a man may err in what he considers important. A love-struck adolescent is virtually guaranteed to be in error about his concerns and interests. His affections are totally engaged; he becomes silly and gawking, mooning about unable to address himself to other activities, unresponsive to everything but his angel's smile. His infatuation is important; his beloved is of little consequence.

A man's interests are what is important to him in the course of his life, not simply as they involve emotion. The seducer Kierkegaard describes, whose life is a continuous movement from desire to satiation, is habituated to his life. His passions are of no moment, since they bear little on his actions. Nothing is truly at stake in his seduction. The object of his acquisitive love could be replaced by any other, and his activities would not change. The seducer exhausts himself in a continual repetition of activities which fully engage his affections and energies, but in no way develop his character. The interest a seducer has in his beloved is not a self-interest, for his person is not involved. Perhaps I exaggerate, for each seduction perpetuates the habitual character of the seducer's life, and plays some role either in inducing change through boredom or in reenforcing repetition. But any particular object of desire is of *minimal* importance in his life.

What is of personal interest to a man is what defines his being, forms his character, and embodies his nature, what is projected from one sphere of action in which he is engaged to another, in which his values, ideals, and character are most heavily involved. A man's parents, wife, and children are of greatest importance to him. His self-interest necessarily involves them, insofar as he manifests who he is through them. A man is, in the most fundamental sense, a producer, a son, a parent, perhaps a moral agent. His interests lie not in objects—though certainly they stand in relation to objects—but in activities, roles, or methods. It is by acting as he chooses, or is forced to, that a man is what he is. His self-interest is an interest directed *toward* himself *through* what he does. What is important is what defines his integrity in his roles as an agent and person. His interests are comprised in his character as projected in what he does.

Ultimately, all human activities end in success or failure. Therefore, all self-interest has a single aim—to reach success and avoid failure. Such a very general characterization seems to mean nothing at all. But that is an error. First, success and failure entail *methodic activity*, and standards which define success and failure. *Self*-interest, then, entails methodic activity directed toward oneself, and further entails continual and analytic self-criticism. Second, the general sense of success and failure is not global in the sense of being vague and undefined, but global in representing a self broadly under consideration. Just as particular objects of desire stand within activities directed toward their acquisition, which define them, so particular activities, methods, successes, and failures are interconnected within a man's experience in relations that give them importance and character. We often take things to be of importance that are not. What is of importance can only be determined from a standpoint of greater generality, in which the self under consideration is evaluated broadly as successful or not. Methodic action always projects from narrower to more comprehensive spheres, especially in terms of ideals and standards to which the agent is loyal. Ideals represent the continuity of action which forecasts success as an agent seeks control over his larger surroundings. Ultimately, a man's interest is in success, thus in maintaining his integrity in everything he does, at least by expanding his abilities and instruments of control. Insofar as a man's surroundings are important to him, as conditions of control and determinants of value, his personal interest is a political interest.

Self-interest is a comprehensive concern for oneself and one's possibilities of failure. A man is self-interested when he addresses himself *as a person,* and seeks what is of greatest importance to him, both within his particular surroundings and extended into new prospects of control. What is important to a person is what has a larger capacity to define his personality and to order his life. It is what threatens failure or provides prospects of success. A man who is self-interested views himself comprehensively (though never totally), in ordered relations to his surroundings, and seeks to successfully expand his control over his surroundings in a way commensurate with his integrity—that is, his character and ideals. A self-interested man seeks a consistent pattern of actions and responding, one that minimizes his prospects of failure and maximizes his likelihood of success. Since a man who fails, if he is honest with himself, must be transformed by that failure, it is in a man's interest to know how not to fail—and that is the same as preserving what and who he is, within the larger surroundings in which he plays his many roles, seeking a consistency of personality that provides control in all circum-stances. A man's self-interest, here, represents his political capacity as an active agent exercising his powers satisfactorily and consistently.

This is not the common sense of self-interest, which is often blind and uncritical, lacking all sense of a person. It must, therefore, be admitted that most men are *not* self-interested, for they are ignorant of themselves. One cannot be affectively interested in what he lacks knowledge about, though it may be of greatest importance in his life. Nevertheless, I believe that most men are self-interested in wishing to avoid failure, in seeking what is important to them and to control it. Unfortunately, they exhaust themselves in objects of desire, foolishly equating their self-interest with what they may acquire. The Stoics captured a profound wisdom in the realization that specific objects of desire may be the greatest possible danger to us; and that true self-interest lies in personal order and harmony, not what threatens our well-being. The simple error of failing to grasp what is truly important can lead directly to the complex failing of not knowing ourselves at all, exhausting ourselves in external objects of little consequence, and in emotions of no substance or endurance. On the other hand, where objects are not desired for possession but as means of control and of maintaining one's values, they are to be sought and treasured—for then they are important. The point is that it is not the object and its possession that is of value, that serves our interest, but means for strengthening our powers and maintaining our convictions.

All men *ought* to seek their self-interest, and that diligently. By knowing what is of fundamental importance to them, what affects their lives and threatens them with failure, they gain the possibility of order and control. Action implicates a man in his future. He may discover at any time that he has failed. It is only by incorporating our surroundings in our judgments that we can hope to avoid failure.

Does this imply that there is no conflict between a man's self-interest and the interests of others? The rest of this essay will be devoted to the complexities of this question. I have been arguing that there is no reason *essential* to self-interest that entails such a conflict. The dichotomy of altruism and self-interest suggests a permanent and inherent gulf between them. This arises from a narrow and distorted sense of self-interest. The very notion of "enlightened" self-interest, which is often introduced to bridge the gulf, suggests a peculiar distortion. Interest is not a simple notion, but one rooted in the most complex and difficult determinations. The *prima facie* case is by no means that interests collide, but rather, as Plato shows, that they mutually inform each other. If togetherness is essential and important to all men, they may share what is important, their ideals, even their interests. Political life represents the attainment of a common order relevant to the interests of many men, and is bound to fail where interests remain in unresolvable conflict. At the very least,

common institutions and ideals are essential within social life if togetherness and social powers are to be realized.

Nevertheless, interests can conflict, as an instance of conflicts in
action. Circumstances bring people together in conflict, duties in conflict,
and even personal interests in conflict. However, three points must be
kept in mind: (1) Conflict is omnipresent in human life; conflicts among
interests are not of particular moment. (2) Conflicts are mediated within
particular actions performed by particular men. (3) A human life is
open-ended, in that ever-new possibilities emerge to be realized for the
agent. This entails that conflicts among interests enter into the decisions a
man makes as a self-interested moral agent, and that such conflicts are
important to him in determining the kind of person he will be—thus
necessarily part of his self-interest. Opposing interests become a fact of
importance, and part of the interests which collide. Methodic consideration of opposing interests, when incorporated into the personal character
of the agent who must act in the light of such conflict, can mediate that
opposition. Agreement can be reached through compromise, especially
where personal integrity and persistence of character is sought. It is
essential that clashes of interests be mediated by cooperation and
adjustment. It is in everyone's interests to do so. This is the heart of social
existence, the foundation of social norms. The avoidance of failure
requires us to cooperate and to work together. Self-interest thus seeks
accord, not aggrandisement at the expense of others—except where
circumstances permit nothing else.

B. *Self-control*

A natural and powerful impulse in men is toward self-preservation.
Hobbes' classical argument for a coercive political force stems from his
version of natural right—"the liberty each man hath to use his own
power, as he will himself, for the preservation of his own nature; that is to
say, of his own life." Spinoza agrees: men seek to live and to preserve
themselves, and all principles of action may be traced to self-preservation.
It is presupposed that self-interest and self-preservation coincide, and that
all rules of life depend in the last analysis on self-interest.

I have already shown the complexities inherent in the concept of
self-interest, and begun the development of a view of the self that
undermines too casual an acceptance of the necessity of conflicts among
different interests. It should be noticed that Hobbes does not presuppose a

principled opposition of interests, but rather the *fact* of conflict among men who seek to preserve themselves in a dangerous world. The right of nature is inherent in human life because men are weak and feeble, threatened by destruction at the hands of others, forced to take protective measures. Hobbes' argument leads from self-preservation to social cohesion. If such an argument has any force, it cannot but be improved by a richer conception of the self and of how it may be preserved.

Plato's entire moral theory may be read as a theory of self-preservation, though *not* as a theory of the preservation of life. In the *Gorgias*, Socrates claims, "I do believe that it would be better for me that my lyre or a chorus I directed should be out of tune and loud with discord, and that multitudes of men should disagree with me rather than that my single self should be out of harmony with myself and contradict me." (482) With the arguments in the *Phaedo* for immortality and against the sheer preservation of life at the expense of justice, we have a powerful case made for self-preservation as a harmony of functions, and against the preservation of an unjust life. We must think twice about the casual identification, as in the line from the *Leviathan* above, of the preservation of one*self* and one's *life*. All too easily, we find the transition made from the impulse towards self-preservation to strictures against suicide. Death is the end, and one has lost oneself. But what of the slightly paraphrased question, "what shall it profit a man to win his life and lose his self?" Self-preservation must be torn from its identification with the preservation of life. In some situations we can remain true to ourselves, and can preserve our integrity, only in death. What is needed is to study the self and its modes of preservation. Is the self one, and does it permit a harmony of functions? It is the burden of this chapter to deny that self-preservation is possible, but to delineate in its place a consistency in action and integrity which may replace it.

Two pathways to a conception of the self are natural to us; and where maintained in the final analysis also as two, give rise to the problem of other minds. The self as mind, consciousness, or subjectivity stands aloof as in Descartes' *cogito*, blind to the self as agent, doer, engaged in the world. Cartesian dualism arises from a natural division of qualities of human life. Nevertheless, it is a confusion. The two elements of a self, subjective and objective, have no analytical correlatives. The subjective cannot maintain itself apart from objects with which it communicates; the objective is unintelligible without subjective dimensions. Since Kant, the metaphysical poverty of the categories of the subjective and objective have become clear. Yet those categories haunt our notions of the self and represent its internal division. Psychoanalytic explorations, rooted in pathological fragmentation, perpetuate the divided self as prevalent, yet hold up as well an ideal of completeness unintelligible within the terms of analysis proffered.

The two paths meet; indeed, they entail each other; they do not, however, define a complete unity of self. The subjective and the objective are dimensions of personality. A person with subjective concerns and interests stands in objective relations. This is by now a truism; what has not been made clear is whether a unified continuity of personality is possible among a man's many roles and adventures. It is this subject which will now be our concern.

1. *The Subjective.* The traditional starting-point in the subjective order of the self is the Cartesian *cogito:* "What is it then that I am? A thinking thing. What is a thinking thing? It is a thing that doubts, understands, affirms, denies, wills, abstains from willing, that also can be aware of images and sensations." (*Meditations* II) It is simple enough to follow the course of any of these dimensions of thought to realize their ramifications—in particular, that they transcend subjectivity. Phenomenologists have shown unmistakably that the consciousness implicated in the *cogito* presupposes a transcendent background. All consciousness is intentional in presupposing an object; all consciousness is transcendent in presupposing a wider domain of fact against which to define its projects.

Thus, doubting presupposes affirmation as a background. Total doubt is meaningless, in providing no correlative. We doubt by denying the legitimacy of affirmation; we presuppose the possibility of affirmation in any doubt at all. And if our doubt is directed toward the possibility of a world larger than our consciousness of it, then that doubt is based upon an affirmation of that same transcendence. I may doubt the shadow in the alley to be a man—but I must affirm the possibility of the shadow's existence and also the existence of men in alleys. Floating in the background of all doubt is what makes doubt possible. The subjective *cogito,* however modest, transpires against an objective order of events.

In the same fashion, imagination rests on a conceptual base of perception and action. Our imaginative constructions reside in a world of hard fact and perceptual demand. We play in our minds against a background of work and necessity. My dreams may come true—but true in fact, not in imagination. The play of my mind can fall short of actuality by inadequate foresight, or by the recalcitrance of events. But *events* are recalcitrant, and *actuality* lurks everywhere. If I am not responsible for my imaginary dreams, it is because I am responsible for what I have done and not dreamed.

The traditional category which implicates the subjective in the world is that of will—will understood not as wish, imagination, or conviction (though all of these entail factuality), but as the act willed, carried through, the will implicated in projects. In willing the performance of an act, I am implicated in the events I wish to change or accommodate, the tools I must employ, the limitations of my body, and my endurance in time. Consciousness in will is the focal heart of a complex process in the world implicated in objects. An agent defines himself in terms of his relations among events and things. In willing, the self is implicated throughout its projects, revealed in them, tested by them, accountable for them. We project ourselves into the world, and it is impossible to say how far. Subjectivity entails not only transcendence, an objective world, but the objectivity inherent in its own character. A man is not a mind alone, nor even a mind conjoined with a body, but an agent implicated through his projects with an indefinitely wide range of events and things. The limits of the self are indefinite, insofar as it acts and is acted upon.

2. *The Objective.* We live among many things in multiple relations. Our various surroundings interact and are what they are by virtue of their interactions. Their character is provided by the processes of which they are a part. Objects give character to events in which they play a role, and are themselves given character by the events which encompass them. Beings which persevere do so by no accident, but conspire with the environment to endure. Nothing exists in itself, but contributes to an environment which in turn defines it. It is impossible to say which came first, the chicken or the egg, because chickens (as a species) and eggs (as a character) mutually inform each other—as does the grain eaten, scattered, and grown. Ecology is the study of natural cycles of mutual formation, wherein specific organisms constitute environments for each other.

A human being is the same. He lives within a multiplicity of surrounding environments, which gives his life structure and to which he makes his contributions. Life is a give and take, ebb and flow, with members providing sustaining character to a social environment, while the environment provides conditions of endurance. Marx's claim that men are determinate consequences of productive conditions, that social environments determine their own character, is true; so is the claim that what occurs in human life is the result of individual activity. They are the same truth when properly understood. Social institutions inform the lives of their members and define conditions for the future; individuals act to bring about the future, but within conditions defined by their surroundings. Men and their environments are coordinated within interconnecting processes.

Human existence is fundamentally social—not so much a similarity of aim or hopes, but personal existence within social environments. Men live among others whose actions create environing conditions. A person develops within orders in relation; and develops by virtue of his relations. The environment is not alone a society of men, but is a multiplicity of systems whose interconnections define the status of their constituents. A person inhabits multiple environments of considerable and indefinite range.

From the side of his surroundings, a man belongs to complex, ongoing processes. He is neither a mind nor body alone, nor even a complex fusion of the two, but is a person by virtue of his environment, which therefore *constitutes* him. By a *constituent* here is meant anything which contributes to character or personality. The many constituents of personality are given focus and order from a point of view defining the individuality of the person.

Given the multiplicity of constituents in a man's life, the many events which shape his character, his manifold and complex relations, the integrity of *a* person and *his* experience is a problem. In what sense is a man one?—in no precise sense. In what sense, then, is personal unity or self-preservation possible? As a project, a work fashioned from the constituents available to him, a man may coordinate what is diverse within his experiences into comprehensive orders. He may expand the range of his control and increase the consistency of his values. Nevertheless, no all-encompassing embrace is possible, for life is too complex and varied. Only a degree of consistency, a range of encompassment, is possible.

There is an integrity to personality, if not for *all* contexts and relations, at least within a given sphere. A person is not a sheer multiplicity. The multiplicity of his constituents is given unity within personal subjectivity. Playing a role in a given situation, a man has an integrity—that whereby his many constituents belong to *him*, insofar as he has *that* role in *that* order. Relations and constituents give us a multiplicity of richness and an indefinite range of inclusion, and many integrities. However, an integrity is nothing without its constituents. A multiplicity of constituents can belong to one life only by virtue of *its* integrity. But this integrity too is relative to a particular environing context in which a man functions. Like everything else in the universe, a person is an order with many constituents, and has an integrity by virtue of those constituents, an integrity different for each order to which he belongs.

The concept of an order is general, an individual being at once a multiplicity within its environment and an integral order of constituents. Every individual is a unity among multiplicity, many become one, possessing many constituents and itself belonging to many other orders.

A person is an order with environments and integrities. But a person also possesses consciousness which creates new possibilities of order. Consciousness makes method and inference possible, from a circumscribed environment to wide reaches of the universe. Consciousness is also imaginative, engendering new possibilities and orders. Even further, consciousness turns on itself, and can possess critical self-awareness. Passively, consciousness merely entertains possibilities inherent in the environing order. However, consciousness can also bring focal control to direct action. Such control may only be a possibility, never actualized. A conscious person may live out his life a creature of habit.

It is possible to define the concept of self-control in terms of the possibilities provided by consciousness. Before doing so, I wish to restate the conception of a person we have defined. The general relation in terms of which interpretation is to be given is the order-constituent relation: to be is *to be an order of constituents;* and also *to be a constituent of some order*—in fact, many orders. *An* order has an integrity as *a* constituent of another order, and different integrities in different orders. Moreover, to be an order of constituents—to have a particular set of constituents—is possible only by virtue of belonging as a constituent to another order. The ontology here is pluralistic: there are many orders, they are interrelated, but not every order is related to every other order. Finally, there is no all-encompassing order. (See the final chapter for a more detailed account of this system).

A person, here, is not one but many orders and has many and different integrities in terms of his different roles in different situations and environments, many of which may be interconnected in complex and ramified ways. A person is unboundable in that his relations may be of indefinite range and capable of indefinite expansion. Nevertheless, control is possible and very important in defining consistency among a man's diverse integrities.

Through knowledge, distant events come before us and define our thoughts and actions. Information can come to us from anywhere; imaginative speculation can move to anything. Even causal influence is of indefinite scope and ramification. A man can be brought to tragedy by distant and seemingly trivial events. Failure lurks everywhere. The human self is as large as the possibility of failure. Our persons are not narrower than our moral accountability. Both are capable of indefinite expansion, to include almost anything, near or far.

But standing before events accountable to them, and methodically seeking success within them, is not submersion in chaos. The specific relations of a man are complexly woven together, but in determinable ways. New relations may be invented and discovered, but they must be elicited from prior conditions. A stone is multiple also, but not creative nor reflective. It too is an order of constituents, and may endure. However, a stone preserves itself by dismissing surrounding events as of little consequence. It preserves itself by exclusion.

A person has not the power of a stone or a mountain to repel influence. Yet he can be almost as blind and unresponsive to his surroundings. Though a creature of his surroundings, he may do no more than gather them within his purview, and subject himself to them. Passive consciousness provides no power to the self; it is but an everchanging mirror of its surroundings. No integral self is preserved in a man within an environment out of his control except the endurance of consciousness and his forthcoming death. A man who is blind to his environment is nevertheless vulnerable to it. He suffers the wounds of existence without instruments for coping with it.

The possibility of a transition remains from the self as a multiple object, which is related to its many environments without adaptation or control, to man as a methodic creature, projecting his powers as consistently as possible upon his surroundings, expanding with and upon them. An individual hermit comes and goes, leaving little trace of himself. The city built by men perseveres in time, defining an environment for future dwellers. Men preserve themselves *within* an order by methodic control—in other words, over *themselves*, their constituents and relations, defining an enduring integrity. Self-preservation is gained by methodic control over oneself—and, of course, over what constitutes him. Control over others is worthless unless incorporated within one's integrity, *preserving* it. We are now ready to explain what this self-preservation or self-control means, to set forth its limitations.

"Preservation" has two senses, which represent two grossly distinguishable processes, though with many shades, distinctions, and qualifications. One is that of massive undifferentiation, a perpetuation without nuance, control, or intent, mere endurance by the exclusion of alternatives. This is inorganic endurance, a preservation over the greatest span of time with little differentiation. A mountain is preserved not only for centuries, but for geological epochs, by remaining inert against the surrounding environment, safe from the impact of possibilities. The environing systems that include a mountain *preserve* it by excluding catastrophes of geological power, by sheer endurance through time. Mountains do not preserve *themselves,* but endure as a primary characteristic of the systems which include them, and which constitute their environment. But all being depends on its environments. Massive endurance is a characteristic of beings whose environments admit nothing which can force them to change, beings which preserve themselves through lack of differentiation and simplification.

Men are weaker than mountains, and cannot manage the massiveness of inorganic endurance. A person is threatened on all sides by forces which can easily destroy him, and must learn to adapt to and with them, or must harness them to his control by foresight and intelligence. A man will not endure for long without adaptive merchanisms and intelligent control, if not his own then by participation in the fruits of cultural intelligence. Man preserves himself by intelligent invention, by the consideration of alternatives, by sensitive response to what surrounds him, by an enrichment of the possibilities of life before him, by an expansion of boundaries and powers.

Undifferentiated endurance is a temptation for all existence, not only where it successfully preserves character, but even where it admits destruction. Massive undifferentiation is the fruit of inertia, and realized in orders that reproduce themselves with little modification, which exclude alternatives and omit possibilities. In Dewey's terms, the force of habit in human life is overwhelming. In Spinoza's terms, all essence provides preservation of being. Men repeat past actions, preserve traditions, and persevere in undifferentiated blindness far more often than they appraise new possibilities and invent adaptive instruments to meet their challenge. The enhancement of powers in methodic control brings ever new prospects of failure. Virtually all forms of mental illness are a preservation of the past, inherent in blind repetition, preservation without directed change. The environment offers new prospects to a man, but he may be blind and unresponsive, preserving his modes of thought and action, excluding the adventure of possibilities in order not to risk the anxiety of change. Psychic defenses promote illness where they concede to the force of inertia and allow massive endurance sway over possibilities of adaptation. Undifferentiated endurance is blind by nature, preserving itself without the consideration of alternatives. Human life is filled with the blindness of inertia and the preservation of mere endurance. Alertness to this blindness is all too often followed by the opposite form—the blindness of willfulness. We may try to preserve ourselves through the exclusion of alternatives. Or we may merely act *differently,* and perhaps fail to preserve ourselves at all, or do so by chance or because of others. In either case, we are blind, able to preserve ourselves only through the controlling force of inertia throughout human life.

In the moral realm, we find the force of inertia at its greatest. The threat of failure brings blindness as natural to avoid threats. What we do not know of cannot threaten us—at least until it brings failure. Blindness makes peace of mind possible, though it increases the prospects of failure. Blind obedience to moral law or customs of action may be safe if one ignores the consequences. Lack of imagination and insensitivity to others provide a protection against the threat of entertained failure—though it also increases the likelihood of failure. A man can attempt to preserve himself by massive endurance, by blindness, automatic actions, by the perpetuation of the past. Such efforts are blind precisely where they require alertness—to the alternatives of change and adaptation. A man may exclude from his purview all awareness of alternatives, of undesirable consequences, of other possibilities. He perseveres and endures through the impoverishment of possibility and the curtailment of imagination. So impoverished, he simply endures, almost by chance. He refuses to consider the likelihood of failure; he endures in a life undifferentiated by methodic controls.

Massive endurance is preservation without consideration of failure. It is perseverance in the absence of a project. There can be no failure, for there is no project and no standards of validation. A complete blindness might blind a man to failure, acting without the possibility of validation, his life mechanical, routine, inhuman in its repudiation of alternatives. However, even the passive consciousness of ignorant men is endowed with some consciousness of alternatives. Consciousness is precisely the entertainment of multiple possibilities inherent in a situation, the proposal of alternatives, at least in imagination. A conscious human life without the consideration of alternatives is probably impossible; it would be inhuman in allowing no adaptation, no redirection, only the sheer repetition of the past, either in endurance or in death. Consciousness introduces the contrast of what is with what might be, and tears asunder the lack of differentiation in massive endurance. The consideration of alternatives makes *decision* necessary, in providing alternatives which must be chosen among. Sheer endurance can exclude all possibility of failure, but by excluding also the alternatives of success. The entertainment of possibilities allows for alternatives to coexist with actualities, and makes failure a genuine prospect.

Self-preservation as massive endurance may eliminate failure by exclusion or confinement, by blindness, ignorance, insensitivity, and lack of differentiation. If everything is of the same worth, nothing can threaten. Failure here is precisely a failure in self-preservation. Some things do matter more than others; in his encounter with them a man is changed. Lear is foolish and old, wanting too much and ready to give too little. Old men, no longer able to face the prospects of failure in action, easily turn to massive endurance. Lear topples with a crash, destroyed in his blindness and arrogance, compelled by failure to know the depths of his own ignominy. If a man aims at massive endurance, he succeeds only insofar as he endures; failure is the cataclysm of self-betrayal, and a compulsion toward self-transformation.

Massive endurance is *amoral,* an inability or refusal to differentiate among alternatives. It is movement without evaluation, not even purposive action. It is inhuman, the attempt of a frail being to preserve itself lacking all the prerequisites. A man has not the power to endure without intelligent foresight. Massive endurance in men is either ephemeral, ending in death, or hypocritical, marked by arrogant self-blindness. It may rest upon a deeper self-denial, where men wallow in ignorance as an excuse for their failures, yet glory in their successes. Massive endurance allows no failure; but it allows no triumph either. It is inhuman and therefore unmoral, blind, and unintelligent—if it succeeds. But men cannot massively endure—they can only remain blind for passing moments.

Lear, like many old men, seeks massive endurance as the prerogative of age. He can claim the perquisites of majesty and of paternity, the respects of office—*yet relinquish the responsibilities of his office.* He is doomed—for though old men may pretend to massive endurance, yet they are men after all, and discover failure in what they do. Men do have aims, sometimes covertly, but nevertheless inherent in their actions, and bringing with them the conditions of failure. Given the peril of events, we cannot blind ourselves without risk, but must learn from Oedipus and Socrates that the quest for truth is the only life worth living, though it may end in disaster. Massive endurance is self-denial. If we cannot escape the risk of failure, then we must abandon endurance, face our prospects openly, and turn to the intelligent use of methods directed toward avoiding failure.

In methodic evaluation, the failure which resides in regret, in the discovery of superior alternatives, in the repudiation of one's errors, becomes the object of methodic activity. The world and its perils are controlled by scientific knowledge and instruments of change. An agent faces himself in his emotional and habitual dispositions, and endeavors either to meet his needs or to coordinate his dispositions with his resources. A moral agent, methodically interrogating the world and himself, reorders both the world and himself to make the prospects of failure slighter.

Most important of all, in seeking to avoid failure, methodic evaluation redefines it. Failure from the standpoint of massive endurance is a failure in endurance: one cannot remain aloof from his surroundings; events are important, and their effects can bring us to disaster. But failure within methodic control is defined by the agent and his resources. His judgments incorporate tests of validity and principles of action. Failure here is the fruit of methods directed at its elimination.

In methodic evaluation, there lies a *double failure*. Failure in endurance is but a failure in hindsight, a regret at one's past actions. One looks backward. But in methodic action, the agent looks forward *to* failure; he holds the risk of failure before him, and seeks both successful action and methods to ensure success. A failure in methodic action is a double failure—not only in the failure to meet one's needs, but in failing to know oneself and the world well enough to avoid failure. One may fail when one cares little about the prospects of failure—that is quite simple. One may fail when one has done everything possible to avoid such failure. The double failure resides both in action and in oneself. One did everything possible; one is then not the kind of person who can succeed. One's deepest being is threatened. Such a failure threatens by calling for a complete self-transformation. What one "must" do is not good enough. The agent himself is a failure. To regret one's actions, given full methodic interrogation, is either to be not responsive enough, not sensitive enough, or not pure enough in one's heart. One's ideals, values, or character, projected from established conditions to new ones, are inadequate. Major transformations are required.

It is this double failure that is the basis of the conviction that death is more noble than an evil life. Failure in massive endurance is merely compelling regret. Failure in methodic action is a sense of failing in oneself and in one's character. The agent must change what he has been—or else remain true to his ideals and, if necessary, die. The commitment to our ideals is the heart of a consistent integrity of self through many diverse situations. In order to preserve a continuous integrity—to remain true to himself and his convictions—an agent may be unable to live through evil times. Death is here no failure—or rather, is the best of the impending failures which are prospects.

Failure in action is a failure in control. One acts as he must, but may discover the inadequacy of that decision later, or in different circumstances. In new spheres, an agent discovers his past actions to be failures, and repudiates himself. To fail, when one methodically interrogates one's actions, is to incur an obligation to change, at least relative to new conditions. The integrities of a man in certain of his roles are inadequate to his new relations.

A man cannot through methodic action be preserved in a static character. Methodic interrogation obligates us to self-criticism and responsiveness to our surroundings. Rigid preservation of order is a form of blindness. Methodic evaluation depends on adaptation and flexible responsiveness, a sensitivity to circumstance and oneself that brings forth the most effective powers to promote success. Even more important, with changing conditions and the accumulation of past failures, action requires imagination and invention, new methods and new opportunities for control and satisfaction. Novel possibilities and the plurality of circumstances make it impossible for a sensitive agent to be permanent in any of his specific traits. Sensitivity entails a responsiveness leading to differentiation and adaptation. A successful man will of necessity be flexible and capable of modifying his behavior.

We turn, then, from self-*preservation* to self-*control,* conceding only to the notion of preservation a consistency and continuity of character and action an agent must possess throughout his manifold relations. Action is a form of control whereby a man orders his conditions in terms of his purposes, where events or his own aims—or both at once—are to be effectively manipulated. Still, it is the agent's own circumstances that are the means of control and the seat of all validity. An action is a mode of influence—or judgment—*from* given conditions to the future, to new circumstances, other situations. If successful, this extension will be a continuous one, a man in effect *preserving his identity* through many different orders.

Methodic self-control avoids failure by making an agent not the kind of person who fails. Self-control, then, is having had the foresight and sensitivity to avoid trouble even in novel circumstances, possessing a continuity of character and skill that ranges from established to new situations. Through time, we maintain a responsiveness and self-knowledge that avoids failure, and endows our life with a consistency given by methodic action, yet responsive to circumstances and environing qualities. Failure is always a possibility. Therefore, self-control is won by arduous effort, and is always at the mercy of conditions. Sometimes only terrible alternatives are possible; self-control can only avoid the worst of them.

In methodic action, we must grow through time, as our past failures change us and make us more aware and responsive to our surroundings. If we are not to become captives of our past failures, we must grow because of them. Self-control cannot mean the end of development, the end of personal change, the achievement of static perfection. In methodic action, life is an adventure, the agent acting as well as he can, seeing the impact of his actions on others, changing in his methods, developing in his powers. Self-control is methodic self-*transformation,* as past decisions constantly bring new points of departure and new decisions. Joseph Knecht, in *Das Glasperlenspiel,* reaches the perfection inherent in each stage before moving to the next, yet can never acquiesce in any stage of perfection. Faust's life is a perpetual surpassing, the surmounting of his prior achievements. No particular qualities of action or character may be preserved over extended periods of time, or through unrelated spheres of action. Only a continuity of action and integrity within the larger order defined is a possibility to be realized successfully.

Methodic self-control is acting so as to define a continuous and ordered progression throughout one's life. Every act reaches out to define a broader perspective within which all one's deeds form a progressive order, in which a past failure becomes an educational advance to new and more comprehensive successes. An action which is an essential element in the subsequent development of a man's life and character cannot be *merely* a failure. On the other hand, an action that does not conform to the developing process, which becomes a mere digression within the agent's life, one which he regrets having performed, is indeed a failure. Once methodic interrogation has become a style of life, with its fundamental commitment to the avoidance of failure, then every lapse in action which does not perpetuate methodic improvement is a failure.

Sophocles understood well the nature of heroic failure. Oedipus reaches failure through earnest efforts to forestall it, though blindness contributes. Yet his willingness to accept his failure, and his understanding that the world goes beyond human ken, make even his incestuous relationship with his mother and his killing of his father stepping-stones within his life. The acceptance of failure can become a redemption—particularly when a man suffers the full magnitude of his crimes. A failure confronted and passed through can bring with it the possibility of redemption. At Colonnus, Oedipus is a new man, steeped in divine wisdom, whose blindness hides nothing of greatness. No one lesser, in ability or in sin, could have his divine madness. His failures have become the source of new possibilities. Redemption through suffering always rests upon the paradox that without the suffering there would be no redemption; yet the suffering is due to the awareness of failure. From a later standpoint, one no longer suffers one's crimes or atonement. A man who lived an undisciplined and wasteful life, who is brought to his senses by a disaster, does not later regret the event that brought him to awareness. On the other hand, he never forgets that the event was his own failure.

Self-control, then, is the methodic *enhancement* of oneself, one's powers or one's ideals. It is not a preservation of character and order throughout one's life—though that is occasionally possible—but the creation of an order wherein the important events of a man's life contribute to a stable and effective integrity of character and skill. A failure can be overcome by a style of life in which such a failure will not occur again. It is difficult to remain alert at all times to the possibilities of temptation. An occasional failure has the virtue of making one alert to further threats. Still, human life is so permeated with prospects of failure that no one need go out of his way to seek it out.

So casual a comment on the educational value of failure is misleading. Moral failure is not a trifling matter, to be sought as a trial and purification. Raskolnikov tests his mettle by murdering an old woman. By the end of Dostoievski's novel, he has learned the enormity of his crime, and seeks redemption through exile. Dostoievski hints that through his punishment Raskolnikov will come to an even greater sense of the goodness within him and the worth of human life. He will thus transcend his failure, *and by virtue of it,* come to a deeper understanding of goodness. One must pass through purgatory to reach heaven. But one may not *seek* purgatory. It would be the deepest corruption to suppose that all men should struggle to sin in order to have something to transcend. The paradox of self-transcendence is that one cannot seek to transcend. Every decision may involve regret; but none ought to. No one can methodically seek the failure which may make him change. Methodic evaluation depends on principles and connections, not on a rare and astonishing magic. The sensitive and responsive man, who methodically interrogates his surroundings and himself in every one of his decisions, *risks* at every moment the discovery of his failure, but is successful only if he avoids that failure. At every moment his ability to persevere within himself is under fire, but he succeeds by persevering.

There is another paradox of failure—that it is no longer a failure once it has been fully acknowledged. With respect to the past it is not changed: Raskolnikov did murder an old woman. But with respect to the future, his action may be the beginning of a new understanding, to the extent that he understands his failure. A later perspective may incorporate past failures within it as part of its development. An action regretted may no longer produce regret, while a failure ignored is a failure to be condemned. Understanding requires a more comprehensive perspective, one developed from the sense of too narrow an ideal that led to failure. A failure can cease to be a failure by being accepted as a failure, *and in no other way.*

This is a notion that allows great confusion. A moral being *cares* for others in the deepest sense. If he knows he has unjustifiably been the cause of a death, he can only hate himself, or else weaken his commitment to the absolute value of human life. Kierkegaard defines the agony of such a choice, and a redemption either through resignation or an unintelligible leap of faith.

As I see it, the paradox of failure is overcome only by continuous methodic action. One must live through the agony of self-hatred and a sense of sin, and be redeemed *thereafter.* Dostoievski is more sensitive to this than Kierkegaard. But he too neglects the *methodic* character of transcendence. Raskolnikov, we are told, will be redeemed through suffering. The working of time is overtly acknowledged. But we are puzzled nevertheless by the accidental character of the redemption. Unless methodic interrogation takes place through time, and a failure incorporated into action, redemption is inexplicable. We can understand an order of possibilities only within methodic interrogation.

In action which is sensitive and methodically critical there is a sense of oneself as a responsible agent whose convictions and knowledge form a continuous order. One sees one's life *under the guise of necessity:* one has always done what he had to, given his character and circumstances. A man preserves himself—even through development and change—as a man capable of effective action and critical enough to act in terms of his beliefs. Ideals are of utmost importance here, for they are capable of a continuous and compelling rule over a man's life, yet, by virtue of their vagueness, they are flexible in their particular interpretations. Loyalty to ideals is one of the most important means—if not the only one—to self-control, especially if ideals are themselves methodically evaluated and adjusted to changing conditions.

Method and the cognizance of failure are critical. A man may see his life as a blind reaction to external events, necessary and even consistent, yet sinful and immoral. The difference between the necessity of reactiveness and the necessity of control is one of method. Only where a man is alert to his surroundings and continuously self-critical—especially critical of his past, alert to the need for sensitive and imaginative responses—is consistency in his life and action a clear good. All human life has some order within it, even if externally imposed. Only when the order of an agent's life is created *by him*, through methodic and interrogative activity, is there a consistency in action chosen and lived. Only this is self-control.

Self-control is the consistency which belongs to a methodic agent who is continually faced with prospects of failure, interrogative in his concern to avoid failure, and effective throughout his life in his commitments and convictions. Only based on a self-knowledge of great depth, and an ordered and consistent set of relations among his loyalties in new situations, can an agent remain alert through the prospects of failure. Consistency in feeling and action is fashioned through dread and torment, failure and success, *created* in terms of circumstances. We have all encountered *some* of these characteristics—a clear commitment to a value lived, not necessarily heroically, but firmly and well. A successful agent is reliable, unswayed by external circumstances, though responsive to them. He can be trusted, for he is secure in what he has chosen to be. He keeps his promises, for he makes only promises he can keep.

The ambivalent, tortured man, unable to decide any course of action without regret, is not trustworthy. Nothing he does gives him a clear character, for he has no sense himself of who or what he is. In similar circumstances, he acts inconsistently. In different circumstances, he defines no continuity of action. He is constantly led to regret his deeds. The methodic agent, who seeks through action always to gain the widest range of consistency in his deeds, is ready for new situations, possessing skills gathered from the past. This is the greatest possible security of action. Such a man may fail—failure is always a possibility. But he will do so as seldom as is humanly possible. He will die first.

C. *Decision*

An action is individual and ineluctable; so is the decision that produces it. A methodic decision unifies into an order the multiplicity of established conditions, an order which fulfills the methodic enterprise and beings it to fruition. A decision leads to action: an agent must decide, given the information available to him, and the principles he espouses, what to do. Nothing can replace his decision or eliminate his trial. His considerations, however careful, entail no action in themselves. Moreover, a decision is implicit in all grounds to accept them as such, a loyalty to principle or to criteria for determining what is important.

The element of decision in action has been addressed throughout the history of moral theory, though with but partial success—addressing but a part of judgment. Protagoras called man "the measure of all things." In the last analysis, each man decides what he will do. An action is a decision of an individual, made by him alone. The principles he accepts, the methods of analysis, the concerns of others, all must be integrated in *his* decision, upon a foundation of knowledge and commitment, but a decision that goes beyond its foundation. This point may be put sceptically—we can never prove beyond a possibility of doubt that our actions are valid, whatever information may be in our possession, whatever principles we espouse. Ultimately, we stand alone and unsure; all action involves a step that transcends the limits of justification. Each man is the measure of his actions—*but only in the final analysis.*

The sharpness of Protagoras' insight is blunted by the obscurity of its consequences. A decision, final though it may be, is no *measure.* A measure entails a standard or criterion, the contrast between a rule and a particular case. The decision provides the standard with force; but a decision without a standard can be no measure. The criterion, not man, is the measure. Protagoras' insight is that no standard comes ready-made, necessarily applicable to a particular case. Men *decide* to apply a standard. The standard then provides a measure. A gulf exists between a principle and an action—a gulf transcended only by decision. In the last analysis, the generality of a principle is overwhelmed by the individuality of a decision.

Kierkegaard deeply considers the nature of a decision. Unfortunately, he treats decision as an independent step, based on a complete loyalty to the ethical, but transcending it finally. In *Fear and Trembling,* Abraham is represented as having taken an additional step beyond the dread of the irreconcilable conflict between God's commandment to sacrifice Isaac and Abraham's supreme love for his son. The narrator tells us that he could understand Abraham's readiness to sacrifice Isaac with resignation, but not the absurdity of his readiness to do so with faith—that is, with joy and peace of mind. Faith transcends the conflict among supreme ideals. Principles do not carry within themselves their own application. The individual must move from the situation to action. Decision is not to be identified with deliberation, but completes it. Therefore, Kierkegaard claims, decision or faith *transcends* reason. A knight of faith takes a step beyond dread, however absurd such a step may be, and teleologically suspends the ethical. Thus, Kierkegaard must face the paradox of repudiating reason in order to surpass it, though the irrational is the sinful.

Kierkegaard's solution to the paradox is dialectical: one passes *through* reason and dread *to* faith. One therefore preserves the rational even while surpassing it. In representing faith as transcendence, Kierkegaard suggests that faith is separable from deliberation, and higher than it. In effect, he defines a mode of judgment based on reason, and *another* mode of judgment based on faith. Any resolution of the conflict between them must be paradoxical, since the principles of reason define justification, while faith transcends reason and all justification as well.

Part of the solution to the problem of the limitations of reason is given by a richer sense of its capabilities, especially a richer understanding of the function of principles in action. Kierkegaard stresses the constitutive and regulative function of principles. Abraham loves his son and owes him protection and security. Ethically speaking, fathers ought to protect and certainly ought not to kill their children. Given so absolute a principle and an absolute obligation to God, reason collapses. Poised between two absolute and conflicting obligations, the rational man is paralyzed; or, if he faces the imperative of decision, may resign himself to action, but arbitrarily, unconvinced of its moral validity. A rational and good man may discern the need for action where no basis can be determined, and may resign himself to an unjustified choice. This is not faith; it may well not even be a decision.

The multiple function of moral principles, however, introduces a complexity into rational deliberation that can blur the force of moral imperatives, but which extends the range of rational deliberation. Moral principles serve a substantive as well as a regulative and constitutive function. An empirical test is entailed in the judgment that a principle ought to be followed, that it generally—and specifically in application—

serves a beneficial purpose. It must maintain a continuity of control relative to the values and needs of those involved, even in new situations. In looking to the consequences of action, we sometimes may break the irresolvable dilemma that a conflict of regulative principles generates. We may come to those broader kinds of generalizations which enable us to move from principles relevant to certain conditions to principles relevant to others. Facts can help us to make moral judgments, particularly when we are in doubt as to the outcome of our actions. We transform moral principles into hypotheses instead of rules. A conflict among absolute principles disappears as soon as we repudiate their absolute character. Through the intelligent *re*appraisal of the principles which paralyze us, we may recover strength of will and overcome our inaction.

The return to substantive appraisal, the consideration of moral principles as hypothetical in nature, is either a dialectical step or a sinful one. In this respect, Kierkegaard is correct. Hypothetical principles—especially those with many exceptions—cannot command our loyalties or regulate actions. In preserving an open mind to a principle, we in effect question its regulative and constitutive force, and doubt its moral imperative. In looking only to consequences, we let history provide moral justification. The end justifies the means. The consequences of action determine its validity. Here moral principles are but efficacious instruments. A skillful workman keeps his tools in good order; a skillful moralist keeps his principles fresh. Loyalty to principles as constitutive of action is then absurd.

However, in a fundamental respect, the treatment of principles as instruments for the realization of predetermined consequences is not the work of intelligence, but blind conformation to unexamined emotional dispositions. Moral ends are not just experienced satisfactions, but satisfactions which merit principled anticipation. Kant's brilliant insight— though weakened by *a prioristic* conceptions—is that moral principles meet criteria of generality and worthiness of respect which transcend a concern for mere consequences and satisfactions. Principles are necessary to endow divergent circumstances with sufficient order for consistency and security. Where moral principles function only as hypotheses, as instruments for the realization of independently determined ends, they cannot also define those ends. The reduction of principles to hypotheses abdicates any concern for the principles themselves, the absolute loyalty to what is good that is essential to security in action. Success is achieved by an order imposed on events given by ends in terms of which circumstances may be directed and controlled. Principles are substan-

tively evaluated in their regulative and constitutive functions—as principles to which we should be unswervingly loyal. Otherwise they cannot
serve moral ends. Our loyalty to them strengthens their regulative
capacities, and makes them more effective instruments for grounding and
attaining important ends.

On the other hand, the regulative function of principles leads to
conflict and even paralysis of will as ultimate loyalties come into
opposition. The instrumental conception of moral principles neglects the
commitment necessary to morality. The regulative function of principles
encourages blindness. Love of mankind can be destructive if it promotes
no consistency of expectation and grounds no generality of principle.
Love of mankind can also be so general as to be devoid of applicability,
grounded in principles but lacking sensitivity to circumstances. Morality
is found in the regulative and constitutive function of principles; but the
intelligence and sensitivity that makes morality beneficial is found in their
substantive function. The three-fold complexity of moral principles
produces a tension within all moral action, and permits only fluent
resolution. Moral judgment may be rigid in adherence to principle, or
flexible in its concern for satisfaction. When automatic, action fails to be
methodic. Most of our routine and everyday actions are directed toward
simple satisfactions, apparently without coming in conflict with principle.
We work for the most money we can get, everything else being equal.
We live as comfortably as we can, everything else being equal. We
attend parties, seek friends, dress as we choose, without moral concern.

Yet every choice can—and implicitly does—conflict with an
important principle. The company that offers me the highest salary may
sell goods harmful to others, engage in irresponsible selling techniques and
misrepresentation, promote wars on foreign soil, or employ agents to
undercut bargaining by its workers for higher wages. Our comfortable
life may gain its luxuries indirectly at the expense of others. It may be
unjust that we are so well off when others are starving. As soon as our
commonplace choices come into conflict with principles, we require
methodic decision among conflicting alternatives.

From the opposite standpoint, a principle adhered to with absolute
loyalty can be useless in a particular situation, even damaging, especially
in unanticipated circumstances. Our everyday sense of moral virtue is all
too often a blind accommodation to principle. Thus a father feels
virtuously righteous in sending his unmarried pregnant daughter from his
door, and a country wages war.

There is a greatness which belongs to loyalty to principle, a purity of motives and a freedom from corruption and self-seeking. Tragic heroes are heroic in their total commitment to duty, at any cost whatsoever. Such heroism, however, can verge on fanaticism. Greatness is not identical with rightness. Often loyalty to principle leads to destruction and death, even of those loved most. Loyalty to principle can be the altar on which a self-righteous man sacrifices others by ignoring the consequences of his actions. The world awaits the hero who will conform to principle by the destruction of mankind. The expediency that is condemned in political affairs is a concern for specific consequences of action unaccompanied by insight into the worth of such consequences. Substantive considerations are often supreme in political decisions, leading to the view that politics is immoral. Without ideals governing ends, even skillful action is blind. We may be grateful that democratic political life affords us interplay between personal moral convictions and political expediency, each informing the other. Sometimes great conflicts arise, fought in civil war or legal battles before accommodation can be reached. The heart of the moral life resides within the conflicts generated, to which we bring methodic analysis and definite decision, neither substantive consideration nor blind loyalty alone.

If the interplay among the relevant aspects of moral judgment promotes conflict, and if methodic evaluation is necessary, then we have a dialectical process which requires synthetic resolution. Blindness can inhibit methodic interrogation. Complete loyalty to principle can blind us to consequences. Intelligent consideration of consequences may blind us to the commitments essential to valid ends. When ends and principles stand opposed, when the ultimate loyalties of the agent bring no resolution, then methodic interrogation is essential to decision. This decision, the outcome of methodic interrogation, is a dialectical synthesis of opposing constraints, and presupposes a basis of opposition and conflict.

The entire account above is misleading in a fundamental respect. The dialectic of action has been represented in terms of a rare concern for opposing commitments. Kierkegaard looks to the story of Abraham who stands before the impossible conflict of disobedience to God or readiness to kill his son. His faith transcends this conflict, and that is a great thing. But such conflicts are rare, perhaps absent from most human lives. Why concern ourselves with situations that are so rare?

However, we may dwell on the impossibility of Abraham's situation, and lose the issue in the rarity of such difficulties; or we may realize that Kierkegaard's concern is with the nature of satisfactory decision, not in substance but in mode. The problem is how *any* decision is possible, given our grasp of its complexities. How are we to overcome despair in action?

We may suppose most actions to be performed without anguish or despair, blind to some aspect of what is at stake. Such decisions are not fully moral. Once we presuppose not only a consciousness of deepest concern, but a methodic awareness of the conflicts among ultimate loyalties inherent in all moral decision, then action seems to be impossible. Blindness affords decision through neglect. If we neglect nothing, how are we to act?

We have here two different kinds of decision: *open* decision, predicated on nothing taken for granted, the outcome of methodic judgment; and *circumscribed* decision, dependent on principles taken for granted or criteria arbitrarily employed. A circumscribed decision is unexamined in some respect, a rule or fact assumed without critical examination. A man who acts in anger, without consideration of the consequences of his actions, acts in a manner circumscribed by feelings out of his control. Such circumscribed decision Plato and Spinoza take to be a form of bondage. A man who goes to war to protect his country against an invader, and who has little knowledge of his government's policies nor those of the enemy, acts in a manner circumscribed by ignorance. This too is a form of bondage, to circumstances and events. The man who calculates actions before him as they promote his advantage, but who is ignorant of himself, also is circumscribed by his own ignorance.

Circumscribed decision is the outcome of a blindness to considerations that would undercut the justification for the decision if faced. Kierkegaard carefully poses for us hypotheses concerning Abraham's manner of action which remove all possibility of simple decision. If Abraham did not love his son, his obedience to God would be a simple thing. If he disdained all worldliness out of love of God, his obedience would again be simple. If he was envious of God, as is Satan in *Paradise Lost,* he might defy God's monstrous commands. But we are to suppose that Abraham loves his son above all else, that he fully knows the monstrous nature of what he is called to do, that he is not only obedient to God but loves his goodness and justice. How then can Abraham decide what he is to do?

A man finds an unidentified wallet in the street containing a large sum of money. If he is wealthy himself and has no need of the money, such a man may do his best to return the money without much thought. If he considers keeping something that he has not earned quite abhorrent, he will have no problem deciding what to do. In proposing little force to his own needs and great force to his scruples, we circumscribe a context of decision that makes of it a simpler thing, one without the need for methodic interrogation. However, suppose the man's child has had no food for some time, or that his wife needs an operation which he cannot afford, and that he has no other way of acquiring the money. Shall he keep the wallet? Once the question is raised in earnest—meaning that there are ultimate loyalties concerning the various alternatives—then a moral agent finds himself in the anguish of an open decision. His love for himself and for those close to him stands juxtaposed against his concern for others and his love for mankind. Opposing tensions are generated by his own methodic interrogation of the situation in which he stands. Only he can reconcile them in his final decision.

I have supposed throughout this discussion that conflicts create a need for methodic interrogation. But the reverse is more the case: once methodic evaluation is undertaken, every situation engenders a conflict. No matter is trivial. Students have been expelled from school for their dress and style of hair. We are told that personal habits of dress and cleanliness may make the difference between success and failure. Great problems of personal life are revealed in the breakdown of the most casual actions. Our tone of voice is too sharp; we forget our appointments; we are constantly late. None of these has grave significance in itself. Any of them may embody conflicts of vital importance. In neglecting anything as trivial, we expose ourselves to ignorance and circumscribe our choices. Nothing can be let pass without question. Once we know of methodic evaluation, we are committed to it; it commands our ultimate loyalties. Yet deliberation seems not to provide decision within itself.

The anguish implicit in apparently trivial judgments is closest to the surface during adolescence. Unfortunately, it is most confused then also. An adolescent must find his own terms of life, and sever himself from parental control. Every trivial decision that bears upon his parent's wishes may be a critical one for his self-esteem and his future. He must fight or surrender. Shall he be neat in his dress and manner of life, or is neatness a fetish unsupportable in a rational life? Shall he conform to parental expectations in his studies, his vocational goals, his dress, or his friends? Or shall he seek his personal differences, his own mode of choice within the context of parental expectations? Adolescence can be a period of torment, for every decision becomes a major one in which to preserve identity or surrender. Unfortunately, the adolescent who is so aware of conflict in his life is least capable of methodic decision. The conflicts he faces bring emotional chaos. His decisions are circumscribed by emotional paralysis. He decides too much by default, and the rest by impulse. He senses the anguish of evaluation but possesses insufficient wisdom to transcend it. His anguish brings disloyalty to principle, for others manipulate the consequences of loyalty better than he. Yet without ultimate loyalties, he has no basis for action. Instead of realizing that open decision comes through the intensification of loyalty to what is fine and good, the adolescent seeks to make his decision possible by abandoning ultimate loyalties, and only paralyzes himself the more.

Many men cannot make decisions. The ones they make come by default, as they do nothing. The Underground Man never makes a decision. He either does nothing, or acts on impulse. He is torn between the envy of others for their ability to act, and his superiority in being too sensitive to act. He sees that too many people make decisions circumscribed by ignorance or willfulness. He fails to grasp the possibility of open decision, once interrogation is methodically pursued. The exquisite awareness of possibilities, coupled with a profound concern for the failure inherent within every possibility, leads to inaction. However, this inaction is not methodic. Methodic evaluation leads to decision. A resolution is implicit within it.

The distinction between closed and circumscribed decision obscures a more important distinction among kinds of decision. This is a distinction between methodic and nonmethodic action, between those which are the outcome of methodic interrogation based on judgments of validity and invalidity, and those which are essentially groundless and without methodic control. The Platonic view that all men aim at the good presupposes that all action is methodic and strives for validity. We note, however, that many actions are undertaken without forethought, without expectation, without the control of method. Intentions can be dissipated to the vanishing point in circumstances of great anxiety. Men undertake courses of action which they cannot understand, as if such actions were forced upon them. We may consider such actions the result of decision, though uncontrolled. A man explodes in anger at his wife; a child smashes his favorite toy; a woman allows herself to be seduced only to feel degraded thereafter. All of these actions are intentional, but without regard for consequences, principles, firm expectations, or goals. If a decision is made in such cases, it is without methodic control, a "nonmethodic decision." But it may be even more accurate to speak of such actions as the result of *no* decision, *no* choice, precisely in being nonmethodic.

We return to the Platonic principle that all actions aim at some good. We may distinguish actions with methodic control, and which aim at validity, from acts which are merely performed, which are part of no method. In lacking a method, actions may have no mode of judgment applied to them, no criteria of validity by which they are to be evaluated. Our unthinking deeds are merely events until methodic analysis is brought to bear upon them. Of course, we may act in an unthinking way and later judge our actions to have been failures. A nonmethodic action may be surveyed methodically at another time. Otherwise we could not evaluate its success or failure. But a nonmethodic action lacks control. That is why we often deny responsibility for such actions.

A nonmethodic decision lacks methodic judgment of its validity. Such an action is no decision *at all* in the absence of justification. A man presented with alternatives may choose among them, but only upon the application of some method. We may explain our decisions only by giving reasons for them. The outcome of the flipping of a coin is no decision—though a man may decide to flip a coin instead of doing nothing. Where no grounds have been established for action, no decision has been made. A man too drunk to stand up does not decide to lie down—though he may have decided to get drunk earlier in the evening.

A man walking in unfamiliar country comes to a fork in the road. He may take either path, or, like the fabled ass, he may hesitate forever. Neither his inaction nor his stepping unhesitatingly down the left-hand road is in itself a decision. He acts, even in his paralysis, but his decision is impotent. Suppose he halts at the brink unable to decide how to proceed—then he decides nothing, not even to stay. Suppose he unthinkingly takes the left-hand road—he may continue to walk along, but he has decided nothing. A man taking a road may strike across country, or stop anywhere along the way. His continuing to move is no decision unless the alternatives posed to him are ordered methodically. Thus, a man may wait for someone to come along to tell him the right road. Here we have a decision. Or he may take either road instead of sitting still, since roads must lead somewhere. Again we have a decision which entails a method—of moving along, of getting from one place to another. Here, the man does not choose to take one fork rather than the other; he decides to take one fork as an experiment, planning to retrace his steps if he goes astray. The experimental method obligates him to take a road, though it is indifferent as to which one.

Decision entails method; we abandon the distinction I have proposed between methodic and nonmethodic decision. Men act without decision when they lack methods of judgment and criteria of appraisal. All decision presupposes an interrogative attitude, and defines an answer to questions posed. To all decisions, we may ask "why?"; and expect not only a ground of decision, but a methodic analysis of aims and expectations. A man may "decide" to build a perpetual-motion machine; but if he possesses no method for doing so, his decision is but a wish or dream, not a genuine choice. The methods employed, and the possibilities inherent within them, define decisions made.

The distinction between open and circumscribed decisions is therefore a distinction among methods. There are methods arbitrarily closed, governed by unquestionable assumptions. There are also methods which are indefinitely interrogative, which presuppose no unquestionable principles, no unassailable facts. The latter methods are those inherent in moral judgment. Decisions reached within such methodic activities are open, rational, and controlled by the agent. An open decision is the result of leaving no stone unturned, no question unasked—in principle, though never in practice.

But if no question remains unanswered, if we face the anguish of indeterminacy and the despair of a perilous world in such methodic activity, how can we ever decide what to do? If we commit our loyalties and deepest concerns to general principles that may have exceptions, how do we choose among alternatives? Our circumstances may be exceptions, or they may demand unswerving loyalty to principle. Rules themselves call for continual reevaluation. Facts may be distorted or incomplete. The more we know, and the more sensitive we are to moral subtleties, the more complex we find our decisions and the less sure we are of our foundations. How can methodic evaluation lead to decision? How can anguish issue in action?

The answer is simple, though incomplete. The methods involved not only *allow* for the making of decisions; they are methods *for* the making of decisions. Their goal is decisive action. Here is where I part with Kierkegaard completely: for Kierkegaard treats the final dialectical step of faith or decision as a passionate, personal, individual decision *separate and distinct* from the rational considerations that preceded it. Methodic evaluation is for action, and is misapplied if it produces paralysis.

Consider a man working with wood. Every cut he makes is a methodic decision. He plans and designs a cabinet; he buys the wood, marks and cuts it to suit his intentions, and finishes it to his specifications. He may, in an excess of sensibility, constantly wonder if his design is very good, if his sandpapering is quite finished, and so forth. These questions, though sometimes valuable and worthwhile, can dissipate not only his ability to complete the cabinet, but the method he employs. He may reconsider his design so often as never to start executing it. He may refinish his work before varnishing it so often as to turn it into a pile of sawdust. Both failures are in the method employed, for the method leads to a finished product, and is abortive if it does not. A method of cabinet-making may produce an inferior cabinet in unskilled hands. But if carried through to the end, it must produce a cabinet. Otherwise, it has not been followed to the end.

Analogously, a scientist performing an experiment must be sceptical about his presuppositions if he is to produce valid results. But beyond a certain point of self-criticism, he abandons the method of science and embarks on a scepticism of little value, one which fails to protect him against error and merely makes his work vain. A scientist must learn at what point scepticism promotes impotence and when it strengthens conclusions. Methodic investigation is for the reaching of conclusions. The scientist who is so careful as never to finish an experiment does not advance science. Here too, methods employed lead to conclusions, and entail the decision inherent in results—even if such results immediately raise new questions which call for new methodic activities.

The most striking example is perhaps that of art, which employs methods from which continuously emerge alternative possibilities. The development of a new technique in a school of painting proposes to other artists the possibility not only of joining that school, but of developing an alternative technique. Forms of art are promulgated only to be transcended. But an artist who continuously transcends his earlier stages, without producing works of art at a particular stage in his development, is no artist. Methods of art issue in invented products. Techniques of criticism and imaginative ventures are means for the creation of works of art, not properly employed if they issue in paralysis.

Methods of action also produce results, and they provide the basis of judgments of validity. These methods aim at action; deliberation is a means of controlling action. It is a fundamental error to assume that, in addition to the investigations undertaken and judgments made in methodic interrogation, there is a separate and distinct decision which follows them. Such a conception beheads the method. Without an aim which provides it with a test of its validity, a method is but an order of judgments and actions without control or direction. Methodic interrogation is *reproducible,* as are the steps undertaken within it. Such reproducibility entails an end which is also reproducible under sufficiently similar conditions. There is no method apart from the action produced by it.

Thus, a man who proposes principles of action, seeks data by which to test his judgments, and considers the whole in the light of experienced satisfactions and regrets, but who makes no decision at the very end, aborts his method in its final stages. He abandons the method as it comes to fruition. We have a case like that of a chess-player, who plays a forceful and aggressive game, but who doesn't want to win, and who resigns when he could easily win. He isn't playing the game, though he goes through some of its motions. If he doesn't want to win, why does he play the way he does? His earlier moves are unintelligible apart from an aim.

This last point has an important converse: a method not only is unintelligible apart from its aim, but has form and structure by virtue of its aim. Not only is a game of chess meaningless except in terms of the goal of winning, but every move in the game is to be understood only in terms of the outcome. The final position of a game is what it is—a thrilling denouement or a foregone conclusion—only as part of a game with specific steps. An action is the result of deliberations undertaken which lead to that decision, and which cannot be separated from it. The principles take on a specific force only as they promote decision. Information provides a ground for decision only as that decision emerges from them. Kierkegaard's sense that ultimate loyalties may conflict distorts the fact that a loyalty is ultimate in a specific case only if nothing can undermine it. Rather, *hitherto* ultimate loyalties are here called into question, and if no decision is reached, no loyalty emerges either. Where moral principles come into opposition for an agent with ultimate concerns, then his claim that no decision is possible is actually a denial that his concern is absolute. The man who cannot act does not care enough to act, in a case where action is required.

Methodic action produces results, but can never ensure against failure. The best the method can do is to provide maximal control in terms of given conditions. Unfortunately, the pluralistic world makes any given conditions perilous, as novelties may come from any quarter. For this reason, we can only act as an extension of ourselves within a given sphere of action, reaching out to other spheres, seeking successful control. The extension always involves us in possibilities of failure. This is the basis for anguish and despair. Deliberation and methodic evaluation cannot prevent failure, nor should we expect them to do so. They can at best decrease its likelihood. Deliberation produces paralysis if certainty and complete security are demanded.

Methodic evaluation presupposes both unremitting possibilities of failure and the unavoidability of action. Anguish and despair temper loyalty and dissuade it from arrogance. Despair is the sense that action is unavoidable, that it is of greatest importance, yet it cannot assure us of success. Despair may torture us—but only if we come to a decision. On the other hand, anguish increases as we seek to escape despair, for we increase the likelihood of failure by our indecision. We may escape despair by increasing our likelihood of failure. We may escape anguish, also by increasing the likelihood of failure. Methodic judgment maximizes our prospects of success in action, and thus produces a local minimum in both anguish and despair, given the perils of our condition. We act as we must, given our integrity, our ideals, and our conditions. We may fail, but we have done the best we could. Anguish remains, but minimized, for all other alternatives produce a greater likelihood of failure.

If one never wishes to be right in calculation, one may never adopt a method. The method brings with it the risk of *proven* failure. If a man remains illiterate, he may never be able to perform simple tasks dependent on calculation; but he also may never be exposed to conscious failure. What a man cannot do is to employ a method of calculation, yet refuse to reach a conclusion. The adoption of a method is a submission to its constraints and its aims as well.

However, methodic evaluation is not just calculation, and it is the difference between them that restores Kierkegaard's sense that a decision is a wonderful thing, not simply entailed by methods employed. This is, however, a truth about the methods involved, not about the transcendent quality of a decision. A method of calculation *entails* the results produced, given only the data required. In all methods, the aim permeates the steps taken prior to its realization, which then produce that aim through their orderly progression. There are, however, methods which minimize the personal qualities of the agent, which entail the same results no matter who adopts the method. An agent needs only to decide to employ a method, and employ it correctly. The result follows automatically. In methodic evaluation, the decision and resultant action do not follow from general considerations alone, but return to the personal qualities of the agent. It is in this sense that a moral judgment involves a personal decision of a transcendent nature.

What I have shown to this point is that Kierkegaard's question, "how is a decision possible?" is not to be understood sceptically. Nor is the question to be understood to call for a further account of decision— methodic evaluation provides whatever grounds are possible for action. Kierkegaard's question, however, calls to our attention the uniqueness of methodic action—that it entails a synthetic resolution of a multiplicity of considerations in which the unique qualities of the agent are of vital significance. The tragic hero may relegate his personal idiosyncracies to irrelevance in becoming the incarnation of a principle. He closes off consideration of the failure of the principle, and becomes the agent of an Idea. The decision follows directly. A rational being may decide to employ a method which constitutes his rationality. Sometimes that method calls for no further decision within it. Methodic action indeed does, a decision of a most personal sort. What Kierkegaard suggests, and what I am denying, is that this subsequent decision can transcend the earlier decision to employ the method itself, even to call it into doubt. The final decision is part of the method employed, would have no meaning without it, and completes the method in application.

Nevertheless, the final decision is a personal one, and transcends the generality of evaluation in two senses. Neither of these is recondite, any more than a method of artistic production. A painter, whatever his education, whatever the constraints of the medium with which he works, whatever his history and development, must determine his own work of art and fashion it as he sees fit. In the last analysis he takes his entire history and makes of it what he can. The methods he employs, however determinate in style and craft, emphasize *his* history and development, and are completed in *his* decision.

The decision which is the outcome of methodic evaluation is personal in the same way, though to a greater degree in one respect. A moral judgment is personal in that, (1) it is the outcome of an individual's life, in which his history and convictions play a vital role. Ultimately he must determine what is most important to him, the standards he must live by. His physical disposition may be of vital significance here, as his inclination toward particular kinds and intensities of feeling will partially determine what he considers important, and partially define his expectations for the future. His upbringing and education too enter determinately into his tentative convictions, the strength of his loyalty to principles, his consistency, his compassion and his dispassion. Loyalties are engendered not found. The reconsideration of fundamental loyalties casts one's entire heritage into question. But it can be viewed only from within itself. There is no external standpoint a man can take toward himself and his past. Therefore, who and what he is enters into his decisions in a vital way.

A moral judgment is also personal in that, (2) it is a decision a person must make for himself, in that something more than general deliberation is required. A man may consider his ultimate commitments, the consequences of various courses of action, the passions which are part of his makeup, his history and qualities. But an action goes beyond these in raising the question of whether he wishes to remain the same or change. His own nature is cast into doubt; his decision must alleviate that doubt. An artist may at any time consider the possibility of developing a new technique, and of abandoning the style he has cultivated before. Either decision leaves him in the domain of art, as does ignoring the whole question. Methodic action, however, makes such a question imperative. An action belongs to its agent, and he is judged by it. He projects what he was into what will be. His integrity and character are at stake. He may act successfully and preserve his integrity or he may find that a failure obligates him to a new perspective, to new values and ideals. A man cannot remain detached from action as he can from science or even art—except when they are viewed as actions of particular agents.

There is, then, a truth in moral relativism, though it is often obscured by arbitrariness and love of obfuscation. Differences among men are vital determinants in moral action. Very different actions may both be valid if they adequately reflect their different agents. A valid decision is one which the agent can live with indefinitely. A hero can live with greater threats than an ordinary man. What is valid for him is not necessarily valid for others—though many men choose cowardice and hate themselves later. The character of a man enters into every one of his actions, and must be taken into account in his decisions. Unfortunately, men err constantly in their sense of themselves, and discover their failures in what happens to them. The element of personal decision in moral judgment in no way undercuts the possibility of error.

Moral judgment is individual in bringing to fruition the particular qualities of a man in his actions. After he has considered his ties to other men through sympathy and to reason through principle, he must fuse his understanding in a decision adequate to his nature as an individual. But the decision can fail if he fails to know himself well enough. Thus a moral judgment must be "true for" the agent who judges; but judgments are not true for an agent merely because he thinks they are.

An action expresses the character of the agent, and it then becomes part of his future development. A work of art also expresses the character of the artist; but it is not urgent, nor does it plumb ultimate commitments. A work of art might have been very different, yet we would not censure the artist for it. (Of course, an artist may consider his work an action, and endow-it with moral qualities.) An artist's work takes on an independent life of its own. A moral decision continues to reflect the man who made it, as the basis for our judgments of him. Where we judge an artist to be a noble or worthless man on the basis of his art, we consider his deeds to manifest him as well, and view art to be of moral import. All actions, including those involved in art, may be judged as acts. But such a judgment is no longer within the province of art.

Where we view a decision as a personal expression of a man, on the basis of whether he fails or succeeds, we establish the need for method in action. Only such a method addresses itself to the rich panoply of a man's relations to the world, his ultimate commitments laid against his personal character. In every decision, he must cast his personal being into question, and either establish it again for the future, or repudiate it. A man may, in consistency with principle and loyalty, act as he would have in the past; or he may repudiate consistency in response to recurrent failure, and remake himself in action. A man decides what he will be in the future, given the alternatives defined by his history and circumstances. A moral decision is personal in that it is the ultimate decision as to what a man will be, once he has taken responsibility for himself.

In the last analysis, then, a man decides what he will be. But his decision is not a further difficult step he must take, after he has deliberated. Rather, it is the fruit of the method to provide action. Nevertheless, since a man's nature and character are at stake, it is never easy to make a decision, and never easy to act methodically. On the other hand, methodic evaluation is the only way a man has of defining himself as he wishes to be, after having taken what needs to be taken into account. We give ourselves to methodic activity in order to find ourselves therein. If we are afraid to take the first step, we will never take the last.

IV

Larger Spheres of Value

~~~~~~

A. Sympathy

Hume's scepticism has often inhibited a clear understanding of his analysis of the fundamentally social aspects of the moral life, his grasp of the broad emotional qualities which underlie moral sentiments. Where Hume's sense of *sympathy* is recognized to be foremost in his analysis, some philosophers interpret it to provide a *ground* of moral judgment—which it cannot do—and criticize it for its limitations. By imposing upon Hume a demand for a *criterion* of moral judgment, such philosopers trivialize his analysis, render his understanding of justice impotent, and manage to avoid the basis of his position.

The criteria of action I consider to lie within methodic evaluation. Principles are discovered to be reliable guides to conduct. They embody wisdom gathered over centuries of human life and provide judgment with its ideal qualities. Moral principles regulate action, yet also embody satisfactory aspects of life. They are the determinate criteria of all moral decision, given substance by methods in which they play a role. They constitute the ideals which make evaluation possible; they are also an outcome of all successful action, ideals which represent the broader values encompassing the larger spheres of action. We act according to our moral principles; our failures are then located in such principles, either in application or as guides to the will. Ideals may fail in the discovery that they are inadequate and imperfect. They may also fail in their appeal to our better qualities. If we do not respect them as ideals, we cannot serve them. Arbitrary and incoherent ideals tend to decline in worth as we respect them less.

Assuming this account of the methods and principles within moral action to be legitimate, we may return to Hume's argument. Sympathy is no ideal; it provides no criterion of judgment. Rather, it endows the circumstances of action with substance. It is the human background against which moral decisions are made, an essential quality which gives moral principles their force. It cannot be appealed to in argument—only the principles to which it gives rise provide appeal. It does not provide the ground of principles—they are evaluated in the concrete results they engender. Nevertheless, a pervasive quality of moral life is the quality of sympathy, which permeates all moral judgments, and makes it possible for moral principles to gain regulative control over our actions.

The role sympathy plays in action is analogous to the role played in science by the sense of vision. Without sympathy, our moral judgments would be quite different; without vision our science would be quite different. Vision is no ground of judgment—rather, it provides the facts which are the grounds of appeal. So also, sympathy itself is no ground of judgment—but it provides facts which condition our loyalties and values. Vision is not our only sense—though it is a powerful one; sympathy is not our only moral sentiment—though it is a powerful one. Both constitute heavily the empirical ground of judgment in their respective domains.

A value derived by an interrogative method affirms what is important to the agent and what will continue to be so in the future and in other spheres of control. Perhaps the ultimate ground of such values is a sense of felt importance. However, such a conception is extremely misleading, for a man may err concerning his satisfactions, especially as he determines his priorities over time. A man may discover through his own unreadiness the weakness of his convictions, and the importance of security, fear, even the feelings of others. Without sentiments, value judgments are impossible. But such judgments are complex developments in methodic activity, not the simple transformation of sentiments into principles. Satisfactions must be transformed into enduring orders of action. Dissatisfactions must be found to be permanent or transitory, embodied in principles of conduct. A man must discover what he can best live with throughout his life, consider the satisfactions available to him and the pain he cannot escape. His methods are complex and elaborate, constantly undergoing modification under the pressure of new circumstances. Employed instruments of control generate their own complexities and conditions, and become part of the problems with which future instruments must deal. Although sentiments provide facts for deliberation, they do so in indirect ways. If sentiments are ultimate, so also are ideals of life and maxims of action. They are interconnected by methods of evaluation.

Sentiments may be classified under two headings: self-interest, and a concern for the interests of others. I have already shown that these are not exclusive headings, that self-interest and love are often two faces of the same concern. A man exclusively interested in himself may come to know that his own worth is a reflection of what others take him to be, and act therefore with a constant concern for the judgments of others. Conversely, altruism entails a concern for one's own interests if he is to be an effective agent acting to promote the interests of others. A doctor who devotes his life to helping cure the ill cannot be effective unless he is healthy himself. Intelligent altruism obligates him to consider his own welfare, if not foremost then insofar as it makes him a more effective agent. Resentments at dissatisfactions can make a man a poor agent serving the needs of others.

Sympathy is inherent in the impulse to altruism, the heart of our concern for others. It is not, however, altruism. Sympathy is the emotional quality within social togetherness. Men are bound together by a sense of their own *commonality,* their likeness, above all their togetherness as men. Nothing is clearer to us than our own humanity—a humanity that is more a social than an individual attribute. Our sense of ourselves as *men* is plural, at once a bond of sympathy and embodying an ideal of achievement. The sentiment of sympathy and the ideal of human achievement are not separable. We are sympathetic toward men because they are *men*—human, frail and noble—not merely because they are like ourselves.

Man is a social being. This means at least the following: (1) men are born into a human society; (2) they are educated within that society to the qualities and expectations of that society; (3) they possess a consciousness of being *human,* among other human beings. It is worth considering the ramifications of each of these headings. We pass, here, from the individually moral to the social and political, from narrower spheres of action to larger and more comprehensive domains of control, from relatively simple and direct values to complex, changing, and elusive values, from what is nearly controllable to what always escapes us, and poses unending challenges.

(1) Men are born into society in their *dependence* on other men and in their generic character *as* men. Unavoidably, men are alike, physically and emotionally. Our genetic heritage is both unavoidable and essential. Our genetic character determines our reproductive expectations as well as

basic physical needs and qualities. All human action takes place in the context of a factual background which defines the alternatives which may be chosen. Our common humanity is a primary fact. It provides us with the greatness of our technological instruments and the powers of being human; but it limits us in our physical abilities as well. We are not birds or lions, able to hover in the sky or run down the antelope. Without the powers developed over centuries from intelligence and social inheritance, men are weak and impotent, born only to die. Because we are men, we suffer our weaknesses and glory in our special strengths. We cannot change our weaknesses into strengths except through the power of our intelligence and the institutionalization of our inventions. Men are social in their humanity in being men *in* society; and they are alike in being men, with common hopes of satisfaction and common powers.

The *helplessness* of men apart from others is manifested in the dependence of an infant on its parents. Men begin life completely dependent, possessing virtually no powers of their own. The sense of individuality as independence is empty here. Independence takes on substance only after a social process of development. However it occurs, a transition is made between infancy and adulthood that is inevitably social, if not within society in the larger sense, then in the microsociety that is the family, or its occasional surrogates the monastery or the nursery. It is reasonable to consider alternative ways of bringing up children; it is absurd to propose none. The growth of a human being to adulthood is necessarily social, instilling within the child a dominant concern for other people and a sense of being related to them. Most of all, the dependence of a young person instills in him obligations he must meet, if he is to develop at all.

The most obvious and the least important of these obligations are those a child senses he owes to his parents for their goodness in providing for him. In certain societies, norms engender respect for parents, and make it unthinkable for a child to defy his parents' will. In the abstract, such norms are debatable, for although parents may sacrifice themselves for their children, it is not clear that children thereby owe anything whatsoever to their parents in return, The parents *choose* to have children; children do not choose themselves or their parents. On the other hand, here we have a clear case where self-interest cannot but implicate us in a concern for others. In a society where children are educated by their parents, then the greater the children's respect for themselves, the greater their appreciation of their parents must be—for having made them worthy of such respect. The dependence of a child on his upbringing entails an intimate relationship between sentiments directed toward himself and toward his parents. Conversely, a child who despises his parents must struggle to find his own value, having repudiated the most natural and intimate source. A great insight of psychoanalysis is that the intimate relationship between a child and his parents embodies not only moral commitments, but the entire sense the child has of himself.

The dependence of the child as an individual on his upbringing leads to another sense of obligation. Not only does a child owe his parents filial respect for what they have done for him—which can also entail hatred for mistreatment—but he owes them his being. This is a bit too strong: rather, every person owes his character largely to the other people in his life, most forcefully his parents, but also his teachers and friends. What men become is inevitably social, *even if they choose to repudiate that society*. Such obligations are only incidentally moral. What is more important is that the eyes with which a person sees himself are the eyes of others; his sense of himself is engendered by the view others have of him. It does not follow from this that he will conform to their wishes.

What does follow is that a man who repudiates his society in his own self-interest largely repudiates himself. One may choose among the conflicting trends within society; but the total repudiation of a society is a repudiation of oneself as a member of that society. It is akin to the arrogant repudiation of the entire world without which we would have no being. A man who lacks any sympathy for other men lacks even a sense of himself—for he is constituted by relations with them. He is not only heartless; he is ignorant and blind, unaware of his own origins, unaware of his debt to others. Of course, the bond among men which is the result of dependence may be interpreted differently: a man who is heartless may be so *because* of his education and upbringing. His being is social; and he is not easily to be blamed by others. Each of these views reflects the same fundamental fact: men are not individuals "in themselves," but are constituents of social and organic interactions. The dependence of individuals on other men creates obligations that must affect their judgments, even in sheer self-interest. The selfish and greedy man must consider the reactions of others to his charitable offerings; otherwise he will wound their pride and nullify his generosity. The consequences of our actions enter a social context in which they are evaluated.

(2) The dependence of a child on others is educationally important. He is taught what he knows, and given a sense of personality through social contexts. We move here to more accidental elements of human life—the particular qualities of a society carried on in its descendants.

Every society finds a way to perpetuate itself and to carry on its traditions. Skills of value within the social order are taught. Expectations and values are inculcated. A society finds effective ways of perpetuating itself in the activities of the men who live in it.

Institutionalized forms of conduct, engendered through the education of children, make a mockery once again of the notion that personal interest stands against social interests—not, this time, as absurd, but rather as impossible. A man may stand against his social order, but his defiance is undercut by his being a member of that very society. His powers are gathered within that society, as he is taught his ideals and given reason to preserve his convictions. An undivided society may well eliminate almost all diversity and opposition. Competing aims reflect important divisions within the social order. The ideals of resistance are not invented anew, but are inherent within the social order which is resisted. Thus, a society may be divided against itself, and part of it may be opposed with hatred. But such hatred is itself a social product, embodied within the institutions of that society, or it is a vain chimera, vanishing as soon as it comes to light.

On the other hand, the powers of individual men to "be themselves," and to oppose a social order, are powers engendered through social interaction and education, as well as powers made effective through social institutions. Inventions are given substance by the education provided within society. Moreover, such inventions are empty of significance if they do not engender social institutions to realize them. We may oppose social institutions and invent others. But such invention is impossible without assistance by the institutions rejected; and the inventions become then the beginning of new orders of society if they are to have value and force.

(3) I have hypothesized all along a tension between social and individual aims, which I have shown is mitigated by their mutual interaction. There is another side to the social dimension of human life, one which embodies that dimension within individual concerns. The consciousness of being human is first and foremost a consciousness of being one among many men, a consciousness of being part of a community of human effort. Other men are objects for us and a stimulus to reaction. The consciousness of our common humanity creates within us a sense of sympathy for other men—sometimes for all men, sometimes for a select few—that has no tension within it between individual interest and the well-being of others. It is sometimes termed "altruism"—but that suggests a denial of one's own interest.

Sympathy is this consciousness of being human *with* other human beings, a man among men, a part of mankind. Marx's fundamental sense of alienation is from one's *species-being,* a failure to grasp how one is above all a *man.* This alienation suggests that one may be ignorant of or deny his humanity. That is absurd. We are unavoidably conscious of other men, as threats or supports, as objects for our control or who try to control us. Sympathy is the consciousness of kinship among men, a sense of belonging to a human order. Sympathy here is a feeling directed toward another individual as a specific instance of a more general sense of being a member of mankind.

This kinship must be qualified: it is not necessarily a bond among *all* men. A man's consciousness of his humanity may place him in a close bond only with some other persons, not with all. Men combine in kin groups, sometimes against the rest of the world. Sympathy is often channeled into itself, as a family stands off the world. Sometimes it is difficult to defend close ties against hostile forces outside. Towns and families must oppose groups which would destroy them. Close social groupings must define themselves as hostile to other men. Prosperity may bring with it a broadened sense of sympathy, diverted from a love of family or tribe to mankind in general. Economic security makes it possible for men to live in peace. Insufficiency promotes robber bands; strangers are hated. Plenty brings with it the possibility of sharing, and makes it possible for men to love one another without restriction.

The force of sympathy is immense. Even in the most inhuman and violent conceptions of human relations, we find some men together. De Sade's characters are never completely alone, but form cults; they respect—even care—for each other. In completely masculine cultures, where women are mere chattels, friendships among men flourish. We yearn for another human being to trust and to love, someone to love more than someone to love us, though we will not admit it easily.

One of the most remarkable analyses of love can be found in *Being and Nothingness*, where Sartre portrays men seeking to define themselves and their freedom under the regard of others. We wish at one and the same time, thus inconsistently, to control other men and yet to have them freely love us. Sartre captures many of the qualities of manipulation whereby we prevent others from seeing us as we really are. But we cannot succeed, for in controlling others, we make them unfree, not a reflection of our own freedom. Sartre develops profoundly the analysis of the master-slave relationship in Hegel's *Phenomenology*. Ultimately, the master, whose superiority is manifested through his slave, is dependent upon that slave for his superiority.

What is lacking in such an account is sympathy. The analysis of human relations in terms of power is of tremendous importance, because so many human relationships are manipulative and defensive. What is missing is the unique quality of *human* relationships. Men control nature and animals also. The particular aspects of power over other men are given form by the sympathy which underlies them. Essentially, we desire to work *with* other men, and to have them join *with* us. We will even compel them to join us if necessary. But we need them, for we realize that we are all human beings. Sympathy is the emotional quality that commonality of humanity provides—namely, similarity of emotional sensibilities and a mutual concern. "There but for the grace of God go I" is the essence of sympathy—our common humanity is great, our differences in circumstance trivial by comparison. As we find others, so we find ourselves, in our sympathetic response to their misery and their joy.

I am not claiming that all men have sympathy for all others, nor even that it is a "natural" characteristic of human life. Rather, sympathy is a quality inculcated through patient education and love, through example and action. Children are often unresponsive to others—though, I must point out, they certainly do not lack sympathy. If one child cries loudly surrounded by others, they may cry as well. In addition, even small children are alert and aware of what other children do. But a child cannot consistently act commensurate with his sympathies. His feelings are often blind in being unrelated to appropriate activities. What we learn as we become adults is how to manifest our feelings. We may learn instead to repudiate them, to mask our sympathies, to become less vulnerable to the misery of others. We inculcate in ourselves a coldness, an insensitivity to other men, so that we are not touched by them. What I wish to show is that this insensitivity is self-destructive, though it is intended to make us more powerful. The selfishness which is an indifference to other men is a defense bred of weakness, useful only in a short run, and deeply injurious to the agent in time. The self-sufficiency of withdrawal is a kind of death. Sensitivity to others is rarely encountered—perhaps the rarest of the great virtues. Yet without it, human life is not worth living. The intrinsic value of others to us in their fullest development is the fundamental moral ideal. It rests upon the sympathy every man feels for other men.

Two facts are necessary to moral life. One is that men are similar in important respects, and can be led through reason to common principles of action. Unfortunately, men also differ among themselves, and sometimes have quite different loyalties. I believe that men share a more common character than is commonly acknowledged, that it is differences among social institutions and norms which promote different needs. Anthropology has shown a far greater similarity among social norms than *a priori* speculation would suggest. Humpty Dumpty suggests to Alice that men all look pretty much alike. Men might differ so remarkably from each other as to make any common effort impossible. Men do differ in important ways, and general principles must accommodate such differences. If we impose an unyielding moral system upon individuals who differ in their ability to conform, it is the system that will break, though not until many of its best members have first been broken by it.

The other fact of human life essential to moral judgment is that of sympathy: men need others. Our similarity to others makes us acutely aware of their passions and torments, not as disinterested observers, but in passionate response to them. Hume emphasizes this aspect of sympathy—that derived from obvious similarities among men. We *identify* with other men, and indirectly feel their sorrows and their joys. As Spinoza puts it: "Although we may not have been moved toward a thing by any emotion, yet if it is like ourselves, whenever we imagine it to be affected by any emotion, we are affected by the same." Likeness of aspect brings with it a kinship of emotion.

The power of this mode of sympathy is limited. Some men revel in the pain others experience: They may enjoy the relief of escape from pain or the sense of power of inflicting it. More important, we can characterize groups of men as beyond the pale, thereby destroying any sympathy we may feel for them. Sometimes this is based upon observed differences—such as color of skin—though it is difficult to see how such a minor difference could undermine a sympathy based upon humanity. But even where physical differences are nonexistent, difference in geographical location, in heritage, class, or economic conditions can undermine the sympathy derived from similarity.

What is far more important is the sympathy men feel for *some* other men with whom they identify, whose passions they share, and who define their milieu. We may not share concerns with all men, but for every human being there are others who are an essential part of his life, either objects of his passions, or at least important objects of his actions. Men do not live alone; nor, but for a very small number, do they want to live alone. Christ went for thirty days into the wilderness, not merely to suffer physical hardship, but to face the temptations of his relationship to other men. His exceptional nature was manifested in his ability to live alone and still to be uncorrupted by that isolation. Few men choose to live completely alone, apart from commerce with others. Such men, if they succeed, do not conform in mind or action to common moral principles. Nor should they, since moral principles reflect our ultimate commitments as we live by them. The abdication of human society of *any* sort should bring with it a completely different set of loyalties. A man whose sole commerce is with things and animals will develop a set of loyalties toward what he loves and lives by, not necessarily an inferior morality, but a less social—perhaps therefore a less human one.

I am concerned here with the sympathy which reflects the fact that men are not completely self-sufficient, that other men are essential to them. The aims men set for themselves almost always include goals for others to be achieved with their help. The evaluation of success almost always embodies within it the judgments of others as well as oneself. We need others, and they need us, not only as instruments of each others' purposes, but because we mutually constitute each other through interaction. Men seek communities to define their existence and to bring them a sense of fulfillment.

Meursault, in *L'Etranger*, is a stranger to mankind because he is devoid of any sense of sympathy. He lives among men, and joins them in activities, not only bereft of their common emotions, but also of an understanding of their personal feelings. He is the dispassionate observer who lives without feelings, who witnesses the actions of others clearly but inhumanly. Lacking sympathy, he lacks morality. He can commit murder as a mere reflex response to the heat of the sun, indifferently and unknowingly. He cannot feel remorse, for he cannot feel the horror of his deed. He has done nothing *wrong*—for without feelings of sympathy directed toward some other human beings, we cannot know of right and wrong. At the end he comes for the first time to share a sense of the emotions of another person—he "understands" why his mother had a lover. He has progressed so far, and it is a significant discovery.

Men who lack all sympathy are incapable of moral judgment. Kant's attempt to base morals on reason *a priori* can be criticized for ignoring the possibility that men may differ so greatly as to make commonality of judgment impossible; but Kant does preserve a common aspect of human life—reason *a priori*—as well as the emotional disposition to respect the moral law for itself. Morality depends upon a sympathetic uniformity of emotional life, the possibility of shared viewpoint as well as deeds.

If sympathy is essential to morality, it follows that morality has a factual character. I do not think that this can be emphasized too much. Methodic evaluation can promote stable ideals and security of expectation only if based on definite facts of human life. If men are *not* similar in their needs and aims, no arguments of moral significance can be offered, and certainly none will have wide appeal. *A priori* moral arguments neglect this aspect of moral life, and promote positions that reflect little of relevance to specific decisions. Rational moralities which presuppose the attitude of a disinterested observer on the part of all moral agents are absurd, unless human beings possess in common *and in fact* a commitment to rational and disinterested judgment in moral affairs. Faith and loyalty transcend reason in this sense—but not blindly or arbitrarily; rather, they are rooted in the real characters of men who reason and who are willing to submit their judgments to methodic analysis.

Even more important, if men neither care for other men, nor respond passionately and deeply to them, moral judgments are absurd. All moral ideals represent a profound concern for other men, what they do and how they feel. The wisdom inherent in moral ideals is an empirical wisdom, about how men must live if they are to realize their common needs together. Ultimately and substantively, morality rests upon an empirical base in facts of human life. *A priori* moralities fail to grasp this ultimate character of moral judgment, and dwell upon the regulative aspect of moral principles without a due regard for the wisdom carried by such principles. Such moral theories do make capital of the profound insight that moral judgment is not *exhausted* in facts about human life; but they have nowhere to go from there, trapped as they are in apodeictic certainty or unqualified generality.

"Man is a social being." This is neither an analytic truth nor an *a priori* principle. It is an empirical fact. It might have been otherwise. Like some animals, men might have been capable of independent activity directly upon birth. Like some animals, men might seek the widest separation from others of their own species. They would not then be men as we understand them. Civilized life as we know it would never have developed. The dependence of the human infant upon adults for his survival brings with it the possibility of education and the perpetuation of a technical and cultural heritage. The sharing of concerns brings men together in mutual projects as well as in the conflict of competition. The identity of aims and emotions, particularly in the mutual reenforcement of sympathy, makes cooperation both a necessity and a joy, even in conflict. Social life is both possible and necessary because men possess the complex quality of sympathy—the sympathy which arises from dependence, from proximity, and as feelings shared with others become love. Where sympathy is undermined, human life becomes unstable and treacherous. German concentration camps are horrifying not because what transpired in them was "wrong," but because of the complete collapse of sympathetic concern. How could one man treat others that way? He must be a *monster*—not evil, but inhuman. No man could so lack sympathy for other men. We can understand murder in fear of one's own life. We cannot understand a man who can murder children without being affected by it. In war, we can tolerate the killing of women and children by bombs dropped from the sky, but are horrified at face to face killing.

Men do commit atrocities, even in highly "civilized" countries. It is essential to realize, however, that such actions are always considered *abnormal*. No doubt much of the force of such a conception is persuasive; abnormality is to be condemned. Monstrous actions are considered *inhuman*—meaning not only evil, but alien, rare, aberrational. Inherent in our conceptions of evil is a sense of a human norm, a general concern for others, a sympathetic love for other men, a sharing of aims, the mutual reenforcement of expectations, hopes, and feelings. We postulate sympathy in our moral judgments. Without sympathy, our sense of human evil would have no foundation.

Selfishness is common; sometimes evil becomes prevalent in social life. These facts do not prove sympathy to be rare, only to be delicate and changeable, and capable of being overwhelmed by other forces. If a man is to be persuaded of the inadvisability of being selfish, he must be shown that his interests involve others. Either he is dependent on the powers of other men, and must consider them if he is not to injure himself; he can satisfy his own needs only by a system of cooperation with others; or he is mistaken about the insularity of his own needs, and requires the affection and help of others. All of these together amount to an argument against selfishness, and in favor of a system of justice which reflects the mutual interrelationship of men. If men were independent entities, neither physically nor emotionally dependent on each other, selfishness would be unchallengeable. Nor would anyone challenge it. We postulate a social togetherness in our very conception of justice. Justice is the system of principles that reflects the real bonds of togetherness—mutual projects, enforced proximity, mutual affections. Men live and work together, either because they wish to, or because they must. Justice is the system that embodies the togetherness of social life, and furthers it where desirable. The bonds of sympathy which bring men together are crystallized in a system of principles that is the intellectual and pragmatic formulation of the forms such sympathy may take.

Justice is the system of principles which enforces the mutual aspects of social life, yet allows individuality to flourish as well. Justice brings the complex and vague aspects of sympathy into coherent form, rendering them clear enough to be followed by everyone, strong enough to satisfy the needs of sympathy, yet open enough in texture not to overwhelm the individual elements that remain. Equity is part of justice to alleviate the competition that promotes corruption. Contracts are given formal sanction in order to foster trust and respect. Crimes are punished in order that trust be secured and security in life be achieved. Fairness is an ideal which manifests the interaction of individual and social interests, an ideal which looks not to the interests of the many but of all men. As countries become sufficiently affluent, they move toward the minimal support of all their citizens as a *right,* fostering the security necessary to mutual cooperation in social life and the sympathy men bear for each other. With prosperity, men are challenged less by the sheer need for survival, and can dwell upon the private aspects of their lives with little interference by others. Unfortunately, it may be that the rewards of private life are much less than we think, and social life may become the primary dimension of human existence. If so, justice in its cooperative aspects will be expanded, if tacitly and without enforcement. On the other hand, with the satisfaction of essential needs necessary for survival, men may be able to abolish most explicit forms of justice, and realize their mutual concerns without enforcement. Either of the alternatives will be successful only if it adequately reflects the nature of sympathy in the social conditions *to be realized.* The exact form taken by justice in human life awaits the discovery of the precise nature of the sympathy men bear toward others in the concrete spheres of action which are governed by those principles of justice. In practice, that discovery will be realized only through the enactment of differing systems of justice, tried over periods of time, and adjusted as they prove inadequate.

All moral judgment ultimately rests in the emotions. Even respect for oneself, which is only indirectly related to sympathy for others, depends upon the emotional force of self-love and fear of death. Men could be indifferent to their deaths, and gain the freedom of action such indifference might bring. Most well-known systems of morality, however, have treated death as a particularly important concern, to be met by specially devised institutions and activities. Personal mortality may be the most pervasive problem in human life, and must be reflected as such in the principles embodied in practice. On the other hand, sympathy for others may promote contradictory tendencies, which must also be accommodated. The complexity of human needs, particularly when given institutionalized garb, is almost indefinite. This makes the search for principles by which to live a perpetual and ongoing one, constantly being realized in agonizing failure.

Sympathy itself is a complex and indeterminate notion. If man is a social being, the forms and qualities of his social nature are unclear, even unformed. Men are bound together in complex and manifold ways. Most important of all, the particular forms in which mutual concern is realized are themselves open to a bewildering array of possibilities. Bonds among men are at once hidden and revealed in the forms of practice. Moreover, if there is an inherent sense of kinship, it is transformed by socializing processes. Sympathy has many guises, none of which appears to take precedence. Men love others, but some are selfish. Men are dependent on each other, but some strive for and attain a considerable independence. Sympathy manifests the interdependence of men, their inability to be completely self-sufficient. But the ways of interdependence are manifold, and vary not only from society to society, but from person to person. Similar principles can be found in many if not all human societies; but individuals within each society accommodate themselves to these principles in their own ways. This is what makes moral argument so treacherous and unpersuasive: individual men define their social relations in different ways.

It is a truism to say that individual men differ, for that difference is their individuality. We have discussed at some length the irreducible individuality in moral judgment. Here I wish only to relate the complexity of individuality to the impossibility of characterizing sympathy in a precise way. Sympathy takes on precise form only in the systems of justice which stem from it, given their character by social traditions, personal aims, and a history of institutionalized principles. Systems of justice and laws can be formulated relatively precisely. The ultimate basis of such laws forever escapes us. Moreover, the promulgation of laws is never a simple matter. Laws reside in a legal tradition. They may be modified, but subject to overriding matters of consistency, expediency, and enforcement. Systems of law are crude instruments serving too many purposes for us to find within them the bonds of true human sympathy. Yet law both enforces and reflects sympathy.

The sympathy that is reflected in law and systems of justice is lost therein. We replace the love men bear for each other by sanctioned threats against hate. We overlay the love a parent feels for his child, and his sense of personal immortality, by promulgated and enforced expectations. We compel men to send their children to school, though they cannot but educate their children somehow. We define general expectations to promote security in action and uniformity of conduct; but by so doing we blur the bonds of human association. Threats become predominant rather than love. Fear replaces cooperative ventures. The few men who threaten social disorder, who either lack sympathy for others or whose sympathy takes peculiar and dangerous forms, must be dealt with in a rule of law. In such a system, the primordial associations of men vanish, perhaps never to reassert themselves. Sympathy in some of its forms is necessary to any moral system; but the system overwhelms sympathetic feelings by its own forms and rules, and imposes on men its own constraints. Sympathy becomes less tangible than its manifestations.

There is no escape from this. Bonds of togetherness among men are manifold and constantly changing. But social order, which is the realization of these bonds, requires a uniformity of character and a security of expectation. Tensions among conflicting interests must be smoothed out by principles for determinate decision. Men differ in the priority of their personal and private interests, in their pleasures, in the value they place on unqualified cooperation, and in the men toward whom they feel sympathetic concern. Only quite general and definite principles of action can bring a uniform order into the indeterminacies of human social life. There are no *specific* and highly determinate feelings common in precisely the same form for all men. Sympathy is too vague to promote the uniformity essential to normal social life.

Justice replaces sympathy as the heart of moral life. Principles which reflect mutual conformation are replaced by principles which enforce such conformation, at least outwardly. Men cannot act jointly from the sheer goodness of their hearts unless they know sensitively and accurately the reactions of others. Sympathy cannot but be felt vaguely. But even postulating a genuine love for others, a man can act validly only by knowing well what others require from him. He must be sensitive and alert to the needs of others, which will not be precisely the same as his own. He can learn what they are only if others will tell him—and since there is often no time to be told in words, since others are not always aware of their own needs, he can be told only in their responses to his actions, in his accommodations, and in their further responses. Justice provides a common order of expectation in which we may be secure about at least some of the requirements of others. Sympathy and even love can be realized only in situations of mutual interaction and reenforcement. Equity is the basis of justice by virtue of the greater security it provides, especially where norms are challenged.

Action is always undertaken in social contexts, in the light of expected and realized responses of others about whom we are deeply concerned. However much we care for others, if we knew nothing of their reactions to what we do, we would have no basis for acting with respect to them. But they do react, we discover our failures as well as our successes, and our sympathy and love make us concerned. Sympathy promotes an impulse to avoid failure in our actions involving others. The system of principles we come to accept, and to which we commit our loyalties in our quest for valid action, is the system of justice through which our concern for others is manifested.

The sympathy which is a concern for others, either as they view us or as they suffer, is indeterminate though strong. Others affect us, but how they do so is conditioned by the common expectations and principles of social life. Our concern for others has no significance in the absence of a clear sense of what they feel and expect. It is in the force and clarity of the reactions of others that sympathy receives its determinate form, and comes to define principles of action. As we come to know what others will struggle for, die for, punish for, what makes them suffer and what gives them joy, our concern for them becomes capable of effective realization. Other men reveal to us what is important to them, and we accommodate ourselves to their needs insofar as we are concerned about them.

Sympathy is often a mode of identification. Other people are similar to us, so they must suffer the same feelings and experience the same needs as we do. This is a powerful mode of sympathy, and of great importance. It is also the source of the most pernicious errors in action. All too often men expect others to be like themselves, and act accordingly, only to discover important differences. Great theories of psychology, especially theories of emotion, may depend upon a small set of fundamental principles identical for all men. But they must also incorporate a principle of diversification that produces very different results in different human lives. The range of diversity among men is perhaps not indefinite, but it is large, and allows for every possible hue and form within its compass. A concern for others which is the expectation that they will be like us, and actions taken out of this concern, can be the source of great evil.

Sympathy which produces action and yet avoids failure is a sympathy deeply bound to a sensitive awareness of the needs and feelings of others. The sharpest awareness of belonging to mankind can be empty without accurate knowledge of other men and their requirements. The most common failing of men who address themselves to the good for mankind is insensitivity to men in particular. Dostoievski captures this in Ivan's remarks to Alyosha in *The Brothers Karamazov*: "I could never understand how to love one's neighbors. It's just one's neighbors, to my mind, that I can't love, though I might love those at a distance." Many revolutionaries sacrifice themselves and others on the altar of a better world in the future, only to discover that their own sacrifice of the present brings failure with it. Blindness pervades human life, a blindness to others that makes some men deny that they belong to mankind, and a blindness that makes even the deepest moral concern devoid of value in its lack of sensitivity. Revolutionaries criticize the present—and well they should, for it deeply needs criticism—by postulating a better future, though that future is often but an idle dream with no pathway to its realization, or sterile in lacking a fullness of sensitive concern for the men who will live in it. From this point of view, the present generation is the sacrifice that will bring the millennium, a sacrifice which requires no sympathetic concern.

Sensitivity is a rare jewel, essential in moral life but all too often absent in judgments of right and wrong. Men of good intentions and great self-discipline fail in their responsibilities because they are insensitive to others, not thoroughly *responsive* to the issues they must judge. Sensitivity is so rare that moral philosophers have abandoned it as a moral virtue, since so few men would be capable of virtuous action were they obligated to be sensitive to others. Philosophers have instead sought moral validity in adherence to law, or in traits of character such as authenticity. Yet obedience to law is evil when blind; authenticity is meaningless if devoid of sensitive alertness to the hidden concerns of men. In practice, we continually discover our failures in reactions of others. We often seek to please those we love, only to discover that we have injured them. Our failure to understand others is often our greatest failing.

In the absence of sensitivity, action is risky and likely to fail. Personal analysis and therapy can provide a possibility of success through greater sensitivity to oneself and others. Nevertheless, sensitivity is not brought automatically upon greater knowledge of oneself and the principles of psychology. Human defenses are based on blindness, and cannot easily be dispensed with or transformed into an open acceptance of unpleasant truths. In the absence of general sensitivity, only systems of rules which define the expected reactions of others, and instill also in others the forms their reactions will take, can provide the likelihood of success in action.

Moral principles play a three-fold role. As substantive generalizations, they express common aspects of human life, not necessarily applicable to all men, but of great value as generalizations, provided we recognize the possibility of exceptions. The exhortation, "thou shalt not kill" substantively reflects the deep concern all men have with death, their fears and hopes. No doubt, there are unhappy people who wish to die, and noble men who understand the value of personal sacrifice. The generalization has exceptions, and cannot be interpreted so as to provide us with truths applicable to the desires and actions of all men. In its regulative role, however, the moral rule "thou shalt not kill" defines our actions toward others and instills in men a respect for life, even their own. A human life is precious even to a man who contemplates suicide. The ideal of life, the expected reactions of others to death, both expressed in a moral principle and enforced by it as well, define the boundaries of his projected action. When we define principles by which to live, we create a greater uniformity of expectation, and gain some control over the reactions of other men to what we do, even lacking a deep sensitivity to them in particular. Our sympathy for others is given form by the principles we follow. Substantively, such principles should capture what is generally true about human needs and emotions. If they fail to do so, they must be modified accordingly. But in their regulative role, such principles provide a structure for the expression of emotional reactions. By following the rules of morality and even courtesy, we make our insensitivity to others less problematic, and gain a greater possibility of valid action.

The regulative function brings with it a willingness to condemn those who disregard principles and even to punish them. Our lives are interwoven with the lives of others, and we find ourselves influenced and affected by them. One of the most important modes of interaction is through condemnation, when we are told unequivocally and forcibly that we have failed. Condemnation is a strong expression of failure, and provides us with a means of accurately coming to know the feelings and needs of other men without requiring a rare sensitivity. Consistent practices of punishment promote a uniformity of expectation that makes knowledge possible of the reactions of others to what we do. A man may not be able to find a consistent relationship in his own life between his self-interest and his concern for others. His knowledge of what rules others live by, and of what actions they are willing to condemn, can sharpen his own judgments considerably. A selfish man must face the prospect of condemnation for his selfishness. Our dependence on others, if they are willing to condemn those who fail to meet certain moral standards, may compel us to conform to those standards. In this way, principles of conduct, especially when embodied within a system of justice, may bring some uniformity of expectation and security of action into the complexities of human life.

Nevertheless, moral principles can persuade, either through regulation or threats of punishment, only if there is a fundamental truth for human existence: that men are inextricably and essentially bound to each other, that human life is necessarily social, that a pervasive trait of human life is the sympathy men bear toward each other in their emotional responses and in their actions. Other people play a major role in our lives, either because we love them, because we identify with them, or because we are dependent on them and what they do. All systems of justice presuppose this fundamental truth—though they also provide different forms for its realization.

B. Political Coordination

The Platonic and Aristotelian sense of political order makes it continuous with individual values. The political ramifications of actions are a continuous extension of individual interests. Such a view is based on the fact that men engage themselves, act, and form their values within the society of other men. Personal interests may be adjusted satisfactorily in the political order. Plato emphasizes the harmony of interests that a well-run society may provide for all its citizens—or at least the greatest number of them. We have reformulated this conception of the relation between social adjustments and individual concerns in the terms that personal interests are often the same, that it may be important to diverse individuals that they inhabit a society with common structures and ideals. Ideals represent the vague but common values in which men may share, though they may differ in specific cases and in particular actions. In Plato's view, the polity provides what is common among men, the typically human, the ideal realized in particular contexts of action. Personal morality is not even intelligible apart from social justice: a man's character is provided to him and also revealed in his social relations.

Unfortunately, justice is made too much the attainment of an antecedently determinable state. The harmony within and without the soul of the just man is a formal condition of human life, rather than an achievement won through dedication, effort, and skill. Politics is made an art of recapturing an ideal value, rather than a creative adjustment of diversity to common enterprises. The harmony of social interests is assumed to have formal reality quite apart from the projects in which it is realized. Here is Plato's fundamental shortcoming: representing values timelessly rather than in terms of projects undertaken and methods employed. If political harmony among diverse concerns is possible, it will emerge as it is *created*, not merely *recaptured*.

In Aristotle, a somewhat different sense of the political may be found. In particular, politics is the highest practical activity—the master art—because of its range and comprehensiveness. The political order is here the larger sphere of action in which particular concerns are pursued. Practical reason guides action; reason moves of necessity from a narrower to a larger compass, taking in wider domains of control, incorporating diverse and separate elements within a systematic order of action. An individual action is relatively circumscribed except where the individual plays a political role.

Aristotle's conception of politics as the master art is not entirely defensible, especially where the political and the moral are contrasted. Governments are notoriously parochial in their concerns, while moral ideals are often of unlimited range of application. Moreover, to the extent that moral and political ideals may be similar—that of reverence for life, for example—they are equally unrestricted in scope, defining ideal principles regulative of actions. We might say that individual *actions* and political (or governmental) *actions* differ in their comprehensiveness, except that governments are often ruled by individuals whose actions have political efficacy, while individual actions as we have understood them often have large-scale ramifications and implications. Finally, the individual and the collective—or the private and the public—are not separable, and overlap in complex and intricate ways. Political measures influence individuals, but individuals sometimes wield political power. All of these complexities indicate that we may not plausibly distinguish the moral and the political as they are commonly understood, nor should we wish to do so. It is rather our purpose to trace the movement from relatively circumscribed spheres of action to the broader and more inclusive concerns that are implicated in most enterprises of great moment in human life. In so doing, we may loosely associate the greater and more inclusive concerns with the "political," though the fit will not be perfect. The virtue of our approach is to show that broad or political concerns are usually implicated in most actions of narrow compass, and enables us to trace the strands of continuity between narrower and encompassing spheres of action.

Nearly all urgent and vital problems have political—that is, large-scale—ramifications. Yet politics is often thought to be steeped in the sin of power, dominated by expediency, not morality. Morality is identified with purity and the ideal; politics is tarnished with compromise and the realities of a harsh world. Moral and political values have here virtually nothing in common. Yet they are both values accruing in action. From our point of view, the gap between morality and politics is absurd, especially if a contrast between ideal values and self-interest. We have seen that individual interests have moral ramifications. So too, societies and governments work in terms of established values and seek controls which affect individual satisfactions as well as social institutions. Both political and moral enterprises seek control over the spheres in which they arise by reference to ideals and principles. And the sense in which control is established looks to the abilities of individual men to act and to gain satisfactions.

Let us not define politics as arenas in which some men exercise power over others, but as those relatively comprehensive spheres of action in which control must be established if failure within narrower spheres of action is to be minimized. The significant distinction does not address the nature of political organizations and their powers—for established organizations frequently take on a life of their own, almost in direct contrast with the concerns of their members—but the interplay between relatively circumscribed and broader spheres of action. Collective powers are required in these larger domains of action, especially where merely individual powers are unequal to the task. It is not merely the *social* implications of action—for and by many men—that are important here, but the diverse powers of men in comprehensive domains of control. Inclusive considerations arise not merely with a multiplicity of agents and their actions, but with the multiplicity of far-reaching components of individual life. They move from the individual to the social, but also from the individual to his encompassing conditions and requirements. In this sense, politics only incidentally is concerned with government—though government and its instruments are among the most compelling of political means—but is rather the larger sphere of relations comprising a diversity of human actions and projected consequences. It is this sense of the political which we will examine, setting aside all other significations, especially those which would emphasize a fundamental disparity between the moral and the political. Political concerns look to measures of comprehensive effects and scope. Politics here addresses technology, economy, science, knowledge—in fact, all areas of human life. Only a part of politics is concerned with the interaction of men in social groups, except as these represent means by which larger powers are exercised.

Traditional moral principles represent social values, the traffic of men with each other. As we treat men in our daily activities, so we may treat others in larger groupings. These principles represent in addition a traffic with life and death, with war and peace, with instruments of life as in medicine and with instruments of death as in capital punishment. Customs of marriage and the family are implicated, but also institutions of property and of kinship. The modes and devices of social relations invoke all the appurtenances of human life, and change with changing methods and instruments of control. A blind morality often neglects the larger concerns, the extension of values to more comprehensive arenas of action. Broader spheres of action often call for different kinds of decision and employ unique instruments of control. To say that politics is concerned with expediency and not morality denies it ideal values, although it is continually involved with the greatest and most vital of human concerns —life, death, love, hatred, war, and peace. The circumstances of comprehensive spheres of action may call for new and different ideals, reflecting changing conditions and the constraints of coordination. Nevertheless, political action requires ideals and principles for regulation and judgment as does all action, and for the same reasons.

Where an established sphere of action reaches its limits, and new conditions emerge which require methodic reevaluation, there action not only extends what is given but synthesizes new ideals and means of control. The established and given must be relinquished and new values created, though maintaining continuity with the past. The established is bounded and delineated, at least in space and time; we must then seek a larger arena of evaluation. Overly pure moralities often protect themselves from the perils of engagement by leaving to politics the entire enterprise of evaluation and the establishment of new values. Yet as we have seen, if we exclude arbitrary blindness, even commonplace situations are evaluative in the same full sense, open-ended and perilous, bounded only by practical considerations. The moral is the locus of all active values, and in one sense the moral and the political are the same. Political concerns are simply more comprehensive in the diversity of elements they seek to coordinate.

We may pause for a moment to consider specifically some of the concerns that inhabit the largest spheres of political action—the most comprehensive domains over which man exercises or seeks control, his entire planet, even the solar system. The most obvious is the social—the relations of men in groupings and in institutions. The polity is often identified with the society—though both notions are flawed by the restriction of relations to persons and by the diminution of the range of political and of social interconnections. In any case, governments exercise control over their citizens and in large nations broadly regulate interpersonal relations. Through law and through administration, institutions are created and regulated; likewise, some of the ways in which men interact are regulated also.

It is unfortunate that we may speak so casually, without being taken to task, of governments *controlling* the actions of their citizens. Certainly all governments exercise some control over their citizens. Yet no government can exercise complete control over all its citizens. The most complete exercise of control, the most stringent forms of compulsion, nevertheless leave room for deviation and for choice. Hobbes argues that law cannot diminish a man's liberty, apparently disregarding the constraints which a power over circumstances may provide. His claim is absurd, for control is indeed exercised by means of conditions and circumstances. Nevertheless, the claim masks a profound metaphysical truth: that in any sphere of action, given conditions cannot exhaust all alternatives. Possibilities reside in every sphere of action. A law making criticism of the government a capital offense nevertheless preserves the possibility of such criticisms and subsequent punishment. More to the point, it may not inhibit critical thoughts and may encourage plots against the government. The most authoritarian government cannot regulate every possibility in the lives of its citizens. However stringent and comprehensive the force of necessity in any sphere of action, alternative possibilities remain. Given any actualities, multiple possibilities prevail.

The more important point, however, is that the function of government is only incidentally to exercise control over its members. Its primary function as a *political* institution is to strengthen powers, to make actions more effective. Individual actions often conflict—not due alone to conflicting interests, but in being uncoordinated actions requiring regulation. A well-run polity is in the interest of all its citizens, a means whereby their individual concerns can be successfully coordinated. Small numbers of individuals may sometimes cooperate easily together without elaborate coordination. Large numbers of men call for administrative measures of a complex and far-reaching nature, though not necessarily stringent and punitive actions. In many cases, the most effective

coordination of diverse concerns and ends is through minimum regulation
and effective compromises. The continuity attained throughout diverse
spheres of action is governed by principles of equity and tolerance. The
important point, however, is that specific coordination must be developed
from and within given conditions. It is not a timeless condition of all
human life.

The fact of increasing population would be enough to justify political
concerns—though we may note that political measures often affect
population. Political action—like all action—influences the conditions for
its own future. Setting aside such considerations, we may note that
individual spheres of action intersect in diverse and complex ways, and
their interconnections must be regulated if satisfaction is to be possible.
Orders of life and action expand from narrower individual, family, and
community spheres to world-wide regions involving great numbers of
men. Our moral principles call upon us to consider all men as moral
agents. Increasing populations strain such principles, requiring continual
adjustment in terms of political and social realities. If modern life is to be
successfully maintained, actions of men in one place must be coordinated
with actions of others several thousand miles away. It might be
argued—and often is—that such large-scale and expansive coordination is
hostile to individual and to community life. This issue is crucial for all
political action, and will be our focus shortly. Here we may note the fact
that individual and community enterprises are not isolated nor wholly
circumscribed. Local industries pollute wide regions. Farms must feed
distant cities. Failure haunts all isolated and circumscribed domains of
action for neglecting their surroundings. Technology brings men ever
closer. Medicine prolongs life and increases population. The entire planet
may today easily be perceived as a single, comprehensive system. Such a
perception is partly a truth about new institutions and means available
now as never before. But it is also a truth about complex interactions in a
pluralistic world.

It is absurd to speak of political affairs as if they concern numbers of
men only. Economy, technology, even science, art, philosophy, and
political institutions and regulations, all comprise simultaneously the
conditions of action and also the means of political control. If economics is
concerned with the exchange and distribution of materials, goods, and
services, then we may at once regard our economic circumstances as
conditions definitive of value, yet also as the means for coordinating values
in large-scale enterprises. Through economic means, new goods are
valued and marketed, thereafter to influence life everywhere, including

the marketplace. The concerns of an individual farmer or craftsman must be coordinated with the needs of a factory worker who dwells in a large urban center. Economic regulations—in the broad sense that includes political measures—are the lifeblood of any communal extension from individual spheres of action and control. The assumption of a free marketplace is that minimal regulation will have the broadest success in establishing cooperative interactions within and among diverse spheres of action. The principle—adhered to by few economists today—is that in the absence of explicit regulation, economic interactions will be successful over wide reaches of social and human life. The goal is the establishment of successful and comprehensive interaction—though the means recommended is that of minimal regulation. It is by no means absurd to think that control may be won by patience and by naturally harmonious conditions—though it is overly optimistic, and reflects a preference for avoiding rather than undertaking action. In a well-established ecological system, minor changes produce compensatory adjustments which maintain the stability of the system. It is important to note both that some changes may not be capable of compensatory resolution, therefore destroying the stability of the system; and also that human life has notoriously been unstable. Men rend the environment and waste resources to expand their powers. If such activities are no longer to continue, political powers have a frightening responsibility to find new modes of organization and control.

Technology represents for us the most compelling and overwhelming means by which our world has been and continues to be transformed. Technology is also the instrument by which control is most successfully established over the environment—and over men as well. Instruments for obtaining raw materials and for shaping them into goods are of utmost influence in all human life—although technology shapes human life more by shaping the forms of activities than through consumable goods. The automobile and airplane have brought men closer together in time; radio and television provide nearly instant means of communication over remarkably great distances, and the range of their use is continually expanding. Even more far-reaching are the prospects that the surface of our planet is no longer a practical boundary to our powers, and that both the inner recesses of the earth and the other planets of our solar system have come within the reach of our practical abilities. Our scientific explorations, from which we gain knowledge without immediate prospects of action, reach out to the recesses of the physical universe. We may expect that industrial processes will move into space, if only to that immediately surrounding our planet, and a new industrial revolution may be in the wings.

Yet science and technology are neither individual nor even community enterprises. We by no means have established consistent controls over our solar system, nor even over our planet. Yet so large is the expanse of our powers, and so diverse are the qualities and ramifications, that coordination of a very comprehensive nature is required. Governments support research and the exploration of space. No one else could afford to, not even major corporations, nor would they have access to the necessary means. Worst of all, they have too limited interests and goals to serve so broad a political purpose. Many discoveries have military applications with political implications. In addition, new technological developments generate their own special problems, which often call for measures of greatest importance and of broadest purview. Nuclear energy, biological discoveries which could stem the spread of disease, pollution by automobile fumes and industrial wastes—all have great ramifications in human life, and require political measures for their development and control. New devices for extending life create very difficult moral problems. Not only are men kept alive regardless of the consequences for their families and society generally, but medicine has great costs which must be adequately met and distributed.

Over the last half-century we have witnessed the rapid expansion of human powers through technology and science, even within the related arts. The arts have become more technological; in addition, art works are often widely distributed. With the rapid expansion of powers, the need for regulation has grown also, and political institutions have become overwhelming in their influence within and without their own societies. Governments exercise control within—if not wholly upon—the economy, technology, science, education, the arts, and upon other governments as well. They also regulate their own measures—though by no means satisfactorily. In one sense, the expansion of political powers is a legitimate consequence of the larger spheres of human concern—a reflection of new powers requiring broad regulation, new and larger environments in which control must be established if human life is to be secured. In the same sense, we may say that the complex, difficult, and insecure aspects of political life are exactly what they should be, for the issues are so intricate, and the need to reevaluate large-scale policies so frequent and urgent, that politics can only be experimental, hypothetical, methodic, complex, even extremely subtle—for that is the character of human concerns in their widest spheres of control. Politics is a matter of influence, of experiment and trial, of give and take, for that is the best we can manage on so broad a scale.

And yet, there is that other sense in which we may lay all evil today at the account of governments. We live in an age of affluence, life extended through medical advances, agricultural surpluses in many countries, all sorts of goods available to a greater number of people than ever before, a range of possibilities and a liberty to partake of them that has never before been present in human life. Yet men seem no happier, many are still poor, there is bigotry, racism, and cruelty; there has been an increase in violence, in the use of drugs, and in a prevailing sense of meaninglessness. Could not the poor be fed by appropriate political action? Could not racism be ended by law? Have not the rich become richer? Civilization may literally be the cause of evils, as Freud speculated, either for reasons inherent in the characters of men or simply by the sheer magnitude of problems facing a large civilization. The alternative is that political measures themselves are in vain, are biased, corrupt, pernicious in their sources and in their consequences.

The answer to the possibility that civilization is the evil, and that men are better off in a primitive society, may be given by a single fact: the average life-expectancy in the United States in 1890 was 26 years of age. Movements which seek a return to primitive simplicity ironically rest on a disrespect for life. The second view—that governments are evil and corrupt, that political practices are destructive—has no direct answer, for it is partly true. Indeed, governments often inhibit coordination and prevent success in individual actions, imposing thoughtless and unresponsive practices on diverse individual concerns. In this sense, governments are often politically unsuccessful, as we have understood political concerns. Nevertheless, the view that governments are evil is partly untrue as well, and that is our problem. For the issues that face governments and political leaders are both immense and rapidly-changing. Measures quickly prove inadequate or of but transitory value. It is naive to suppose that there are straightforward solutions to all our problems. It is equally naive to suppose that tinkering within the established system is the best we can do.

We will shortly return to the broader aspects of political power from the standpoint of the continuity to be established between political and circumscribed actions. Before doing so, we may undertake a brief consideration of some of the central elements of political controls, especially to emphasize the complex nature of political measures. It is important to be clear that no aspect of social and political life in its broad character is either an unqualified good or evil. There are anarchists who find all governments evil and destructive, and who advocate a government-less polity. Yet there is no way of avoiding the interconnection and regulation of diverse spheres of action. Means must be found to coordinate disparate actions. Anarchists believe in management and administration, though not in the exercise of power over men. There is no way of escaping the movement from narrower values to broader concerns, with the attendant risks of enormous failure.

We may conveniently classify the broader institutions of social and political organization under three headings: government, law, and custom. It is important to realize that each provides mixed values, that there are significant and important benefits provided by all phases of political organization. We may, for example, note that one of the most essential functions of government is administrative—to coordinate and regulate diverse elements of social life into a coherent and harmonious, or at least non-antagonistic, system of relations. We must note here the importance of administration without coercion, simply coordinating the multiplicity of events and concerns which require attention. All bureaucracies— though they are the source of many problems—provide instruments for effecting broad policies and for ameliorating specific conflicts. As for the coercive elements of government—especially the direct force of armies and police—though certainly often destructive, they contribute to security in action. And although violence nearly always breeds further violence, it is not a simple matter to find alternatives that maintain individual security. Finally, governments have educational effects, and influence the ways their peoples act and react. Government actions generate values and encourage common expectations and ideals. Here again, the educational influence of governmental controls may often be pernicious, but education is necessary and valuable. In fact, the educational effects of political measures may be their most important role in terms of common policies and cooperative modes of action. The entire panoply of controls and results provided by governments is quite mixed, and its values are difficult to sort out.

Law provides a similar complexity in political structure and organization. Unlike governments, who are responsible for direct coercion when necessary—including enforcement of the law—legal prescriptions are only mediately coercive. A large society without regulation by law would be impossible, even a society whose every member possessed a perfect sensitivity to the thoughts and emotions of his fellows. Conflicting emotions would require resolution, and one based on comprehensive principles and broad instruments of coordination, not merely individual decisions. Law here represents the political form of principles of action, as well as regulations through coercion and fear when coupled with enforced sanctions. In addition, law has a deeply educational effect—far greater than governmental influence—upon the expectations and values individuals will come to have through time. We may note that legal regulations can be educational both in generating a respect for established values— where laws prove successful—and also in generating disrespect and contempt—where nearly everyone is led to disobey the law.

The values of law also are mixed. Law is the primary instrument of coordination among manifold and diverse spheres of control. Coordination requires legislation and dissemination. Whatever legislative forms are followed, we may debate whether coercion and punishment are necessary in law, but not whether regulations can be dispensed with. They define the means of coordination, represent the ideals to which coordination looks, compel some obedience—even where overt sanctions are absent— and educate men to the broad values essential to social cooperation. It is sometimes said that all civilized societies must come under a rule of law. If this means that political coordination essential to beneficial social interactions requires law, that is certainly true. Also, laws are generally to be obeyed—for that is what regulation by law means. But no regulative principle is necessarily *always* to be obeyed without question, without exception, having no room for individual decision, judgment, and interpretation.

It may be that *generally speaking,* a political order will be the more beneficial and stable whose citizens seek legislative remedy in the face of difficulties and obey established laws until they can be changed. Certainly administration would be improved under such conditions, and where simple cooperation is required, such a conception of the rule of law would be most effective. However, when ideals come into conflict, it is by no means obvious that a citizen ought to obey an unjust law. Were a minority group to be severely oppressed by legislation, they and members of the majority as well might decide that exceptions were required to the general regulations. The two extremes are that all laws should be obeyed until repealed, and that an unjust law imposes no obligation on an individual to obey it. The first is a repudiation of individual decision, and may be rejected forthwith. All principles of action require interpretation and individual decision. The second is repudiation of the loyalty that principles must be given in action—here the loyalty to law that is required if broader spheres of control are to be established.

Our general theory of principles and ideals of action defines a theoretical solution to the problem—though the practical question of when disobedience is required remains for each man to determine in his particular circumstances. From a substantive point of view, laws are to be obeyed, regardless of coercion and prospective punishment. Law is the primary instrument by which political action is undertaken and compromises established among diverse spheres of action. Hobbes' recognition that an enduring and satisfying society rests on a general respect for law and for sovereignty is a great substantive truth—though we may sharply differ with him concerning both the nature of the sovereign and the implications of our respect for it. In general, history has shown that obedience to law is obligatory within a stable and successful social order. It has shown also, however, that law can be stifling and immoral. It follows that the principle of obedience to law is substantively established and therefore regulative in spheres of action to which it has application. Nevertheless, any particular case may be an exception to a general principle, based on specific substantive considerations. Such considerations are not lacking in political contexts. It follows that obedience to the law is always an obligation, but there may also be overriding obligations relative to other ideals. Here we come to the most important truth about political considerations: that the broader coordination provided through government, law, and custom may be incompatible in specific cases with other ideals, and that individuals may be obligated to oppose their governments when this occurs.

It is not the case that every unjust law must be disobeyed—Thoreau notwithstanding. A law which coordinates diverse actions may indeed conflict with other ideals. Loyalty to law can overpower loyalty to moral ideals and to individual powers. However, to disobey an unjust law easily is to make narrower ideals dominant over political concerns, and to sacrifice comprehensiveness to specificity. To challenge a law for failing to serve a narrower sphere of action may be to sacrifice all prospects of coordination and compromise. We may be too morally pure to compromise, and remain aloof from all coordinating action. The balance is treacherous, constantly shifting, and extremely difficult to establish even temporarily. But its general goal is clear: to ensure that broader domains of control and more specific ideals relative to personal interactions are compatible with each other where they come into direct relation.

We may consider briefly our third aspect of political order—moving from explicit regulation to the implicit regulation of *custom*. Hume makes custom the entire basis of norms and values. Though his view is flawed by too narrow a conception of reason, Hume is insightful concerning the fundamental nature of implicit regulations and traditional modes of action and feeling. Custom is the general conformity within human life, the maintenance of tradition and community. It is the repetitive and conservative quality of communal action even in the absence of government and law. It joins with sympathy in many cases, producing patterns of action of great endurance and influence. Here we may note that government and law—though explicit and capable of far more effective and rapid direction and control than inertial habits of custom—of necessity rest on custom themselves. No government has so great a force that it must be obeyed by all through coercion and fear. Some men—the militia, the many, the ordinary—must obey by custom; and their loyalty forms the basis of government power. Law too, though coercive, possesses its effectiveness in terms of customary obedience by the ordinary man. The common patterns of life, conservative as they are and as they gradually change, may be modified by government and by laws as well as by changing conditions. Yet they retain their regularity, and are an important basis for collective modes of action and control.

The implicit nature of custom does not in any way alleviate the thoroughly mixed values which may be found within it as in all political regulation. The controls and stability custom affords have great benefits but can also lead to great evils. Custom represents communal values, the prevalence of norms common throughout a social order. In this sense, it is the heart of political controls and the goal for which all comprehensive orders reach. Custom represents the coordination within and among diverse spheres of action to produce common norms and established modes of collective endeavor. Nevertheless, custom is too often regularity and stability without flexible adaptation or rational control. Though methodic action—like all norms of action and thought—rests on a foundation in custom, methods can be delicate and responsive where custom is thoughtless. The standards of custom may be effective and coordinative, yet unfounded in substantial truth. Customs can be blind and nearly purposeless. They may also generate a conformity and regimentation that breeds both mindlessness and dissatisfaction. Custom verges on the blindness of habit—though there are customs of thoughtfulness and inquiry. Custom is a conformity that is less imposed than a fact. It can attain a uniformity alien and hostile to individuality.

We come, then, to consider political orders and the comprehensiveness they may attain relative to the diversity of manifold spheres of control. We have examined the notion of diverse and antogonistic interests and have found that a stable and comprehensive order is in no sense intrinsically hostile to its members. It is illegitimate to conclude from the plurality of individual spheres of concern that interests conflict. Nevertheless, there can be too great a conformity in human life, a regimentation hostile both to individual satisfactions and to discovery and creation. Custom provides conformity without coercion—or with minimal sanctions. It may be suggested that men yearn for a stable and uniform social order—for they often act as if they do. Were it true, nevertheless we should still be convinced that too great a conformity—though desired by all—would be a danger and hostile to man's present and to his future. John Stuart Mill emphasizes the diversity of individuality, claiming that the greater value is not the social good but deviance and originality.

It becomes necessary for us to consider more carefully the extension through action of control from individual to political orders. We have noted that established modes of control are hypothetical means for extending an order through action, and that action extends such control by seeking values that are not yet established—either in the future or in new provinces of experience. Either action moves from established orders to new and perilous circumstances to gain control within them; or it moves from discordant and partly controlled domains to new spheres in which control has been established, however temporarily. In both cases, values are projected under the omnipresent peril of failure. Control is established by means of successful action—or at least, actions which reach into new spheres of concern without encountering failure. In the complexity of political affairs, the likelihood of failure is increased, and prospects for satisfactorily coordinating the great diversity of relevant concerns are slight.

From this point of view, political devices are at once part of established conditions and of means for realizing future possibilities. Regulative and coercive institutions as well as principles of law are part of the conditions for action. It is tempting to claim that only individuals can act. Nevertheless, there are collective actions: a country goes to war; a parliament legislates; a mob lynches an innocent man. We must admit that groups can act, even that they can be brought to account and held responsible. In a sense, they may even regret their past deeds, and learn from them. A legislature may reconsider its actions, and repeal a law. A country may pay reparations on the grounds of failure.

It may be that collective regret is significantly different from the regret felt by an individual that is the mark of failure. But collective actions are different from individual deeds in many respects. Groups as well as governments can learn from their past actions and act methodically on the basis of what they have learned—though they may act and experience regret only through their members. However, just as groups require their members for action, so individuals act through their social and political groupings. Politics affords a means whereby individual men gain in their powers to control the future through their actions.

Organizations and groups which are established for political control take on a life of their own—though they are inevitably related to their members. It is true neither that groups are "merely" aggregates of individuals, nor that individuals are "merely" instruments of social interaction. Individual and social concerns are diverse—which does not mean that they are necessarily antagonistic, but only of distinct purview and subject to disparate conditions and judgments. Individuals and groups cannot be harmoniously coordinated—not entirely, not without loss, for there would then be but a single and uniform political order, a supreme and comprehensive order of human functioning, including all men and all their concerns.

Pluralism is not a theory of conflicting individual interests, but a theory of diverse concerns—both individual and collective. Groups and organizations as well as individuals are all—in the language of our final chapter—*orders*. They are interrelated, but each possesses a distinct integrity. The organizations and instruments devised to provide coordination among individual concerns come to possess their own conditions of endurance and stability. Governments protect and aggrandize themselves, not always their members. Organizations may demand loyalty from their members, but may not reciprocate. Created structures for maximizing individual satisfactions may decrease such satisfactions as they develop their own conditions of endurance.

If the structures for political control can undermine individual powers, and if they can embrace their own conditions of validity, then a normative principle is required. Marx points out correctly that individual men are both weak and inefficacious in their capacity to control events, while social powers control the lives of men. Classes and groups exert power and move in part of their own momentum. Nevertheless, they are comprised of men, so that circumscribed and comprehensive spheres of action are inevitably related, though not the same. Following Marx further, we may seek a normative ideal for political action, one rooted in the relation of comprehensiveness in action to individual spheres, repudiating political orders except as means to individual fulfillments. We may acknowledge the forcefulness of political organizations, yet repudiate their powers except as conditions for action and as means to individual control. If so, we may formulate the following moral and political ideal:

The purpose of political organization is to provide such controls over the broader and more comprehensive orders within human life that individual control is maximized, both within the narrower and the more inclusive spheres of action which are implicated. All action looks to further action. Political action subserves the individual powers of men. Of course, it also influences them, and provides both conditions and principles for individual actions. Nevertheless, it is only in terms of individual acts and powers that political action can be judged a failure or a success.

It is important to understand the grounds for such a normative principle. We may discern three distinct but interrelated considerations:

(1) Political action depends on the actions of individuals, who must evaluate what they do in terms of the criteria and methods appropriate to all rational action. In this sense, the test for the individuals involved of comprehensive measures resides—with all action—in the success and failure of the actions undertaken. Either political measures subserve individual concerns and powers, or an individual will define his ideals in terms of collective considerations. He will give his greater loyalties to the suprapersonal. Although men may do so, sacrificing themselves from patriotic loyalty, we may find substantive grounds for their doing so only within individual spheres of action. We have interpreted the substantive ground of ideals to be ascertainable only in terms of success and failure *for the individuals who conform to those ideals.* Either patriotism promotes satisfactory acts or it does not. Either such acts are found good by individual men, or they are a failure *for those men.* It is of course true that individual goals are tested in terms of their consequences for other men also. The interconnection of diverse actions and goals requires political coordination, whose validity depends on its consequences for individual men.

(2) Failure is the omnipresent condition of all action, possibilities of failure haunting all conditions and circumstances. The methodic considerations which underlie an open awareness of possibilities of failure, and which may lead to felt regret, are significantly different relative to collective and individual actions. Although groups and organizations may both act and repudiate their actions, only individuals can *feel* regret. A legislature may repeal legislation, but only in virtue of the felt regret—the *sense of failure*—experienced by its individual members. As for the converse condition, that men experience regret only in the context of

collective conditions, that is incorporated within the circumstances of action and evaluation. The ultimate test of failed action resides in the regret of individuals. Political groups cannot experience regret in the same sense, or in an analogous sense. In this sense, only individuals are agents. In return, however, only groups are efficacious, and efficacy is far more valuable than agency. Nevertheless, to judge political actions valid apart from the ends of individuals is to introduce a radically different mode of evaluation, one which makes the political radically incommensurate with other moral values. Political and moral ideals here have virtually nothing in common. Commerce between social and individual values is severely inhibited, if not abolished. Action is even rendered unintelligible, since circumscribed and comprehensive spheres of action cannot in fact be separated.

(3) The theoretical question of the relationship between circumscribed and comprehensive concerns is resolved by two simple conditions: (a) that no spheres of action are clearly bounded, but stretch indefinitely into other spheres; and, (b) that larger spheres encompass individual concerns, which are relevant to their evaluation. Having said this, we may note that diverse spheres may be interrelated—though not all are related to all others—but are also to some extent disparate. Just as diverse individual concerns can only be coordinated and compromised, but not fully reconciled and interconnected, so comprehensive and narrower concerns can only be coordinated, but not fully harmonized. The specific question, then, is always whether a given action of a comprehensive nature coordinates as successfully as possible the diversity of individual concerns with constraints of an inclusive nature. Often individual concerns and powers seem lost in the powers of large organizations. In return, individuals without the powers provided by organizations are relatively helpless. The exact adjustment is difficult to determine, and must avoid failure generally for members of the society. Yet they are members of *that* society, with its encompassing conditions. As always, we can have at best an ideal in terms of which particular actions are required, but an ideal to be interpreted within specific actions. All we can do is to coordinate narrow and comprehensive spheres of action toward success and away from failure, as they are understood above. The details are a problem for specific decisions. The political ideal does no more than to reiterate the function of comprehensive concerns relative to action and felt regret.

The natural question is whether it is *all* men whose powers are to be strengthened or simply the majority, even perhaps just a few? At one extreme, we may note how often political systems extend the powers of a minority of men, either the politicians themselves or a wealthy and privileged group. Far too often, governments serve the narrowly defined wishes of a specific class. Political organizations are extremely corrupting, not only in exercising great powers, but in the range of individuals who rule and who are benefited. Shall we then turn to the majority, as democracy would have it? A minority can be very badly served through political means. Instead we may note that politics serves the powers of men indifferently, and that the specific decision to serve one group more than another is a decision like all others, to be judged in terms of the problems and conditions at hand, and perhaps to be evaluated differently by different agents.

Political actions subserve the powers of men—not some men, not even the great majority of men, but men indifferently. Where powers are lacking, and failure is common, there political action has failed—relative to the needs of the men involved. Political action is constantly failing, constantly faced with the need for adjustment and improvement—and constantly finding how elusive is the goal it pursues. But that is no intrinsic problem: it simply shows that the overarching ideal of political activity requires continual action in its service, that there is no ultimate polity, no supreme human life, only activities and methods from which ideals emerge to guide action and to capture loyalties. There is no one ideal compromise among diverse concerns, no one ideal coordination of diverse activities, but a dynamic and responsive interplay of diverse activities. The powers of men may conflict; many may be powerful at the expense of a small minority. They must protest, if necessary loudly, and political forces must respond, if only by minor adjustments. Laws that restrain important appetites generate unrest and resistance. Laws that lead to war may be destructive and opposed. Practices that enforce the poverty of the many and the affluence of the few are perilous—not to say unjust. The ideals of individual interrelations, guided so often by love and consideration as well as charity, are too often harshly confronted with political favoritism and impotence. Here the ideals of individual life are not aided by politics but warped by it. Here political action proves that it has failed.

The founding fathers of the United States understood the principle of political action—not the advancement of the state nor even the attainment of happiness, but the *right of individual men to pursue happiness*. If happiness were not so elusive, such a formulation would serve. But it seems to address a state of mind and being, not the activities which subserve it. We have amended it to the principle that politics serves the end of maximizing individual controls over their spheres of action. Political power is the exercise of collective administration to the end of individual powers *over their own lives, attained through their own actions*—though of course, actions in the context of and utilizing political instruments. John Stuart Mill defends a related ideal—that each man has the right to maximum liberty so long as he does not harm others. This is probably the guiding ideal of all government and communal life. But it is not very useful in practice, since all individual actions have a tendency to affect other men in propitious or disadvantageous ways. Both Mill and the framers of the *Declaration of Independence* understood that government serves its people, whose powers and satisfactions are the measure of its success. They understood also that a plurality of individuals makes a perfect political system quite impossible. They supposed that minimal government was the most compatible with pluralism. Subsequent events have proved them wrong. Sometimes individuals can be effective in action only within the context of powerful, even coercive political organizations. Coercive measures may sometimes be necessary to coordination among conflicting groups. It is our task here to sketch an alternative approach to political pluralism.

It should be noted that *On Liberty* and the *Declaration of Independence* both postulate a plurality of interests and the desirability of maintaining it. We have noted that interests may often be common—that it is rather spheres of action which are plural. Nevertheless, in Mill's view it is important that diversity be encouraged. In the view of political action presented here, *diversity is a fact*. Mill argues that too uniform a society would be destructive of individuality and an evil. In the view presented here, political action which is too confining ceases to subserve its function. It pretends to establish a comprehensive order of action and control as if diversity were not a fact. A fearful price is paid for over-conformity in political action—and it is paid in the spheres of individual action. Instead of becoming more powerful, men are made less so, whether conformity be the result of coercion or custom. Here, institutions do not enhance individual powers but stifle them. In the Grand Inquisitor's society based on miracle, mystery, and authority, men are tended like sheep to eliminate care. The actual result is powerlessness: they cannot function as effective agents. Failure is not eliminated by political measures which induce conformity at the expense of sensitivity and judgment. The only solution to anguish is greater power and the avoidance of failure, not a flight from action and responsibility.

We may turn for just a moment to the level of ontology to enforce the pluralism upon which our theory of political action is based. We will develop the ontology in greater detail in the final chapter. The fundamental premises for our purposes here are few: there are many orders—and only orders: everything is an order. Every order is an order of constituents; and every order is itself a constituent in other orders; the constituents of an order belong to it by virtue of its integrity within some other order. One conclusion that follows is that every order is related to many other orders and indefinitely so; but not every order is related to every other. There is no world order. The universe is no order and is not all-encompassing. Analogously, there can be no all-encompassing political order. There is no supreme political system in which every individual concern has a well-defined place. Diversity is a fact, as is relatedness. Action is continually needed to accommodate diversity within order and relations. There are more or less comprehensive orders, and there is a permanent movement within action from narrower to broader spheres of action and control, as well as a return within individual powers.

There is but one way to understand comprehensiveness in such a pluralistic system. If there is no world order, there is no all-encompassing order. It follows that a more comprehensive order seldom will encompass all the constituents of the orders belonging to it. Given many orders belonging to a more general order, it may not have as its constituents all of their constituents. This should be no surprise, since if every order is related to some other orders, but not every order is related to every other, it follows that not all relations are transitive. The point for our purposes, however, is that a more comprehensive order may not encompass all the detailed and many constituents of its own constituents. A comprehensive order may gain in generality at the price of specificity. In this sense, the philosophical category of Being includes everything—but says nothing specifically about anything. In the same sense also, a political order may only be comprehensive in terms of broad ideals—at the expense of a vagueness which leaves individual decisions quite open to individuals who must make them.

Individual actions take place within relatively circumscribed situations, and it is the control of these situations which is sought in action. However, spheres of action intersect in complex and ramified ways. Men may come together in families or towns. The actions of one man affect many others. Broader spheres of control are thus engendered, and controls must be established which coordinate individual constraints, specific circumstances, and relevant ideals. Were a town to provide such coordination by making one member absolute ruler, whose controls everyone followed unthinkingly, then coordination would be achieved at the price of uniformity and at the expense of individual spheres of action. The ineluctable role of individual men as agents who undertake decisions and actions is undermined. Distinct spheres of action are abrogated and their plurality also. The fact remains that there are many men in the town, each with his concerns and spheres of action, each an agent able to act and make decisions. This diversity is a fact, and if so, must be accommodated. As for whether the diversity might be eliminated within some political systems, that is theoretically impossible and at best an ideal to be approximated—though an ideal without a substantive basis in individual and political experience. It is assumed in despotism either that all actions are *for* the ruler—which is arbitrary; or, as Hobbes argues, that by establishing such a ruler, there will be greater individual security of action. Hobbes' position is in fact pluralistic: it is but a simple matter to determine whether an absolute ruler maximizes individual powers and achievements. The evidence works against Hobbes' extreme position, if not his concern for stability and security.

It makes no difference whether conformity is imposed or merely comes to pass. The diversity of individuals within a society—and of individual instruments and varying surroundings as well—cannot be entirely incorporated into a comprehensive political order. Diversity entails some differences; no authoritarian system, however total, could succeed in treating all its members indistinguishably as instruments of its control. Total uniformity would abolish individual integrity; each person would be a token to be replaced by any other. Decisions would lose their individual character, and individual acts would be abolished, as would moral responsibility. Men would be no agents; only the polity would act, by means of its members, yet lacking all sense of individual success and failure. Political action which abrogates individual judgments, with all of their disparities, is blind to its primary measures of validity. Uniformity can strengthen individual powers—but it may also undermine them. A genuine and efficacious diversity of individuals is to be accommodated in all political orders. It may vary with time and circumstances, from great diversity to minimal differences. The test of success resides in the impact of political measures on the effectiveness of individual agents and their satisfactions.

We have learned from our experiences that many institutions and social structures sap the powers of men, compelling them to act collectively but with minimal satisfactions and control. The powers of men over their own lives are few, especially in the context of modern social structures and organizations. Economic, religious, political, and social structures all confine the powers of men. They also, however, represent the means whereby individual powers may be effective in larger spheres of action. On the one hand, coercive forces generate conformity —sometimes stifling to the point where individual powers are nearly destroyed and individual decisions are impotent. On the other hand, effective institutions strengthen the powers of some men, if not all. Too great a conformity, and individual powers are undermined. Too great a disparity among individual concerns, and effectiveness in action is nearly impossible. The only remaining possibility is that of a political coordination that maximizes individual powers without too great a sacrifice in diversity. As to what constitutes an acceptable sacrifice, only time, effort, and will can tell us.

Democracy is a political system—or many such systems—founded on plurality. Dictatorship sacrifices the many to the ruling orders of control, as if individual diversity could be overcome. The result is either claimed beneficence, though no one can fully control another's needs and act for him; or obvious exploitation, whose oppressiveness is at the expense of the powers of individual men. Totalitarianism would abolish individual differences and their relevance to decision. Yet it cannot; and worst of all, depends for its effectiveness on the powers of some individuals. No polity that would be adaptable can afford to be wholly autocratic. When all is said and done, a political order needs its responsible and effective agents, and is quite self-defeating where it seeks to overwhelm them with regimentation.

Democracy remains as the political system in which individuals act within their particular spheres and thereby exert control in the broad political arena. Yet the particular democratic system which would most effectively attain political ends while maximizing individual powers is undetermined. Corrupt officials serve narrow interests. Property restrictions effectively prohibit many men from exercising even minimal controls upon their lives. Under threats from without, governments become repressive and confining. Contrasted with the complexity of diverse issues relevant to political action, many forms of government— even many forms of democracy—are tried, each with its virtues and its faults. And what would be successful for one country might not be successful for another with a very different history and different circumstances. Even here, diversity requires coordination. Mankind will of necessity move toward a world political system—if not a world government—insofar as our concerns have world-wide ramifications.

Ironically, many dictatorships of the past have been oppressive and fearful, but could not greatly restrain individuality and diversity. Men exercised great influence upon their lives, though some activities were forbidden with fearful penalties. Today, we have the semblance of great democratic institutions, yet individuals exercise little influence over their lives. As so much of life has become institutionalized—food, the economy, education, work—most ways of life become indistinguishable. Few important choices remain. Particular choices make little difference. A large-scale democracy may leave little room for significant decisions, practically abolishing individual spheres of control. However democratic the forms of such a system may be, it has attained its controls at the expense of individual agents. They may become passive and inert, accepting atrocities in the name of social order. They may rebel arbitrarily and without apparent justification, yet aware of the absence of powers they may exercise. The forms of democracy are not the goal. Rather, it is the end of democracy to preserve and enhance individual activities and powers, extending them and rendering them more effective by political means. Instead, our larger institutions have become grossly manipulative of individual spheres of action, inhibiting individual powers rather than enhancing them. Political institutions today would define and implement a best life for *all* men to live, as if such an embracing order might be created in human experience, rather than providing a coordinative arena in which men may maximize their individual effectiveness. Some of the most important discoveries of the last hundred years are that political and social orders preempt individual decisions and powers even where seeking to maximize them. Marx's point is that our political orders enslave us, and must be destroyed if individual powers are to be liberated. Nevertheless, we must discover more satisfactory political orders if our liberation is to be achieved.

We may note again the major quality of ideals of action—that they are quite vague, yet serve to guide action when given specific interpretations. Their vagueness is essential to their comprehensiveness, since they can be very general only by virtue of a lack of specificity. They are general without reducing all actions which they govern to a single all-embracing system. They serve their general and relational function without sacrificing individual decision. We may postulate, then, that a satisfactory political order will rest a large measure of its comprehensiveness on broad ideals of action—fulfillment, life, and individuality. If expediency means lack of principle, then governments fail altogether when they turn away from ideals. It is through the great ideals, in continual reexamination and reformulation, that political action may attain its most effective comprehensiveness. In this sense, our ideals represent the broadest values we have found to live by, politically and morally. There will then be a permanent and dynamic interchange between the greater ideals and the specific practices required by the political order to bring about satisfactory controls. Here philosophic ideals have a vital function: to maintain comprehensiveness without sacrificing individuality. Political action may then render such ideals within the lives of individual men without overwhelming the character of individual decisions. Ideals without political implementation are impotent. Political action without comprehensive ideals is blind and oppressive.

As our final consideration, we may turn to the question of revolution, of the appropriate actions to be taken *against* an oppressive political system. The complex and disparate values inherent in any system so large and diverse as a political order suggest that violent opposition is especially perilous and nearly impossible to justify. Violence is morally proscribed. In addition, the values in terms of which opposition is proposed will almost always be drawn from the society in question. All societies profess to benefit their citizens, and to some extent all do so. Setting aside dictatorships for the moment, we may well wonder how a democracy could be considered a system to be destroyed—though we often find revolutionary rhetoric looking to this end. If mundane and daily activities are perilous, and if failure haunts us in all our actions, then political actions, which may destroy an entire society and the lives of many men, seem too awful to contemplate. Often revolutionaries are blind and fanatical, not methodically sensitive to the desperate situations at hand with all of their risks. The oppressed may rebel from sheer desperation—but this is no rational basis for action.

It is important, however, to realize that revolutionary rhetoric is itself a form of action and one to be distinguished from active rebellion. In an oppressive society, or in one merely inequitable to a significant minority, individual powers are quite limited. Revolutionary demands may be the only mode of action capable of eliciting favorable responses from the powers that be. The principle that *the squeaky wheel gets the grease* is an important principle of democratic political action. Groups out of favor may find it necessary to obtain some power by threatening wholesale destruction. The threats may not lead to overt action. Finally, if men lack nearly all control over their lives, they may have nothing to lose by rebellion. No failure could be worse than their desperation.

We may summarize the situation: It is the purpose of political orders to maximize individual powers and to minimize as much as possible prospects of individual failure in action. Deprived individuals are not being served politically, and have the right to protest. If their situation is desperate enough, they may justifiably rebel. Far more important, their plight when made known is a responsibility for the political powers to ameliorate. And if government and law will not meet this responsibility, then the political system has failed. Nevertheless, there may be situations which have no known resolution, difficulties which a country cannot dissipate. Here rebellion is difficult to justify, even in suffering. But where there is injustice and inequity, where some men suffer poverty while others are affluent, where known measures would advance the cause of the many at slight cost to the few, then the political system is a failure. Where political institutions do not enhance individual powers but stifle them, the political system has failed.

It does not follow that we may overthrow it. No action follows *automatically* upon a failure condemned in another as it does for oneself. Rebellion might cause more harm than good. The clear and open sense of political failure may be enough to generate change, especially in a relatively open society. Still, a great enough moral failure normally leads to punishment. A political system too insensitive to severe abuse and suffering deserves to be condemned, its rulers punished, and an alternative created. As a man may be brought through failure to change his way of life, a society may be brought to change its political system. It involves a frightful risk—but so does all action. Revolution is like all action except in the scale of its risks and benefits. Political action is vastly more consequential than circumscribed action, with great and terrible consequences. Having considered them in the appropriate scale, a man can but act according to his decisions. Each citizen of every country is responsible for the actions he takes or fails to take relative to his comprehensive concerns.

Nevertheless, valid action must be methodic. With respect to violence in opposition to a social and political order, this means that grounds be established that justify the success sought through revolution. Revolutionary action moves from given political and social conditions to successful results established after the overthrow of the present system. Desperation, though understandable, hardly may be thought to establish significant controls. What is needed is the prevalence of conditions and institutions which may be harnessed to the service of new controls. What is required is that the given oppressive system be divided in its character, not only oppressive but employing means and furnishing ideals which may provide powers in action. What is essential is that the complex political order furnish the means to its own demise and to the new and more successful order. Revolution is but one form of action—and a drastic one to be sure—moving from given to new conditions, realizing possibilities inherent in actual circumstances, employing means available to establish more comprehensive controls. All of this is akin to Marx's conception that a revolutionary condition provides within the situation to be abrogated the seeds of its own destruction; that the means for overcoming alienation must precede its elimination; that socialized production precedes socialized appropriation. But we abandon his sense that dialectical movements of necessity bring the tensions from which greater controls emerge. Political action is of greatest moment, and extremely perilous. Its greatest danger is the source of all its ills, conservative and revolutionary: that a momentous political action will sacrifice some individual concerns, while the concerns of individuals are the end of all political enterprises.

V

Active Judgment

~~~~~~

As Aristotle says, "every action aims at some good"—not, however, as he thought, a specific end given antecedently, but often an end undisclosed until its realization. Action projects from one complex sphere to other spheres, seeking the establishment of a new and more inclusive order in which the agent and his circumstances are effectively related. As Aristotle suggests also, the end of action must be *comprehensive*—for so complex a world as ours admits of successful action only when founded on inclusive and far-reaching ideals. Ideals represent the range of our control over action; their precise interpretations establish specific actions in relation to the ideal which broadly encompasses them. Action is always a means of control—the manipulation of conditions to attain success and to avoid failure as measured in terms of results attained. Success depends on the establishment of comprehensive spheres of action ruled by encompassing values and implemented by large-scale—that is, political—measures.

Validity in action resides in its consequences, not only in time and for physical objects, but consequences in imagination, for diverse points of view, and for theories. Control through action may be projected into any sphere in which further action is possible, there to be assimilated. Even a suppressed thought has the consequences of curtailed imagination, consequences not only for other men but for knowledge and truth. Any deed evaluated in terms of its results for assimilation is an act—even a claim to be widely disseminated or suppressed, or a work of art in its impact on men, on other art, or on the range of human imagination. Psychology has been deeply affected by both Freud and by Skinner, each in his own way, each exerting the impact of his actions *as a scientist* upon the science of psychology. Such acts change human history, but they also change important spheres of judgment.

In looking to effects and consequences, an action is always an extension from what is established to the unknown, from given circumstances to what remains to come, from the actual to the possible, from one order to another. Possibilities are the extensions of actualities in their interconnections, and the validity of actions resides in the possibilities which are actualized. Failure haunts all action because of possibilities yet to emerge. Action is one of the prominent sources of new possibilities, created by the extensions of spheres of action. A failure is an abortive or discordant extension of agency, the discovery that an action compatible with prior conditions will not serve in new circumstances. The standards and conditions of agency which ground action in the given sphere are discontinuous with the constraints of new situations emerging from the old. The impact of separate processes can be the wellspring of a new process, engendered by the old yet pragmatically discontinuous with it. Success is adequate extension, the continuous preservation of effective powers. Values established in narrower spheres of action serve well when projected into more comprehensive spheres; or else, action brings about new standards which serve broadly throughout the vital contexts of life. A man divided against himself is an incompetent agent, since his judgments are inconsistent and uncontrolled. Yet a man psychologically whole and consistent in his actions may find himself in circumstances to which he is inadequate. His vision may be narrow, his knowledge limited. He may encounter conditions so new that he is not prepared to meet them. Action runs the perpetual risk of failure. Nevertheless, some failures may be opportunities for experimentation and growth, not just disasters.

Evaluation is the methodic control of conditions to maximize prospects of success and to minimize the likelihood of failure. Comprehensiveness is required by the condition that actions have public effects, in new and unexpected situations. Rational methods can at best project controls from established spheres of action into new domains which have not been brought under control. Comprehensiveness is required so that the extension of control should retain continuity with its established conditions. This is provided by the substantive function of principles as they move toward the comprehensiveness of ideals. To avoid failure, it must be considered a prospect from any quarter. Means must be developed which comprehensively order actions and results so that failure is avoided. Success expands the domain over which standards and principles hold sway, extending the dominion of a general principle to new conditions and spheres. Comprehensiveness thus resides in our ideals in their capacity to guide actions in a wide variety of circumstances, undergoing modification with new conditions, yet retaining sufficient continuity with their origins to be the "same" value or ideal. Comprehensiveness also resides in a pervasive responsibility to all events as they might be relevant to our actions. The threat of failure from any quarter makes every action a peril that presupposes an unending commitment to greater comprehensiveness, a pervasive responsibility to whatever might be relevant to failure, a commitment to seek the new and to expand the range of controls. Pervasive responsibility is here the primordial condition of agency—that actions project into new domains, that failure lurks everywhere.

Finally, comprehensiveness resides in the synthetic encompassment of new experiences through action and evaluation, often realized in new principles of action or in scientific laws, but especially in comprehensive styles of life, patterns of action consistently applicable in wide domains of experience. Methodic evaluation is comprehensive in attaining new and more general ideals, facts, and attitudes. To be ready to act—and to do so—in new and changing circumstances, in situations alien and unexpected in terms of past experience, is to be comprehensive oneself through all this experience, consistent with oneself yet successful through heterogeneous conditions. A successful act in trying and confusing circumstances is a synthetic and comprehensive achievement, the overcoming of opposition, thus an encompassment through adjustment.

Ideals await interpretation by an agent in his particular circumstances, and are determined by him in his acts to apply there. The consistent interpenetration of acts and ideals, each providing the other with tests and conditions, is a *life-style*—a way of acting relevant to and potentially successful within a wide range of diverse contexts. In the final analysis, comprehensiveness in action turns on the continuity of a given style of life—defined both by loyalty to principles and consistency of interpretation—as acts are projected into new situations requiring control. The interfusion of assimilation and manipulation that is success in action is a dynamic interplay where the significant elements of the agent's experiences are brought under a dominant order of values and character. What is assimilated contributes to further action; what is manipulated has continuously satisfactory results both for further action and in terms of assimilated consequences for other aspects of experience as well.

No order can be all-encompassing, for ontological rather than moral reasons. Nature forms no total system encompassing all things. (Properly speaking, there is no "Nature.") Were all the world a single order, then morals would be univocal, and principles and ideals wholly determinative of the right action in given circumstances. Not surprisingly, so comprehensive a conception of a world-order is often found devoid of value, rather than the source of absolutes. In the great cosmologies based on a supreme world-order—Plato's, Spinoza's, even Kant's—values have no diversity within them. Action is not a creative achievement but a faithful rendering of the order of the universe. What is and what is good become one. Here is the fundamental difficulty faced by all cosmic religions and by all cosmological philosophies as well: that action and the permanent possibility of failure through action become consequences not of the world and the difficulties of human life, but of human frailty and of original sin. Were men not basically sinful, or ignorant and helpless, they would conform to the values at the heart of existence. Failure is always here to be blamed, rather than a consequence of the great difficulties action faces in the complexity of the world. Evaluation here is conformity and faithfulness, not the synthetic attainment of new and more comprehensive orders.

If there were a comprehensive world order, either values would be inexplicable, the fruit of human ignorance and finitude as Spinoza would have it; or they would conform to what is. A comprehensive order simplifies reality so that truth and supreme principles of action fuse. What is is good; the first principles of the world are also the ideals of value. The Enlightenment understood this possibility, though they sacrificed action as a mode of judgment to truth and to science. Kant preserves the modes of judgment in distinct human faculties—the understanding, the practical reason, and the imagination. He does so by repudiating the world order as beyond rational encompassment, beyond *cognition*, and by restricting the understanding to possible experience. Practical reason and the imagination transcend possible experience—but are not then forms of cognition. The transcendence turns on the permanent conditions of reason. Kant substitutes one permanent value for another, the formal conditions of law for the first principles of the world.

The world is more complex than this, even more complex than Plato and Spinoza understood it to be—though Spinoza manifests his awareness of this complexity in making substance *absolutely infinite*, with an infinite number of attributes. The conviction that the universe is one is unfounded, certainly unprovable, but unintelligible also, since whatever its unity, there is a multiplicity of beings as well belonging to it. The faith that all things have a single essence, defined by their role in a comprehensive world order, is only a faith. It suffers from implausibility; it is also indefensible relative to the complexity which nature manifests to us when taken seriously in all her guises. No plausible world order includes the number three, a very large number taken at random, *Hamlet*, Polonius, Orestes, Zeus in all his roles, and the actions by which we make our way through our everyday experiences. The physical world is either too narrow—not then including numbers and imaginary creations—or includes everything in some fashion, in effect begging the entire question, since so many of the items mentioned are not physical, though they are related significantly to some physical beings. Imagination is worth special attention—whether scientific, moral, or artistic—for it creates new beings, relative perhaps initially only to specific spheres or orders, but thereafter influential and effective in other spheres. Works of art and their constituents influence and inspire us. Noble actions also inspire us and give us great satisfactions. Theories and discoveries transform the physical, the emotional, the imaginative, the political, and the scientific realities in which we live.

A great and illuminating insight—whether a new scientific theory, a way of life, a political order in which the diverse elements of human experience are collectively organized, or a creative artistic construction of comprehensive range—is either an imitation of antecedent reality or a new synthetic ordering of diverse elements. Antecedent reality, however, was not so complex as to include the subsequent insight. A new theory is then truly new, and a creative synthesis brought to pass. Synthesis is either mere imitation or created. In a comprehensive world order—such as Spinoza's—all essences of all things, possible or real, are ideas in the mind of God. Either all essences persist timelessly, including the forms of complex and new human creations, or else creation is genuine, emerging from but going beyond given conditions. A new theory moves from what is given to facts and principles organized into a new and more comprehensive form, bringing into a coherent scheme what was not so ordered before. A methodic action brings together past conditions and the vicissitudes of what awaits, and if successful creates an orderly transition from one set of conditions to another. A work of art is the creation of a new being containing diverse elements, a fashioning of the new from the old.

In a comprehensive world order, there is nothing truly new. Novelty is either incompatible with some of the past—thus engendering diversity; or it is itself a creation and encompasses in a new way. In a comprehensive world order, conflict and resolution make little sense. If action can bring about a resolution from conflicting elements, either the resolution was implicit all along, merely hidden, or it is a new complexity and a synthetic realization. Emergent values, created through methodic evaluation, are synthetic achievements. From given principles and conditions, new values emerge, created by methodic deliberation, more comprehensive than prior ideals, since these could not include the new conditions. Ideals of life relative to modern medicine are very different from ideals relative to times of disease and poverty.

The theory of active judgment developed here is founded on the principle that action—especially when intelligent and methodic—is an *achievement,* and when successful produces a greater comprehensiveness of values. Ideals are expanded either in their purview—as in the extension of a known value to new spheres—or in their specific applications. If there is no world order, no system of the world relating all things to each other or even including all things, then action is a way of bringing into relation. It moves from given conditions and relations to new conditions, relating them in spheres of control. Every action takes place within a given sphere and moves from it to other spheres. Every action projects from the order of what is given to other orders, creating some of them, and successful either when the values of the new order are continuous with the old, or when a new continuity has been produced among the manipulative and assimilative dimensions of experience, preempting prior values. Most actions preserve only some continuity with the past. Others break deeply with the past under the impact of new conditions. Only rarely are new and more comprehensive ideals established continuous in many ways with values of the past—though not all—yet promoting rich and satisfactory controls within new situations. The function of ideals is to make such successes in action most likely, by providing broad values capable of diverse interpretations and applications. We turn now to some of the ontological considerations which provide a basis for such a conception of action.

The fundamental relation in terms of which experience may be interpreted is that of order and constituent.* Whatever is is an order of

---

* This ordinal theory is derived from Justus Buchler's *Metaphysics of Natural Complexes.* The systematic pluralism defined by the theory of orders is the ontological basis of the theory of active value presented here. My debt to Buchler is immense, and I can acknowledge here only a small number of ways in which I have been influenced by him. The ordinal theory is basically his, with some major qualifications. In particular, Buchler maintains that every natural complex has a *contour*—the *totality* of its integrities. I deny that such a totality is compatible with radical pluralism. Action is then one of the ways in which comprehensiveness is created relative to some orders.

constituents; every order is itself a constituent of other orders; there is no all-encompassing order. There are more and less comprehensive orders, and orders overlap in complex though determinable ways. The world is no single, all-embracing system. It is pluralistic instead, containing new and sometimes more comprehensive orders provided by imagination, investigation, and action, as well as by novel interactions among established processes. A new theory may be more comprehensive than an older one—though it cannot be so comprehensive as to include itself and everything else as well. A new work of art is the fruition of prior conditions, but is not merely within them. A successful action coordinates what was not so coordinated before, and provides new conditions for the future.

There are only orders of constituents; but not all constituents belong to orders in the same ways. An order is to be understood in terms of its constituents; but so also, a constituent is to be understood in terms of the order to which it belongs. Thus, orders and constituents are complementary categories. A constituent of an order is whatever contributes to what it is. Yet because there is no world order, there are always orders irrelevant to a given order. No order has every other order as its constituents; for every order, there are orders which are not its constituents. What an order is depends on its constituents, but not on what is irrelevant.

Constituents are not *parts* and are not necessarily *smaller* or *simpler* than their orders. A man's country, or at least its social institutions, make him what he is, and are among his constituents. This is clear from the testimony of many of the social sciences. Not only is a circle a constituent of geometry—as one of the figures which geometry addresses; but geometry is a constituent of a circle, in being the system implicated in its particular characteristics.

Every order has constituents—that is what being an order means. Every order is also a constituent in many other orders, to which it contributes some definiteness and in which it plays a role. Here we have a complex relationship, for in many cases the constituents of an order belong to it by virtue of its being a constituent of some other order. A finger belongs to a hand so that the hand may function effectively for a

Buchler's theory of possibility and actuality is the inspiration of mine, but his is quite different, and is not so wedded to the multiplicity of possibilities relative to any actuality. In effect, I consider myself to be a more radical pluralist than Buchler—if that is possible. Finally, the theory of judgment touched on here is similar to Buchler's, though the details of active judgment are mine, and are not Buchler's in any respect. (Cf. his *Toward a General Theory of Human Judgment, Nature and Judgment.*)

man. Thus, many orders are complexly implicated in each other, and related by virtue of their constituents in common. They are related *so that* they may have these constituents in common; and *because* they have these constituents in common they are related as they are.

Nevertheless, there is no all-encompassing world order. This means that not all orders are related to all others. There are no constituents common to all orders. There is no order containing all orders as its constituents. Nor is a given constituent common to two different orders quite the same in each of them. Pluralism entails that constituents function as constituents of their orders, and they are specific there. A constituent has an integrity within its order, and an integrity somewhat different for each order to which it belongs. The role a constituent plays within an order is its integrity. A man has a different role in his home and at his work; and we often acknowledge how *different he is* in his different roles or integrities. In some cases, where there are orders related by common constituents, a given constituent may have the same integrity in both—for it functions in one order so that it may function as a constituent of the other. The finger mentioned above is the same finger relative to the hand and to the man. Nevertheless, a given order has an indefinite multiplicity of constituents, and there are always possibilities for new ones—not to mention the possibilities which are themselves constituents of orders. That there is such an indefinite multiplicity is the fundamental principle of pluralism. In a world order, each order would have an all-encompassing integrity, its complex essence, its total character. Pluralism entails a multiplicity of interrelating integrities, yet an irreducible lack of continuity or completeness among them collectively.

What then of the identity we ascribe to beings amidst their multiple integrities? How may we speak of an order with multiple integrities as *an* order? Here we come to the fundamental condition in terms of which we may speak of synthetic achievement in art, in action, or in understanding. A continuity among many integrities is what we may call the *identity* of an order. Sometimes it will be a continuity of common form, a given constituent common to its many integrities. Sometimes we may ascertain a continuity of character and no more—as in complex and ongoing processes. A cell is a single order through its divisions and its transformations only in terms of a continuity of character in time and place—though nothing may remain quite the *same* over many years and epochs. Finally, there are often complex interrelations among integrities such that a continuity prevails among some of them, another continuity among others, an overlapping similarity among many of them, but no single and continuous order among them all. Here we have separate but interconnected orders.

Yet the connections and similarities may be striking and nearly irresistible. The project may then be defined of comprehending diverse orders in a larger embrace. A continuity of integrities entails an order comprehensive enough to include all of them—for this continuity of integrities or identity is also an integrity in an order. Two interconnected integrities are diverse, each relative to a different order. Where we can find another order comprehensive enough to make the diverse integrities continuous—or simply *more* continuous and interrelated than they were before—we have generated a new order of greater comprehensiveness, an order in which diverse constituents are shown to be the same, to have the same identity. We have created—and only in some cases discovered— identity amidst diversity. If in science, we have understood separate items as belonging together by virtue of our created theory. If in art, we have created a work in which diverse elements function together successfully, a work with its unique integrity. If in action, we have defined principles, ideals, and ways of life in which discontinuous conditions and values have been merged into the larger embrace of a more comprehensive value. Action projects from a conflict of disparate integrities to the synthetic realization of a new order. If successful, the action provides a new continuity of personality, of ideals, or of values and applications.

Diverse integrities may be coordinated only within an order sufficiently comprehensive to include them all. Where no such order can be found, there may be disparate orders which overlap sufficiently to pose the problem of an over-arching identity, though it is not a problem we can resolve. Here we have the identity of an order called into question, either by perceived disparities or suggested continuities which have not been fully elucidated. The identity of most complex orders is nearly always in question in one of these respects. The great human enterprises all seek the continual expansion of powers and orders, seeking to create continuity and to define encompassing identities which may resolve disparity and engender synthesis. Yet there can be no synthesis of all discontinuities within an all-embracing order. The project of seeking greater comprehensiveness among orders is bound to fail—though it may often succeed in a restricted context.

As agents, men function within surrounding environments which are never the entire world, only circumscribed and limited orders. An agent, then—like all things—has an *integrity* within an environment, the role he plays within it, comprised of what within that environment defines that role. He also—like all things—has an impact on that environment, a *scope,* comprised of what he affects significantly in his surroundings. In any order or sphere of action, a man has an integrity or role, but also a scope or an impact, all those other constituents of which he is a constituent. A man prevails within an order both in terms of his integrity there and insofar as he exerts an influence. Integrity and scope are interrelated by virtue of the larger order and its constituents, though each is a distinct aspect of what it is to prevail within an order. Integrity and scope correspond loosely to assimilation and manipulation: an agent assimilates his surroundings in virtue of his character, and manipulates some of them as well. However, a man's character as agent always involves some manipulative elements. A man's character includes *what he does,* the effects of his action. Some of a constituent's relations are part of both its integrity and scope. Some of its powers define its role in the order. In the case of action, manipulation and assimilation must be distinguished, though they greatly overlap. A man acts as he must, in terms of his integrity, but may fail in terms of his effects, eventually in terms of what he must assimilate. Integrity and scope are related but distinct in orders of action. Moreover, the agent's scope is constantly shifting with new circumstances and changing orders. Therefore, failure is always a prospect.

Men are agents in a variety of environments, both simultaneously and sequentially, and their integrities differ in each environment—sometimes greatly, sometimes minimally. To act methodically is to act within a situation, to act according to one's role in that situation, responding to what one assimilates. But an act will not remain within a given situation; it belongs to orders in which the agent has other integrities as well. A broader consistency and continuity is then required for successful action, a comprehensive integrity—or self—which can avoid failure in many and widely different spheres of action. Action projects the integrity of the self and its ideal values from one situation to another, seeking a broader continuity, a consistency of character through diverse conditions. Action seeks control through encompassment, the *ordering* of what is given as diverse and distinct into comprehensive spheres in which broader values have been established. Successful action is then the creation of new and inclusive orders, *bringing* comprehensive order into one's surroundings. All action implicitly looks to that encompassment provided by political action.

Total comprehensiveness remains impossible, and failure remains on all sides. In part, this is a function of changing and novel circumstances. Partly also, it is a consequence of the multiplicity of spheres of action, a given deed being satisfactory in some domains and not in others, some respects and not in others. Most difficult of all is the insecurity of the scope of action—the most expert and stringent controls over one set of conditions nevertheless being insecure relative to others. A man has little control over how he will appear to other men. Diversity of interconnecting spheres of action, especially in their ramifications for the scope of personality and of action, makes total control quite impossible. This is the basic source of conflict in action. And it is why a successful action is a comprehensive achievement, coordinating opposing constraints within a single embrace. Yet there is no all-inclusive order of action, and success can be but localized within those orders important in the agent's life. In this sense, a methodically successful action is the continuous extension from the integrity of a man into a new situation. Where a discontinuity or inconsistency is revealed by action, then there is failure.

Another distinction is essential here—between actuality and possibility. Of those constituents within an order, some are *actualities;* others are *their possibilities.* Such possibilities are not to be confused with so-called logical possibilities, which are fruits of discourse and of conceptual orders. Ordinal possibilities are an expression of the interconnection of orders, the extension of an actual constituent of one order into other orders. In this respect, possibilities are always *of* an actuality—*its powers.* We follow Aristotle here. In addition, possibilities are always many for any actuality—the plurality of alternatives which it possesses by virtue of the interplay of orders. There are no actualities without powers, and a multiplicity of them. Finally, though actualities must be logically compatible within a single order, contradictory possibilities may prevail for an actuality within a given order.

Possibilities represent the extension of actualities from the orders in which they are actual to other orders—whether more comprehensive or merely related alternatives. A weight lifter is actually strong, and the possibilities prevail for him of using his strength, lifting one hundred pounds, two hundred pounds, straining to the utmost, or refraining altogether. It is no possibility that he may lift twenty thousand pounds. Science emphasizes actualities, and addresses possibilities only as they lead to actualities in other orders. Art revels in possibilities, and is concerned with actualities only to attain the maximal interplay of possibilities in the imagination. Action is the projection from given actualities through possibilities to other actualities, emphasizing the specific transition through which a possibility becomes an actuality. Action is the manipulation of possibilities in their multiplicity as they pass into actuality. Nevertheless, all actualities have multiple possibilities, and that is the peril in all action. Successful action transforms possibilities in intricate diversity and conflict into the actualities of a coherent and more comprehensive order—only to evoke the challenge of new possibilities which have emerged. Possibilities and actualities together define the interplay of orders, actualities and possibilities both continually new—not only in time, but in orders confronted, new even in the structure of orders. A fundamental constant still unknown is a prevailing actuality in the order of events and may be a possibility within the system of known constants and laws. Action is both the control of and at the mercy of emerging possibilities, stumbling over them at all times, even in established orders. Possibilities reside in all established orders, quite apart from merely temporal conditions, insofar as actualities are projected into new orders. Orders continually intersect, even unknown. Action is always in peril, even in apparently secure circumstances.

The plurality of possibilities relative to any actuality within a given order—plural by virtue of the complex interplay and manifold ramifications of diverse orders—is the ontological condition of both novelty and the freedom which is autonomy. Possibilities are engendered within orders by prevailing conditions—both possible and actual. In this sense, novelty belongs not only to actuality but to possibility as well. There is no timeless realm of essences, whose lawful relations comprise a permanent condition among all actualities, all orders, all constituents. Determinism is a theory of pure actuality, lacking all possibilities in the sense here described. Determinism presupposes that the world is a total system all of whose constituents are actual. Actualities stand in actual relations; no genuine alternatives belong to such a system. With plural possibilities, alternatives always prevail.

In the pluralistic theory of orders defined here, any constituent belongs to many orders and has diverse constituents. Its integrities too are diverse, and the interconnection of integrities engenders specific possibilities. The actual constituents of a given order may have definite and distinct relations; but the interplay of diverse orders, diverse actualities, diverse interrelations of any actuality, produces a variety of possibilities. Given any actuality of any order, there are possibilities for it. The number two is actual within the order of integers, and its actual integrity then includes its relations to the other integers. But the scope of the number two includes the possibilities of diverse pairs of objects—boots, persons, dreams, even paintings. Possibilities lurk everywhere, and with them lurks failure and a lack of control as well. It should be clear, however, that such possibilities are not indeterminate, but may be quite definite and specific in their character. Definiteness and indefiniteness are traits belonging to both actualities and possibilities in their complex interplay.

If the plurality of orders is the source of the peril of failure, it is also the ontological basis of freedom, autonomy, and moral responsibility. Possibilities represent alternatives within any sphere of action, alternatives awaiting selection and control. Action projects from actualities into diverse possibilities, establishing some of them as actualities. The intersection of diverse conditions is harnessed through action into a coordinated sphere of control. Multiple and alternative possibilities are transformed into compatible actualities.

Nevertheless, the plurality of possibilities can be arbitrariness and chaos unless directed and controlled. Ontological diversity becomes autonomy and responsibility only when harnessed by methodic evaluation. Even in the absence of men, possibilities are transformed into actualities through the passing of time and the working of events. A man is a responsible agent only when he has maximized his control over possibilities to be actualized. Autonomy is equivalent with methodic action: the controlled transformation of available alternatives into means most likely to produce satisfactory results in terms of the values engendered. Autonomy is the directed transformation of spheres of action in terms of given conditions and ideals, directed toward maximizing the likelihood of attaining values. The agent's capabilities and ideals jointly work upon conditions given, maximizing the prospects of success. An autonomous agent is free in that his own methods maximize the range of possibilities confronting him, but also strengthen to the utmost his powers for dealing with them. An autonomous agent may still fail, for failure is always a prospect. Nevertheless, he is responsible for his actions in terms of his consistency of self and methodic controls and free to the extent that he controls possibilities before him to the fullest extent.

Action is one of three modes of judgment—the others being assertion and construction. In assertion, claims are made and coordinated with principles of consistency and facts of experience. Assertion seeks a faithfulness to actual experience, and attains it by general laws which represent possibilities for extremely comprehensive orders of events as well as actual interconnections among such events. Science seeks the most comprehensive orders of understanding possible by formulating laws which are simultaneously actualities of events and possibilities for other events. Science seeks the conditions in which actuality and possibility are nearly one, thus severely circumscribing its domains of understanding, emphasizing the general and diminishing its emphasis on the precariousness of specific events. A specific occurrence is an instrument for understanding and no more. Alternatives generated by unknown orders are set aside if irrelevant to general assertions.

In construction, new orders are created in which constituents play a role at once both diverse and unified. The interplay of diversity and order, continuity and discreteness, is the interesting character of art. Something new and comprehensive is made, and its value resides only in what is made—the diverse and the continuous integrities of its constituents in contrasting and remarkable relations. The perfection of a work of art is a contrast with the imperfect and unfinished; its originality is a contrast with what came before. Aesthetic value is always the interplay of excellence with originality, the creation of a new work of an exceptional and noteworthy character, in terms of its diverse constituents and their interplay. It looks neither to consequences nor to faithfully represent another object—though it may do both to its specific end of intense contrast.

In action, consequences and effects are controlled, successfully or not in terms of the agent's perspectives, but subject to the responses and judgments of others. A successful action endures through time, through changing circumstances, through novel conditions, through the diversity of alternative possibilities, and through the reactions of other men. A valid active judgment sustains the integrity of the agent, as a man whose actions are satisfactory within new and different orders, for other men, and in terms of the values and ideals, as well as the methods and instruments, which together define his character as agent. As for how dissatisfaction and criticism is to be shown, that may be in terms of any of the modes of judgment—even by simply displaying consequences, by revulsion, or set forth in constructed works. Any of these may expose discontinuity—or rather, may provide such a discontinuity by evoking new and significant possibilities.

Ethics is to active judgment as science is to assertive judgment: a man may assert anything, but if he is concerned with validity, assertions must be methodic and systematic; a man may do anything, but if he is concerned with validity, actions must be methodic and systematic. Self-criticism in science is unending but controlled. Self-criticism in ethics is unending but controlled. Self-criticism in art also is unending and controlled. Any truth—even fundamental laws—may be overturned as new discoveries are made. Any principle—even fundamental ideals—may be overturned as new activities are called for. Ideals may be quite valid for their spheres of action but invalid for others. Comprehensiveness remains as a project and as a threat in all active concerns.

All of the methodic modes of judgment are universal in scope and unbounded, though none is all-encompassing. Any subject matter whatsoever has facts concerning it, and may be studied for what may be claimed about it. Any subject matter whatsoever may be relevant to action, and may be acted upon. Any subject matter whatsoever may be used as an element in a work of art, or judged in terms of aesthetic criteria. Even a scientific claim may be judged actively, in terms of its consequences. A claim may be true but its effects disastrous: men may not be ready for some truths. Conversely, lacking truth we may develop hypotheses based on their instrumental and pragmatic effects in political life. An action has factual aspects and may be judged as interesting or not. Active judgment is a concern for results, instrumental connections. Methodic evaluation is active judgment in maximal control, as science is assertive judgment with maximal validity. Both rest on a ground of principles—but principles which are continuously being modified with new orders of action.

Not only are the modes of judgment of universal applicability; not only may any item in human experience be regarded in terms of each of the modes or all of them at once: in addition, the significant enterprises of human experience are unavoidably mixed modes of judgment. Science seeks faithfulness and truth, but is guided by practical considerations relative to future discoveries and by structural restrictions. Art often maximizes intermodal interplay, producing works which make claims, which have moral implications, and which are of aesthetic value, all nearly indistinguishably and certainly inextricably. Action too, though seeking control over events, requires facts and even elegance of style. Science and art, as enterprises, are great both in their fruits and in their fascination. Among the greatest human satisfactions are such activities. Science may be loved both as a means and as an end to be participated in. Nevertheless, no case can be made that science, art, and ethics fuse into an all-encompassing enterprise. The complexity of the world strongly suggests otherwise. However, it is important to realize that the inexhausti-bility of nature does not entail that there is no supreme human activity—that the many modes of judgment may not be coordinated *for men* into a most perfect unity of methods and judgments. Philosophy is often postulated as such an enterprise. Pluralism only suggests that a diversity of values is the likely prospect within human experience, that even metaphysics will find success only within a multiplicity of comprehensive systems.

Any order whatsoever, including particular judgments, may be further judged in any of the modes. A work of art may be judged in terms of its utility, an act in terms of its aesthetic values. Yet the modes of judgment are distinct though interpenetrating. The only rational response is a methodic one—methodic within each mode of judgment, and methodic in coordinating various judgments in larger and more comprehensive orders. Here philosophy is of importance, as the most comprehensive ordering in human life. Yet the comprehensiveness of metaphysics is attained at the expense of detail, and provides no all-inclusive or superior orders. General metaphysical categories may be precisely formulated and of broad purview; but they sacrifice specificity. In this sense, they are not *all*-encompassing. It follows that reason within a human life is the continual and unremitting reflection upon the conditions and fruits of judgment, the continual interpenetration and synthesis of judgments—art viewed morally, but not morally alone; science studied in its elegance and simplicity and in terms of the consequences it produces, as well as in its evidential foundations; action supplemented by the sciences and by the arts, especially where instruments for new modes of action are possible. Nevertheless, the various orders synthesized comprehensively within human experience are of direct value to action only when consequences are of primary importance, and where the agent is himself judged in terms of his actions. The multiplicity of orders entails that no action will then be quite secure, since there always may be found or created new orders of judgment challenging it; while whatever security is possible comes from unceasing control and vigilant activity. Success in action is fairly rare, but a great achievement when realized. It is even rarer and a greater achievement in the comprehensive arenas of political action. Experience haunts us, but it stimulates us also to new and more comprehensive orders, whose creation calls upon all our powers, individual and social.